CINEMA OF CONFINEMENT

diaeresis

Contents

Acknowledgments

The introduction and chapter 2 contain material from an earlier publication of "Big Window, Big Other: Enjoyment and Spectatorship in Alfred Hitchcock's *Rope*," published in *Quarterly Review of Film and Video* in August 2014. Chapter 5 is based on an earlier publication of "'It's Just a Show?' Paranoia and Provocation in Oliver Stone's *Talk Radio*," published in *Quarterly Review of Film and Video* in April 2017.

Many thanks to my colleagues Jennifer Friedlander and Mark Andrejevic at Pomona College for their support and kindness. Thank you to Hilary Neroni at the University of Vermont.

Much gratitude to Annalisa Weaver-Zox for her comments, suggestions, and overall editing expertise of an earlier draft of this book.

Chapters 6 and 7 were completed while I was teaching film theory in the spring of 2017 at Pomona College. I would like to thank my students Ariana Callan, Ben Del Vecchio, Hannah Grobisen, Sawyer Henshaw, McKenzie Nagle, Bridget Payne, and Adam Soll for all of their thoughts on confinement cinema and the numerous films they recommended.

Love and thanks to my brother, my sister, and my mother for your support. I especially want to thank my father, who unexpectedly passed away while I was finishing this project in the summer of 2017.

Love and thanks to the Thompson family for their kindness and support.

Anthony Tinelli, thank you for your friendship, support, and encouragement.

Thank you to Paul Biagiotti for our numerous discussions of film, especially *The Shining*, which we have yet to exhaust.

Thanks to my dog Beatrice for your presence within the confined setting, and for keeping your barking at a minimal audio level.

Much gratitude to Henry Krips for your friendship, support, and guidance. I am extremely thankful to have taken your amazing course "The Eye and the Gaze" at Claremont Graduate University.

I am tremendously grateful to Trevor Perri at Northwestern University Press and Diaeresis's series editors, Slavoj Žižek, Adrian Johnston, and Todd McGowan, for supporting this project. Tremendous thanks to Nathan MacBrien at Northwestern University Press for guiding me through the editing and production phases of the book. Thank you to Paul Mendelson for your insightful questions and editing expertise.

The seeds of this book began in the summer of 2006, with a graduate paper I had written on *Rope* for Todd McGowan's Alfred Hitchcock course at the University of Vermont. Tremendous thanks to Todd for your friendship, guidance, support, and kindness. I am so grateful that you allowed me to audit "Ethics and Cinema" in 2004, a course that began my journey into theory.

Lastly, I would like to thank my loving wife, best friend, and confined partner, Katie, for her emotional support and listening to me as I developed this project.

CINEMA OF CONFINEMENT

Excess, the Gaze, and Cinema of Confinement

> After *Fight Club* (which had nearly four hundred scenes and almost two hundred locations), the idea of doing an entire story [*Panic Room*] inside one house appealed to me. . . . The whole place, a three-story apartment, is all built on stage and we have cameras that can go literally anywhere. They can move and follow the actors from the third floor to the first. All over the place.
>
> —David Fincher, director of *Panic Room*

Since the birth of cinema, filmmakers have explored different ways of telling stories across multiple settings within the length of one film. From the early editing experiments of Edwin S. Porter and D. W. Griffith, to the current globe-trotting of James Bond and Marvel movies, shifts in location continue to fascinate filmmakers and audiences alike. Aesthetically, many of these movies articulate cinematic space as fluid and continuous, since the image is subordinated to the narrative even when the story changes locations. As such, the mode of production for the classic style of narration is to naturalize and integrate space by not drawing significant attention to the mechanisms that create the illusion of cinematic reality. This process is often referred to as the invisible style of narration, which involves composing and editing space that directs the viewer's spectatorship towards the narrative and the actions of the characters. These films offer the spectator a cinema that displays the unlimited power of the camera, showing all perspectives of the events throughout a variety of settings.

But how do films that take place in one location make for an engaging and suspenseful spectatorship? How do filmmakers make a confined setting such as a living room, a car, a phone booth, or a fallout bunker attractive to audiences over a long stretch of time? Excess is the key concept to answering these questions.

Films such as David Fincher's home invasion thriller *Panic Room* (2002) are what I refer to as the "cinema of confinement" because the narrative tension focuses predominantly within one location. The quotation above addresses one of the ways in which excess is depicted in the film. As Fincher explains, he makes up for the film's confined setting by constructing the home within a controlled environment so that the camera can potentially be "all over the place."[1] But how do we account for confinement films that do not employ an excessively visual style and are just as narratively suspenseful as *Panic Room,* such as Lenny Abrahamson's *Room* (2015), Dan Trachtenberg's *10 Cloverfield Lane* (2016), and Doug Liman's *The Wall* (2017)? This raises a number of questions in understanding the theoretical aspects of excess. How does excess function in cinema in relation to spectatorship? What are its effects in relation to characters and their environment? How does excess serve the cinema of confinement in the articulation of space? What ideological, political, and social insights does excess offer?

Excess is not only about hyper-stylized cinema. Excess also involves what is in the film space more than the film space itself. It is something that at once eludes our looking and elicits our desire to look into the film's narrative or plot. That is to say, excess entails a psychical force in our viewership. Consider Alfred Hitchcock's bomb theory. Rather than having a bomb randomly explode, such as the café explosion scene that opens Alfonso Cuarón's *Children of Men* (2006), the logic of Hitchcock's suspense involves showing viewers a ticking bomb placed on a train.[2] By sharing this secret information with viewers, a common conversation or everyday chitchat on the train becomes freighted with dread and tension. Slavoj Žižek describes Hitchcockian suspense in relation to the phallic stage as something that stands out within the ordinary. For Žižek, the phallic stage "is precisely the detail that 'does not fit,' that 'sticks out' from the idyllic surface scene and denatures it, renders it uncanny."[3] This unordinary detail is surplus-knowledge—it is the excess that unhinges the signified (meaning or mental image) from the signifier (the object or referent to which the meaning or mental image refers), such as the ticking bomb stuffed in the trunk of a car that opens Orson Welles's *Touch of Evil* (1958). Long takes are often associated with slowness, pensiveness, and duration. One would think that employing long takes would frustrate viewers by emphasizing the passing of time. After all, Hollywood films do not want to draw significant attention to a film's system of mediation. The long take in *Touch of Evil* is anything but slow as the vehicle makes its way through the border city in Texas. The suspense of the car bomb sequence is attributed to Welles letting us in on the secret (surplus-knowledge). Allowing excess to "stick out" not only builds incredible suspense—as demonstrated in Hitchcock's bomb theory—but also can transform cinematic space with unsettling effects, as in the long take in *Touch of Evil*.[4] Even when the long take moves away from the vehicle, introducing us to newlyweds Mike Vargas (Charlton Heston) and Susan Vargas (Janet Leigh) walking along the street, the scene continues to have an unsettling effect upon our spectatorship—because desire functions on what we do not know. The logic of desire operates on lack and absence, not on mastery and plenitude. For example, when Mike and Susan first appear within the moving long take, they are obstructions. The camera tracks Mike and Susan as they walk along the city while the couple in the vehicle with the ticking bomb drives off-screen. The introduction of Mike and Susan both intensifies our spectatorship and demonstrates how our desire distorts the visual field of perception within the scene. As such, the bomb as surplus-knowledge radicalizes our perception of the city, as objects, conversations, and events become charged with uncertainty. Our knowledge of a ticking bomb, combined with the real-time movement of the camera, elicits our desire to look as we anticipate the explosion.

Cinematic excess is intimately connected to Jacques Lacan's concept of the "gaze": a limit of looking within the visual field of perception. The gaze is a point of failure within the film's visual plane, which causes our looking to falter. At the same time, the encounter with the gaze reveals the film's hidden excess; this is not to suggest that excess defies interpretation. Todd McGowan importantly explains that early film theorists such as Roland Barthes, Kristin Thompson, and Stephen Heath understood excess as a *limitation* of a film's narrative. Excess, in this regard, exceeds the narrative and eludes narrative analysis. If we can recognize cinematic excess, then we can explain its potential meanings. As McGowan observes, "Even as the excess resists signification, it does so within a world of signification—or else we would not even be able to register it,"[5] because excess is not external to the narrative, but rather "internal" to a film's narrative structure.

My claim is that excess energizes space within the cinema of confinement as well as builds narrative tension. The gaze is a visual manifestation of excess that underscores our looking *within* the picture, not outside it as a transcendent viewer.[6] Depending on how filmmakers deploy the gaze, it can have varying effects upon our spectatorship. To encounter the gaze in confinement cinema is to experience its excessive dimension as both shock and attraction. In the first case of excess, the gaze manifests as an unknowable force that disturbs our sense of looking. Here, the encounter with the gaze arises with shocking or traumatic effects upon our spectatorship. The force of the gaze is unknowable because we do not fully realize how our desire to see initially distorts the field of perception until we encounter the gaze's excessive presence. In other words, the encounter with the gaze as an unknowable force apprises us that we cannot see everything. Moreover, the excess revealed by the gaze underscores that cinematic space is not inherently neutral but is constructed by the filmmaker. The gaze realizes something that does not fit within the order of our looking. At the same time, the impact of the gaze reveals how our desire distorts the visual plane. As such, our encounter with the gaze manifests a blind spot in our desire to see. In the second case of excess, the gaze is primarily enunciated within the visual field by the filmmaker showing us too much information as a distorting presence, such as David Fincher's approach to shooting *Panic Room.* As I will explain in further detail in chapter 1, the filmmaker's rendering excess visible diminishes the traumatic impact of the knowability of the gaze.[7] This is not to suggest that films which exploit excess are not exciting to watch or lack desire. All narrative films, to some degree or another, incorporate the logic of desire. Thus, the goal of this project is to map these two dimensions of the gaze in films that primarily take place in one setting.

The Gaze

To explain how these two dimensions of the gaze work in confinement cinema requires a brief sketching of Lacan's triad and interrelation of the imaginary, the symbolic, and the real. The imaginary is the register of images and appearances. The imaginary involves not only how one sees and perceives objects within the world, but also the subordination of processes or structures that constitute what Lacan calls the symbolic order. The symbolic structures our experiences of everyday life. It is where laws, languages, and systems of communication take place. The symbolic is where we can try on different identities that are already there for us. For Lacan, the subject's entry into the symbolic order requires the sacrifice of enjoyment, or what he refers to as *jouissance.* Here, it is important to stress that enjoyment (*jouissance*) is not the same as pleasure. Enjoyment is what is beyond the pleasure principle and is prohibited by the symbolic order. As such, the grounding of the symbolic order for Lacan is loss. Without the symbolic's prohibition, society would cease to function. The imaginary level, however, entails the illusion of wholeness as a respite from the prohibition of enjoyment that the symbolic order imposes on the subject. Although the imaginary provides the illusion of a functioning symbolic system, it is not a complete and totalizing order. For example, I can imagine what it is like to be a Hollywood movie director, bringing my life story to the big screen. Yet, what I do not recognize is the stress, anxiety, and economic challenges that directors encounter in creating a feature film. Here, the deficiency of the symbolic is the third register: the real. The real is non-symbolic; it is non-sense or non-meaning that breaks down the symbolic. The encounter with the real, as Lacan states, "eludes us."[8] If the symbolic provides the basis for expressing and structuring ourselves and the world around us, the real is a point where those systems collapse. Yet the paradox of the real is that the very limitation it imposes also offers us a challenge, for example, to create works of art or develop new technologies. As such, the real reveals cracks in the social order and, at the same time, is the stage for the possibility of the new.

The gaze is a visual manifestation of the real. It is a point of non-sense within the visual plane. Yet our experience of the gaze can only be detected through our investment of looking. Lacan's premise of the gaze demonstrates the split subject (between conscious and the unconscious) within the field of visual perception. The gaze as a stain or distortion marks a point of failure in the visual field. It is a point where the subject's looking reaches the limits of the visible, where the space between object and subject collapses. Here we must stress that Lacan is not using the term "gaze" in the traditional sense. The gaze, however, is not from the subject, but of the object, as illustrated in Lacan's example of Hans Holbein's painting *The Ambassadors.* The painting consists of two ambassadors, symmetrically framed and surrounded by their riches as they look directly at the observer. But, toward the bottom of the painting there appears a strange smear interfering with the painting's sumptuous presentation. Looking at the painting awry reveals the warped image as a human skull staring directly back at the observer. Lacan states: "we are literally called into the picture, and represented here as caught. . . . [For] the secret of this picture is given at the moment when, moving slightly away, little by little, to the left, then turning around, we see what the magical floating object signifies. It reflects our own nothingness in the figure of death's head . . . to capture the subject, an obvious relation with desire which, nevertheless, remains enigmatic."[9] Lacan's description of *The Ambassadors* raises two points of discussion in relation to the gaze and the subject of desire. First, the painting enacts two types of looking. Holbein's painting invites the observer to explore all of the different objects that surround the ambassadors, and to interpret their symbolic meaning. Lacan describes this type of looking as being a "pacifying, Apollonian effect of painting."[10] The smear, however, arrests the observer's attention, interfering with the painting's world of images, and revealing an excessive element that cannot be incorporated into one's looking. This type of seeing is associated with a disruption, or what Henry Krips describes as having "Dionysian effects."[11] When revealing itself as a human skull, the anomaly produces a failure in the visual space where one has to readjust one's looking. The skull is not the gaze itself, but rather a lacuna or distortion in the painting, an excessive element that cannot be incorporated into the picture. This anomaly is the real—the nontextual thing that disturbs the order of reality. The gaze emerges as an effect of the real within the visual plane.

Secondly, the importance of *The Ambassadors* is that it visually displays desire. According to Lacan, desire is generated by the absence of the object cause of desire, or what he terms *objet petit a* or *objet a.* Paradoxically, it is the very "loss" of the object that sustains desire's energy. For Lacan, once a part of the symbolic order, the subject's desire situates itself with the desire of the Other, as he states: "desire is the desire of the Other."[12] But one's desire can never match or live up to what the Other wants. Therefore, the subject's desire is never satisfied. This is how the symbolic order binds us together: namely, our shared sacrifice of enjoyment. As such, there is no escape route for one's desire. The engine of desire is fueled by not obtaining "the lost object" (*objet a*). When the subject tries to capture *objet a,* it will always miss it and proclaim "that's not it." Žižek offers an example of the soft drink Coke as *objet a* (surplus-enjoyment). Coke's once famous slogan was "Coke is it." By why do we keep drinking Coke? Because Coke is not it.[13] There is a failure in the taste of Coke that keeps one coming back for more. The failure of desire is due to its own impossibility. Lacan notes, "Desire, more than any other point in the range of human possibility, meets its limit somewhere."[14] As long as *objet a* remains absent, desire continues to desire.

The gaze is *objet a* in the visual field. The gaze is what lures us into the picture—it entices our desire to look within the frame. Desire operates on absence and lack. It operates by what we cannot see. When we encounter the gaze, we are encountering how our desire distorts the visual field. Films that elicit our desire to look lay a trap for the gaze. But we must first become involved in the film in order to experience the shock of the gaze as an unknowable force. Our desire must be called upon, as Lacan states, "by pouring ourselves, as it were, along the veins through which the domain of vision has been integrated into the field of desire."[15]

The attraction of cinema is that it allows us to see how our desire distorts the visual field. Cinema can show how an encounter with the gaze not only unsettles our spectatorship, but also unravels the unity of narrative space. Consider the final sequence in Ridley Scott's confinement space horror thriller, *Alien* (1979), when Ripley (Sigourney Weaver) frighteningly encounters the creature in her escape shuttle. After she blows up the mother ship, *Nostromo,* we believe that Ripley, as the last survivor, has safely escaped the alien's terrifying wrath. But when she discovers that the alien has snuck onto the escape shuttle, it is not only traumatic for Ripley, but for us as well. This moment of shock can only emerge because we have invested our desire to look into the film. Indeed, the alien emerges as a blind spot in our looking, with terrifying and "Dionysian" results. Moreover, the alien, as an embodiment of the gaze, unsettles the escape shuttle's fabric of reality. The emergence of the alien forces us to reevaluate our looking. At the same time, Ripley's encounter with the alien illustrates why cinema is such an appealing art form—namely, the shock and attraction of the gaze. The gaze not only realizes one's investment in the film, but permits the spectator to enjoy. Fantasy is key to understanding our enjoyment of cinema and to how we experience the excess of the gaze.

Fantasy and the Gaze: *Alien* and *Carrie*

To understand the gaze as a moment of rupture requires that we consider Ridley Scott's depiction of the scene *before* Ripley encounters the creature in the escape shuttle. We need to understand how fantasy scenarios are constructed in order to explain the traumatic impact of the gaze as a visual manifestation of desire. The gaze emerges as a blind spot within the visual field of representation, causing viewers to lose control of their looking. Part of understanding the impact of the gaze is desire's relationship to fantasy. Like the concept of the gaze, Lacan does not use the term "fantasy" in the traditional sense, such as the imagined worlds of *Star Wars* or *Star Trek*; nor is it an illusion of reality such as "life is just a dream." Fantasy sets up the coordinates of desire. It is a framework that permits the subject to make meaning within the world. As Lacan states, "The phantasy is the support of desire; it is not the object that is the support of desire."[16] Through fantasy, the subject learns how to direct his or her desire. As such, fantasy allows the subject to relate to his or her impossible "lost object" without repercussions. Cinema is powerful in this regard because it can supply a scenario that one may not experience in the everyday world. We can experience characters that can defy the laws of gravity, as in the Marvel movies such as *Iron Man* (Jon Favreau, 2008) and *Doctor Strange* (Scott Derrickson, 2016). At the same time, many Hollywood films forgo the disturbing impact of the gaze. These films create fantasy scenarios that function much like ideology, by neutralizing cinema's excess, a method Todd McGowan terms the "cinema of integration," where desire and fantasy work together, subordinating the traumatic effects of the gaze. As McGowan explains, the gaze in the cinema of integration is not depicted as an impossibility or a disturbing intruder into the film's narrative or plot.[17] According to McGowan, these films satisfy our desire through fantasy scenarios of satisfaction, while reducing the gaze's disturbing effect and thus transforming it into an ordinary object.[18] Indeed, the cinema of integration permits us to experience the object cause of desire in ways that we cannot relate to it in everyday life. This is most notable during spectacular endings in films, such as the slow-motion death of Hans Gruber (Alan Rickman) in John McTiernan's *Die Hard* (1988) as he falls from the Nakatomi building, or the destruction of the death star in George Lucas's *Star Wars: A New Hope* (1977). In both examples, viewers achieve satisfaction in the hero overcoming the narrative's main obstacle. Moreover, directors John McTiernan's and George Lucas's imagining of these endings are visually and audibly fulfilling. They offer an experience that we might not find in everyday life. At the same time, they are pleasurable scenarios because they limit the gaze's disrupting presence. The appeal of these movies and many other Hollywood films lies in the notion that they incorporate the gaze without its intruding impact.

The examples from *Die Hard* and *Star Wars* normalize the excess of the gaze as a cinema of integration. But this is not the case in the final scene in the escape shuttle in *Alien*. So how does the gaze function in regard to desire and fantasy? The gaze emerges with disturbing effects in what McGowan calls the "cinema of intersection."[19] Here, desire intrudes into the film's fantasy space as an unknowable force. When desire and fantasy collide, viewers experience a traumatic encounter with the gaze. That is, viewers see the impossibility of the gaze directly rather than at a distance, as in the cinema of integration, which is why Žižek argues that fantasy is on the side of reality. As he explains, "When the phantasmic frame disintegrates, the subject undergoes a 'loss of reality' and starts to perceive reality as an 'irreal' nightmarish universe with no firm ontological foundation; this nightmarish universe is not 'pure fantasy,' but, on the contrary, *that which remains of reality after reality is deprived of its support in fantasy*."[20] Without the fantasy screen, we do not see reality as *reality truly is*, but rather a nightmarish form of reality. Fantasy renders reality in a meaningful way for the subject. In the collision of desire and fantasy, the subject, however, experiences a loss of reality which, paradoxically, provides a pathway to experiencing the impossible object.

Alien's frightening final sequence in the escape shuttle is not only attributed to the shocking twist that Ripley did not kill the alien aboard the *Nostromo* by blowing that ship up, but also to how Scott constructs a peaceful fantasy scenario *before* Ripley realizes that the alien is now aboard the escape shuttle. After the explosion of *Nostromo*, we believe Ripley has defeated the alien. Here, the escape shuttle not only functions as a space of safety, but as a point of relaxation for her and the viewer. While watching the *Nostromo* explode, Ripley softly says: "I got you. You son of a bitch," reinforcing her safety. Even the way in which the scene is shot and edited, as well as the peaceful score, offer the impression that Ripley has achieved her goal and is safely installed aboard the shuttle. But when the alien emerges from its hiding place in the shuttle, it destroys any sense of respite that the escape shuttle had once provided for Ripley and the viewer. The emergence of the alien deforms and cripples the setting of the shuttle because the fantasy screen has collapsed. Cinematic excess is no longer integrated and normalized within the shuttle's confined space, but is now problematized by the alien's presence as an embodiment of the gaze. This is emphasized by Ripley hiding in the locker as she watches the alien through the door's glass panel. Here, the locker window performs two functions: it physically protects Ripley, and is a protective screen between reality and the eruption of the real as an embodiment of the alien.[21] Knowing the alien is aboard the shuttle, both the viewer's and Ripley's control of looking falters. The intensity and suspense of the scene allow the viewers to experience the gaze *directly*. As such, the sudden appearance of the alien in the escape shuttle renders the gaze into the visual field of representation as an unknowable force that must be defeated.

The shocking twist in the final sequence of *Alien* is a common trait that is often found in horror cinema. Perhaps one of the most infamous endings is the dream sequence in Brian De Palma's *Carrie* (1976). Carrie (Sissy Spacek) is a teen who has telekinetic powers. After her classmates play a prank on her at the school prom (dumping blood on her after she is crowned queen), she unleashes her power and a massacre ensues in the gymnasium. Returning home from the prom, drenched in pig's blood, Carrie has a horrific showdown with her mother (Piper Laurie). Carrie kills her mother and uses her powers to cause the house to cave in on her. In the film's final scene, one of Carrie's bullies, Sue (Amy Irving), visits Carrie's grave, feeling ashamed of the way she treated her. De Palma photographs this sequence in luscious slow motion as Sue slowly approaches the gravestone. She is dressed in white with a flowing gown, holding a bouquet of flowers. The music is tender and swelling. As Sue bends down to lay the flowers near the grave, a bloody hand emerges out of the dirt and grabs her. The image immediately cuts to Sue waking up in her bedroom, wailing as she clutches her wrist. The trick ending is shocking because of the manner in which De Palma lures us into the image as a fantasy scenario. But as Sue reaches the grave site, elements begin to stick out within the serene setting. The grave site is located on a patch of dirt with a makeshift cross that reads: "For Sale" in big red lettering. Over the sign, black lettering reads: "Carrie White burns in hell," with an arrow pointing to the ground. Like the blot in *The Ambassadors*, these elements perform as stains within the picturesque setting, furthering our investment to look within the scene. As such, the grave site does not fit within the picture that leads to Carrie's bloody hand shooting out of the ground, destroying the quaint scene that De Palma constructs for us. Thus, the excess of the gaze invades with disturbing results through the intersection of fantasy and desire.

The Post-Effect of the Gaze, Showing Too Much, and Ideology

Encountering the gaze realizes the subject's desire of looking. But what are the lingering effects post-gaze? How is cinematic space articulated immediately after the encounter with the gaze? At the end of *Carrie*—when Sue awakens in her bedroom—we learn that she was dreaming of Carrie's hand shooting out of the grave. Here, the lingering effect of the gaze is visually captured in the slow-moving camera that glides away from Sue as her mother tries to calm her. The ethereal movement of the camera articulates the deformation of space as a result of the gaze. The crippling effect of space coincides with Sue's psychosis. The camera movement is an example of not only how cinema can show us the traumatic effects of the gaze directly, but can also depict its lingering effects *after* its initial encounter. As I will explain in chapter 2, in Alfred Hitchcock's one-room thriller *Rope* (1948), fantasy coincides with Brandon (John Dall) and Phillip (Farley Granger) hiding their secret from the dinner party guests. The secret is the dead body in the trunk, upon which Brandon and Phillip serve dinner. Once Brandon and Phillip's professor and guest, Rupert (James Stewart), discovers the body, desire slowly begins to undo the fantasy space. This is visually displayed in a panoply of lights outside the big window that penetrates and deforms the penthouse setting. Rupert's exposure of the lie coincides with the logic of desire. Once fantasy and desire intersect, cinematic space in *Rope* is rendered with uncertainty to depict the excess of the gaze.

The aforementioned scenes from *Alien* and *Carrie* exemplify the gaze as an unknowable force. The shock and horror we experience derives from our investment in seeing and looking in both films. At the same time, we do not fully realize how our desire distorts the visual field until we encounter the force of the gaze, as in the case of Carrie's hand exploding out of the grave, or discovering that the alien has clandestinely boarded the escape shuttle. But this should not suggest that an excessive style of cinema is not important for the analysis of the cinema of confinement. Excess can be disarming, as when films show viewers too much, or what McGowan terms the "cinema of fantasy." The cinema of fantasy, according to McGowan, reveals "little concern for producing desire. They focus on disturbing spectators with moments of too much satisfaction rather than reminding spectators of their dissatisfaction."[22] De Palma's use of the split-screen format (the division of separate spaces shown simultaneously within one frame) during the prom massacre sequence in *Carrie* exemplifies the cinema of fantasy.[23] After the pig's blood splatters all over Carrie in slow motion, we hear her mother's voice repeatedly say: "They're all going to laugh at you." Carrie suddenly unleashes her telekinetic powers and entraps everyone in the gymnasium. Panic ensues as Carrie water cannons the students and faculty with a firehose. One student attempts to take control of the hose, causing the stream of water to gush upwards at the lights and explode, causing an electrical storm. Fire engulfs the students and faculty as Carrie creepily exits the gymnasium. Unlike the grave sequence at the end of the film, the prom massacre scene overwhelms us with too much satisfaction. The inundation of visual information is reflected by De Palma displaying a large portion of the sequence in the split-screen mode, as if to suggest that one frame or image is not enough to show us the hell storm unleased by Carrie. The prom massacre sequence is an example of what I will refer to as the excess of the gaze made knowable within the field of vision. It is a moment when a film disturbs and shocks us with too much satisfaction.

The excess of the gaze not only demonstrates the attraction and appeal of confinement cinema, but can provide insights into the mechanisms of power and ideology. As explained previously, the symbolic order provides the systems of language for communication in everyday life. The symbolic is where we construct an experience of reality in shielding us from the disturbance of the real. To encounter the real demonstrates the vulnerability of the symbolic order. As Jennifer Friedlander observes, the purpose of "reality" is "to protect us from the Real, by providing us with a symbolic framework that covers over the Real's disruptive effects."[24] The symbolic order functions by masking excess in order to present the illusion of the world as harmonious and whole. From this standpoint, ideology needs fantasy as a supplement in order to exercise its power. This is because fantasy provides the subject with distance from the antagonism that underlies the symbolic order. Here the excess of the gaze can unmask an obscene underside of fantasy. In Stanley Kubrick's Vietnam War film *Full Metal Jacket* (1987), Pyle (Vincent D'Onofrio) gets too close to his fantasy as the model Marine during the boot camp training segment, which causes him to suffer a mental breakdown.[25] Pyle kills Sgt. Hartman (R. Lee Ermey) with his M14 and then kills himself. Kubrick shows viewers a dark underside of how authority is exercised in war and its damaging effects by having Pyle literally malfunction. As Todd McGowan explains, excess in Kubrick's films reveals "the hidden enjoyment of symbolic authority itself."[26] The exposure of excess in Kubrick's films is not simply an assault on ideology itself. Rather, as McGowan explains, Kubrick's films undercut "ideology's fantasmatic underside" by revealing the symbolic authority as excessive.[27] In *Full Metal Jacket*, the excess of the gaze is rendered visible and knowable as a means for viewers to see the mechanics of power and authority and its obscene underside. From this perspective, fantasy can have both peaceful and horrific results. In the case of *Full Metal Jacket*, fantasy shows viewers an obscene underside of how military power is exercised during the Vietnam War. A number of the films under analysis in this project explore the ideological dimension of excess, including post–Cold War anxieties and paranoia in *10 Cloverfield Lane*, neo-Nazism in Oliver Stone's *Talk Radio* (1988) and Jeremy Saulnier's *Green Room* (2015), war and trauma in *The Wall*, and screen culture, surveillance, and news media sensationalism in Joel Schumacher's *Phone Booth* (2002).

Chapter Overview

The goal of this project is to explore how the excess of the gaze is articulated within the confined setting. Although the ordering of the films under analysis (chapter 2 through chapter 7) has a historical trajectory, I have not set out to give a historical analysis of confinement cinema. Confinement films are not exclusive to one genre—they are often found in horror films, thrillers, and dramas. Some confinement scenarios include characters who are trapped or marooned: *Lifeboat* (Alfred Hitchcock, 1944), *The Poseidon Adventure* (Ronald Neame, 1972), *Open Water* (Chris Kentis, 2003), *I Am Legend* (Francis Lawrence, 2007), *127 Hours* (Danny Boyle, 2010), *Gravity* (Alfonso Cuarón, 2013), *Life of Pi* (Ang Lee, 2012), *All Is Lost* (J. C. Chandor, 2013), and *The Tunnel* (Kim Seong-hun, 2016). Other confinement scenarios feature characters who are held captive: *Misery* (Rob Reiner, 1990), *Buried* (Rodrigo Cortés, 2010), *Captain Phillips* (Paul Greengrass, 2013), *Grand Piano* (Eugenio Mira, 2013), *Don't Breathe*

(Fede Álvarez, 2016), *The Beguiled* (Sofia Coppola, 2017), *Spilt* (M. Night Shyamalan, 2017), and *Get Out* (Jordan Peele, 2017). Confinement can result from weather or a force of nature: *The Shining* (Stanley Kubrick, 1980), *This Is the End* (Seth Rogen and Evan Goldberg, 2013), and *The Hateful Eight* (Quentin Tarantino, 2015); or entrapment due to a supernatural force such as monsters, vampires, and/or aliens: *Night of the Living Dead* (George Romero, 1968), *Alien*, *Quarantine* (John Erick Dowdle, 2008), and *Train to Busan* (Yeon Sang-ho, 2016). Confinement can be due to physical and/or mental disorder, such as in *Rear Window* (Alfred Hitchcock, 1954), *Whatever Happened to Baby Jane?* (Robert Aldrich, 1962), *Lady in a Cage* (Walter Grauman, 1964), *Wait Until Dark* (Terence Young, 1967), *The Passion of Anna* (Ingmar Bergman, 1969), and *The Bitter Tears of Petra von Kant* (Rainer Werner Fassbinder, 1972). In some cases, confinement is a film's experiment with a real-time depiction of the event, such as in *Rope*, *Russian Ark* (Alexander Sokurov, 2002), and *Locke* (Steven Knight, 2013). Of course, confinement can be imposed by the law and the stripping of one's personal freedom, as in the prison narrative. Given the vast number of prison movies, which arguably can be considered their own genre, they will not be explored in this study. Rather, I want to provide a survey of films, tracking how each film under investigation engages with excess.

Chapter 1 explores how the knowability and unknowability of the gaze operate in two recent confinement films: *Room* and *Green Room*. The remaining chapters will examine how these two dimensions of the gaze perform in each film under analysis. Some of the movies I have chosen to analyze have received little scholarly attention, such as chapter 3's analysis of Ingmar Bergman's *The Passion of Anna* and chapter 5's investigation of Oliver Stone's *Talk Radio*. Although *The Passion of Anna* is the only non–English language film explored in this study, I believe it is important to consider one of Bergman's films for this study because the term "chamber play" comes directly from his works, such as his trilogy *Through a Glass Darkly* (1961), *Winter Light* (1962), and *The Silence* (1963), as well as his Faro island films of the 1960s, such as *Persona* (1966), *Shame* (1968), and *Hour of the Wolf* (1968). Chapter 5 analyzes *Talk Radio*, a film that has been overshadowed by Oliver Stone's Vietnam War movies in the late 1980s. Here, I explore the connections between excess and ethical action in relation to the disembodied voice, or what Michel Chion terms *acousmêtre*. A technology that plays a vital role in the cinema of confinement is the phone to communicate with the other outside of the confined space. Chapter 6 takes up the relationship between excess and the disembodied voice and telecommunication in *Phone Booth* and *Locke*. It should be no surprise that many films of confinement are characteristic of the horror/thriller genre. Chapter 2 examines Alfred Hitchcock's *Rope* as an early example of how excess operates in confinement cinema as a mode of suspense. Chapter 4 explores the relationship between excess and Stanley Kubrick's depiction of the supernatural in *The Shining*. Chapter 7 focuses on the logic of desire and symbolic fiction in *10 Cloverfield Lane* as what can be described as a sci-fi containment captive narrative.

Lastly, except for *Rope* and *Locke*, the films under analysis are not purely confined to one room or setting. There is often a lead-in to the chamber space, or where the majority of the film's action will occur, such as in *The Shining*, *Phone Booth*, *127 Hours*, and *10 Cloverfield Lane*. In some cases, the film will briefly cut to another location and return to the confined setting, as in *The Shining* and *Misery*.

Certainly, there are numerous films one can draw upon in examining narratives that take place in a limited setting. Notably, there has recently been a surge in confinement cinema, particularly the emergence of torture porn films, such as *Saw* (James Wan, 2004) and *Hostel* (Eli Roth, 2005).[28] In the conclusion of this study, I address a larger, perhaps speculative question of the recent increase in confinement cinema in relation to digital media and cyberspace. Here, I attempt to connect the recent surge of confinement cinema to the ease of crossing boundaries within virtual reality. The internet has allowed one to traverse the digital ether, whether it is shopping on Amazon, Skyping with a friend, or accessing databases of movies and television titles through services such as Netflix and Hulu. The cinema of confinement appears to have an attraction in connection to digital technology because it imposes a limit or impossibility on the characters' movement within space. The smartphone enables us to always be in contact with the grid. We have GPS technology to help us if we are lost. It should be no surprise that many of the recent films of confinement—particularly movies involving characters who are trapped or held captive—are about making contact outside of their entrapped spaces. In the concluding thoughts of this project, I consider the attraction and surge of recent confinement cinema, specifically plots that involve the inability to use digital technologies to communicate with others.

1

Excess in Confinement in *Room* and *Green Room*

> Visually, shooting such a large proportion of a film inside a single, small room might seem like a problem—after all, don't films rely on scale, movement, shifting locations and so on? . . . In general, the tone of the film [*Room*]—across the entire story—should be low-key and natural; shifts in emphasis, moments of suspense, pathos, horror, catharsis have to achieve without the viewers' attention being drawn to the mechanics.
>
> —Lenny Abrahamson, director of *Room*

> I designed a cluster-fuck of eight people stuck in a room against an army of Nazi skinheads.
>
> —Jeremy Saulnier, director of *Green Room*

The above quotations refer to two highly acclaimed movies of 2015 that focus on characters trapped in a room. A drama/thriller, *Room* tells the story of Joy (Brie Larson) and her five-year-old son Jack (Jacob Tremblay), who are held prisoner for seven years in a shed converted into a room. *Green Room* is a crime/horror/thriller about a hardcore punk rock band called The Ain't Rights who discover a dead body in the backstage room called the "green room," located in an Oregon club run by Nazi skinheads. In both films, escape is the primary objective. In *Room*, Joy must outwit her captor Old Nick (Sean Bridgers) in order to save herself and Jack. In *Green Room*, The Ain't Rights must battle Nazi skinheads outside the door of the green room, or die. Although *Room* and *Green Room* are representative of confinement cinema, they differ in their stylistic approaches to building and sustaining suspense and narrative tension over a long duration of time.

This chapter examines how the gaze operates in both films as a mode of shock and attraction. In *Room*, the gaze emerges as an unknowable force that threatens the boundary between reality and the real. After Jack and Joy defeat Old Nick, Jack struggles to adapt to life outside of the room. I argue that in order for Jack to fully transition into "outer reality," he must surrender his fantasy of life inside the room. *Green Room* demonstrates the distorting presence of the gaze as a knowable force by showing viewers too much satisfaction, as demonstrative in Saulnier's quote above.[1] Yet the film's visualization of the excess of the gaze reveals a tension pertaining to neo-Nazism and the American hardcore scene. I argue that the excess of the gaze provides insights into what Robert T. Wood terms a "subcultural schism," factions within a subculture. Lastly, what ties these films together is that the captives both utilize a fictional scenario to overcome their captors.

Inner Reality: *Misery* and *Room*

Abrahamson's quotation comes from a letter he wrote to author Emma Donoghue trying to convince her why he was the right director to adapt her novel to the screen. Abrahamson's letter expresses the challenge of stylizing the first half of the film, almost all of which takes place entirely in one room, while staying true to the novel's integrity. He states, "Any film version of 'Room,' which imposes an over-energized camera style, or any other self-conscious visual device, in the mistaken belief that the physical constraint of location needs to be somehow compensated for, will fail because it will lose the taste of reality on which the power of the novel depends."[2] Indeed, constraint is key in capturing the horror of Joy's situation. But we should not think that Abrahamson's aesthetic choice makes for a boring or dull experience in watching the first half of *Room*. The challenge of a limited-location film is to prevent what can be best described as a filmed stage play. This is not to suggest that movies based on plays are not pleasurable to watch. Rather, my question is: how do filmmakers articulate cinematic space and build narrative tension within a confined location without falling into the fixed-tableau space of early cinema? If *Room* is filmed in a low-key manner, then why is this section of the story—which takes up almost the first half of the movie—so unsettling? How does Abrahamson render cinematic space that both narratively engages the viewer and visually reflects Joy's dire situation?

My claim is that *Room*'s single-room suspense derives from Abrahamson's engagement with excess. Consider again Abrahamson's concern regarding stylizing camerawork as a means of compensating for *Room*'s limited location. Certainly, frantic camerawork and fast editing constitute excess within the confined space. But this is not what Abrahamson aesthetically and emotionally envisions. How does he achieve suspense and narrative tension within the confined space of a single room if he is relying upon traditional photography and natural shifts? Wouldn't this potentially bore the viewer? Certainly, the first half of *Room* does not lack narrative suspense.

Abrahamson's choice to not utilize hyper-stylized camera work demonstrates how the unknowability of the gaze operates in *Room*. *Room*'s narrative suspense derives from Abrahamson allowing the gaze to emerge with disquieting results, where the realms of fantasy and desire collide. This raises a question: how does Abrahamson create a peaceful and spirited fantasy space when Joy is held prisoner? Wouldn't this simply be a film of desire and lack? Abrahamson creates a fantasy space through the eyes of Jack. Fantasy operates in the room through Jack's perspective, such as the different scenarios he comes up with and the parts of the room that have their own magic, particularly the skylight. For Joy and the viewers, the skylight window connotes freedom and safety. But for Jack the skylight is outer space, a limit to the world. The skylight for Jack is the boundary between reality and the real; it is his protective screen that keeps him safe within the room. But when Old Nick enters the room, it is a tense moment for both Joy and the viewer. Joy instructs Jack to hide in the closet because she knows that Nick is going to rape her. As such, Jack does not fully realize that Old Nick is a threat to his fantasy of the room.

Old Nick's first appearance in the room is seen through Jack's eyes, framed through the shutters of the closet, and we are unable to get a good look at him. The captor or villain in captive films is often introduced as a mysterious figure. For example, in Rob Reiner's *Misery*, Annie Wilkes (Kathy Bates) is first shown in fragments as she rescues her favorite writer, Paul Sheldon (James Caan), after his car slides off the road during a blizzard in Silver Springs, Colorado. We never see Annie's face, just fragments of her body, in order to create a mystery about her character as she pulls Paul out of his crashed Mustang. In *Room*, the partial reveal of Old Nick closely coincides with the distorting presence of the gaze. Through Jack's perspective, we are unable to make out who Old Nick is, demonstrating not only his uncertain status, but also our inability to master cinematic space. Not unlike the locker in which Ripley hides in the escape shuttle in *Alien* as explained in this book's introduction, the closet for Jack is a space that protects him from Old Nick as the embodiment of the real. Old Nick's first arrival reveals what is in the room more than the room itself. He is excess and disturbs the fantasy scenario that Jack paints for viewers. As such, Old Nick not only endangers his mother, but is a threat to Jack's fantasy space within the room.

A trait often found in the cinema of confinement is character resourcefulness. These tactics often entail characters finding objects within the confined space, which are then turned into tools or weapons to escape their setting or to defeat their captor. Just as cinematic fantasy can visually manifest the excess of the gaze, the character held captive can create fantasy scenarios, enticing the captor's desire and, thus, setting a trap for him in planning an escape. In *Room*, Joy tells Jack that she once used the toilet bowl cover to attack Old Nick. Such ingenuity is often the case in captive-confinement films. The first move of the character held captive is provoked by instinct rather than logic. In *Misery*, when Annie forces Paul to burn the only copy of his manuscript for his new novel, he realizes his life is in danger and he must escape the room or possibly die. He instinctively tries to flee the room, even though he cannot walk. When he reaches the bedroom door, he discovers it is locked from the outside. Worse, Paul cannot get back into the bed. In order to escape, Paul turns to logic and reasoning as he begins to hide painkillers in his bed, one of the many steps he plans in order to escape Annie's house. In short, Paul has to trick Annie. To do this, Paul has to, using Joan Copjec's expression, read Annie's desire by sustaining her fantasy of him as her favorite writer. Annie, as the obsessive fan, treasures Paul and his *Misery* novels. In order for Paul to plan his escape, he has to keep up this appearance as the writer of *Misery*. Likewise, the only way for Joy and Jack to escape the room is to "trick Old Nick." This involves Joy telling Jack the true story of the room. But learning there is a real world outside of the room is shocking for Jack, because it involves removing the fantasy screen that protects him from the exterior world. As Jack forcefully says to Joy, "I don't believe in your stinky world." Later in the film, Jack witnesses Old Nick and Joy fighting. In response, Old Nick turns off the electricity and heat in the room. Witnessing a dark dimension of Old Nick, Jack no longer trusts him. Old Nick is not only a threat to Jack's mother, but also a danger to his fantasy space within the room. Here, Joy comes up with the plan for their escape. Jack will pretend to play dead as a result of Old Nick turning off the heat in the room. She will roll Jack in the room's carpet with the hopes that Old Nick will bury him by driving his body far away from the room. Jack's job is to unroll out of the carpet and flee Old Nick when the truck stops. Once Jack finds help, he must deliver Joy's handwritten plea for help. Here, an ordinary object, a carpet to roll up Jack, loses its primary meaning, becoming a signifier of escape. The irony is that Joy and Jack trick Old Nick not by resorting to violence or force, but by using a fiction or fantasy scenario. The key to Joy and Jack's escape is not to physically attack Old Nick, but to elicit his desire by creating a fiction within a fiction, a topic further explored in chapter 7 on *10 Cloverfield Lane.* Jack and Joy have to create a scenario that engages Old Nick's desire, to catch him in a trap. In order for Old Nick to sustain his fantasy of keeping Joy captive, he must get rid of Jack's body. Likewise for Annie in *Misery*, once she reads that Misery dies in Paul's last novel, she burns his latest manuscript, a personal story based on Paul's life. Annie forces Paul to write a new novel that resurrects Misery. Indeed, the return of Misery is the return of Annie's fantasy. Paul has to sustain Annie's fantasy while planning his escape. In other words, Paul has to keep the excess of the gaze at a distance in order to play a fiction within a fiction. Paul must perform Annie's fantasy as her beloved romance writer. When Paul fails to sustain her fantasy, Annie becomes a violent force, as when she breaks his ankles in the gruesome "hobbler" scene. Paul's survival depends on preventing Annie's obscene underside from emerging. Indeed, Joy and Jack's escape derives not from physically attacking Old Nick, but from playing on his desire. Joy knows that what threatens Old Nick is losing his fantasy of controlling and violating her at will. Removing Jack's dead body wrapped in the carpet keeps Old Nick's fantasy of Joy alive.

Outer Reality

In the first sequence outside the room, Old Nick drives to dispose of Jack. Abrahamson does not cut back to Joy waiting in the room. We only hear Joy's voice telling Jack: "truck, wiggle out, run." The narrative stays exclusively with Jack's perspective as he rolls out of the carpet. He looks up and sees the sky, trying to perceptually process the outer world. Once the truck stops, Jack plops down on the truck's flatbed, which alerts Old Nick. Jack escapes as Old Nick goes after him. Jack trips and falls. Old Nick bumps into a man walking his dog. Jack yells for help, holding Joy's message. Old Nick yanks the message from Jack's hand and tells the man to mind his own business. The man says that he is calling the police. Old Nick drops Jack on the ground and speeds off with Joy's message. Jack remains on the ground with shock as he looks up at the sky, overwhelmed by the immensity of the outer world. He grabs a leaf from the ground and looks at it with wonder. Later, a police officer asks Jack questions. Her voice is processed with an unusual amount of reverb to underscore Jack's distorted perspective in processing the world outside of the room, as if reality itself has been suspended. Jack has trouble answering the officer's questions. But when the officer asks what his mother's name is, he removes Joy's tooth from his mouth and says: "A bit of mom." Indeed,

Joy's tooth is a reminder of the room so Jack can cope with the vastness of the outer world. Joy's tooth demonstrates the paradox of the real. The tooth is a piece of the real that does not traumatize Jack, but comforts him. The real is non-sense and, at the same time, enables Jack to render this non-sense in order to cope with the outer world. On the one hand, the real reveals a fissure within the symbolic order. On the other hand, the real operates as an empty screen upon which to project our fantasies.[3] The same can be said of the cinema screen itself. The screen presents the moving-image itself and what is absent or lacking in the moving-image. The screen does not function like a mirror by offering the viewer an image of plenitude that can only be undone by revealing the film's processes of mediation. Rather, the screen operates as both plenitude *and lack.*[4] It is the absence or lack that elicits our desire to see (what we do not know). At the same time, our desire to see sets a trap for our potential encounter with the gaze—our blind spot within the field of vision.

Once the police learn where Joy is held captive, Abrahamson stays with Jack in the police vehicle as he looks out the window. Out of the darkness, Joy appears, running in slow motion toward the police vehicle. The audio drops out as we only hear the piano of the score as Joy and Jack reunite. The uplifting score and slow-motion photography highlight the success of the plan. Yet we are left with uncertainty when Jack asks Joy if they can go back to bed in the room. In order for Joy to enact her plan of escape, she had to ensure that Jack no longer trusted Old Nick. But Jack's belief in the room has not receded. Indeed, the escape and rescue sequence captures Jack's experience of the outer world without its fantasy frame. As Matthew Flisfeder puts it, "When the [framework of] fantasy breaks down, 'reality' becomes too Real for the subject to bear."[5] The outer world is freedom for Joy. But for Jack, the world outside the room is the real. The moment Jack enters the outer world, the film's visual and audio registers radically change in order to reflect the breakdown of the barrier between reality and the real. Rather than utilizing a hyper-stylized cinema to energize cinematic space, the suspense in the first half of *Room* operates by Abrahamson employing excess as a traumatic and unknowable force that unhinges cinematic space.

The last half of the film explores Jack's transformation in the outer world. At the end of the film, at Jack's request, they return to the shed to visit the room for one last time. Jack opens the door and is confused to see that the room is much smaller and different than when he was held captive. Here we have a complete reversal of the first half of the film: the room is now real—destroyed of its fantasy space. The shed is none other than a common thing—deprived of its luster for Jack. The shed has been transformed into what Žižek describes (paraphrasing Lacan) as "a gift of shit."[6] When Jack says goodbye to the objects that made up his world for the first five years of his life in the shed, he is, in a sense, traversing the fantasy. By traversing the fantasy, Jack frees himself of the fantasy he had invested in the shed. For Jack, the shed is the real with which he now identifies.

The Gaze as a Knowable Force: *Green Room*

As explained in my introduction, an excessive style of cinema can be disarming, as when films show viewers too much. For example, overstylized and extremely violent films, such as Tony Scott's *True Romance* (1993), Oliver Stone's *Natural Born Killers* (1994), and Park Chan-wook's *Oldboy* (2003), render and tame the gaze. Here, the gaze loses some of its disturbing impact because it is made knowable within the field of vision, rather than as an unknowable and invading force that breaks down the barrier between reality and the real. These films allow us to see and experience excess by showing us too much satisfaction, such as Mickey (Woody Harrelson) and Mallory's (Juliette Lewis) cartoonish violence in *Natural Born Killers*, or the long take of the hallway fight sequence in *Oldboy* where Oh Dae-su (Choi Min-sik) takes down a group of henchmen with a hammer.

At the same time, allowing us to see excess as a knowable force can reveal fantasy's obscene underside at a political and social level. Ideology functions by not revealing its excessive dimension. The power of ideology is not to proclaim itself as ideology, but rather to appear natural and spontaneous, or what Antonio Gramsci terms "common sense."[7] Here, the excess of the gaze as a knowable presence within the field of vision can be deployed to uncover the workings of power and authority. This brings us to Jeremy Saulnier's *Green Room*, a film that explores a dark and obscene underside of the American hardcore music scene: Nazi skinheads. The Ain't Rights are a struggling hardcore band made up of members Pat (Anton Yelchin), Sam (Alia Shawkat), Tiger (Callum Turner), and Reece (Joe Cole). Like many hardcore and punk bands, The Ain't Rights try to get by from gig to gig with little or no money. This struggle is clearly signaled at the start of the film when Sam and Pat siphon gas from other vehicles to fill their van in order to make it to their next gig. Early in the film, after one of their gigs is canceled, Tad (David W. Thompson), a local radio host in the Pacific Northwest, contacts his cousin Daniel (Mark Webber) and arranges a show for The Ain't Rights in Portland. When The Ain't Rights arrive, they shockingly discover that it is a club full of Nazi skinheads. Here they meet Gabe (Macon Blair), who is in charge of running the club. He tells them, "The owner doesn't fuck around with the fire code." Keeping the fire department (or any municipal department) away from the club serves to shield the Nazi skinheads' secret place from unwanted attention and thus allowing it to remain off the grid. Moreover, this admonition suggests that these Nazi skinheads are organized. The Ain't Rights play their set, which includes a cover of the Dead Kennedys' "Nazi Punks Fuck Off." The performance of the song is both hilarious and frightening because it angers many of the Nazi skinheads. Indeed, covering the Dead Kennedys' song demonstrates The Ain't Right's courage to resist the Nazi skinheads, in spite of being an unwelcome presence in the hardcore community. At the same time, their performance disrupts the Nazi skinheads' fantasy space as a place of gathering. We are unsure if The Ain't Rights will make it out of the club alive. Surprisingly, they are able to complete their set without any acts of violence, suggesting that the Nazi skinheads cannot afford to bring unwanted attention to the club. As we later learn, the club is also a place where they make heroin, which is the source of the group's income.

After their set, The Ain't Rights are paid by Gabe, and all appears well. But as they are about to leave, Sam realizes she left her phone in the green room. Pat enters the room to retrieve the phone and discovers a young woman named Emily (Taylor Tunes) dead on the floor with a knife in her head. In the room are Nazi skinheads, Werm (Brent Werzner), and Emily's friend Amber (Imogen Poots). Emily was killed because she and her boyfriend, Daniel (who arranged the gig for The Ain't Rights), were planning to escape the Nazis' group. Pat calls 911 and contacts the police for help. Immediately, Big Justin, the club's bouncer (Eric Edelstein), confiscates the phone and scolds Werm for not locking the door to the green room as instructed. Werm's inability to follow Big Justin's instructions illustrate that the Nazi skinheads must be organized in order to sustain their power while not attracting attention to their place of gathering.

Emily and Daniel's plan of escape reveals an unwritten law of the Nazi skinhead club: when one becomes a member of this club, one is a member for life. Leaving the group threatens the power of the club. Saulnier exploits this unwritten law of the Nazi skinheads as a cinema of excess and extreme violence. This begins with The Ain't Rights overpowering Big Justin, stealing his gun, and blockading the door. They hold Big Justin hostage as a means to bargain with the Nazi skinheads outside the door. Darcy (Patrick Stewart), the bar owner and head of the Nazi skinheads, is called in as a negotiator to "mop up" the mess. Darcy is frighteningly cunning and operates rationally as he puts forth a plan to cover up Emily's death and dispose of The Ain't Rights. Darcy pays two young Nazi skinheads to stab each other in order to take the blame for Pat's 911 call. After the police arrest the two Nazi skinheads, Darcy gathers a group of Nazi skinheads to kill The Ain't Rights. At the green room door, Darcy requests that the band surrender the gun, telling them that the situation is under control. Both Darcy and the band go back and forth in terms of negotiations. Neither the band nor the viewer can see Darcy during the negotiations; we only hear his voice off-screen. Similar to Old Nick, who is first shown in fragments, Darcy's disembodied off-screen voice demonstrates his power as well as his unreliability. Even though Pat is skeptical of Darcy's terms, he and the other members of the band agree and slowly hand him the gun through a slight opening of the door. Amber warns them not to negotiate with Darcy. But The Ain't Rights do not trust her, for they believe she is also a Nazi skinhead, which she outright denies. Amber is correct about Darcy's motives. This is confirmed when the skinheads outside the door slice up Pat's arm. The band re-barricades the door, knowing that Darcy does not want to negotiate but to kill them. After the attack on Pat, Big Justin attacks the band. Reece chokes him to death as the war with the Nazis skinheads begins.

Darcy's violent attack on Pat is the moment when the film becomes what Todd McGowan terms a "cinema of fantasy," where the excess of the gaze overwhelms the viewer with too much enjoyment. The Ain't Rights must put a plan into effect in order to safely escape the room. Their plan, however, is fraught with problems because they are not organized. They do not think logically to overcome their captors. In their first attack, three members of the band instantly die, leaving Pat and Amber as the only survivors. Whereas *Room* allows the gaze to emerge with disturbing effects, *Green Room* exploits the excess of the gaze through hyper-stylization and an excess of violence. After the attack on Pat, *Green Room* presents the gaze as knowable, disturbing viewers with too much satisfaction. Even though, as Saulnier points out, "there are no gratuitous close-ups when there's a death,"[8] the film provides little respite in terms of its violence. Whereas Joy uses her skills to trick Old Nick in *Room*, The Ain't Rights operate instinctually within the moment, grounding the film with explosive violence. As Saulnier explains, "The band members [The Ain't Rights] are not idiots. They're just real people. When you see a wrap-up of real life news stories or incidents where there are humans trapped in a pressure cooker environment or things go wrong where there's chaos, people behave in very stupid ways."[9]

Space, Fiction, and Subcultural Schism

The chaotic articulation of cinematic space in *Green Room* reflects the film's excess of the gaze. The ordering of space is not depicted as continuous and fluid, as we typically find in many Hollywood films. Rather, space is rendered excessive, making it difficult for viewers to master their looking. This last point is key in terms of understanding the different ways in which space is articulated in the cinema of confinement in relation to the excess of the gaze. The deployment of excess is vital in energizing a film's confined space. The fact that many filmmakers (particularly those from classical cinema) have articulated space as stable does not mean that space is inherently neutral. It is how the filmmaker depicts the image's excess information. Tom Gunning makes this point in his analysis of narrative discourse in early cinema. As he explains, "Although a filmmaker can make images relatively abstract, they will still contain a plethora of information compared to a verbal description."[10] For Gunning, it is a matter of how the filmmaker renders the image from showing to telling through discourse. For example, the classical narrator mode of Hollywood typically subordinates space as a vestige for narrative meaning. David Bordwell points out that the principle of subordinating space for narrative thrust is most notable in the "bad" cut.[11] The jump cut or imbalance of space edited between shots draws attention to space itself. From this perspective, space in the classical mode of narration strives toward neutralization of the excess of the image, as is often seen in the shot/reverse shot technique. Here, the cross-cutting between characters does not violate the established axis line between two characters talking. The editing between character A and character B functions through eyeline match edits. When character A glances at character B, the cut of the reverse shot must match what A sees. Bordwell explains that objective reality "of the action independent of the act of filming is analogous to that stable space of proscenium theatrical representation, in which the spectator is always positioned beyond the fourth wall."[12] The director must establish the 180-degree line, so that the edits between the two characters occur frontally. Certainly, recent films, particularly action films, often violate the 180-degree rule in attempting to depict space from a 360-degree perspective. Steven Shaviro goes so far as to claim that the new "stylistics" in the articulation of space in recent cinema is "post-continuity," where big blockbuster films such as *Transformers* (Michael Bay, 2007) are preoccupied "with [how] immediate effects trump any concern for broader continuity—whether on the immediate shot-by-shot level, or on that of the overall narrative."[13] From this perspective, the violation of the 180-degree rule closely corresponds to the depiction of the gaze that overwhelms the viewer as a knowable force within the field of vision. This is one of the primary effects of the gaze in *Green Room*: space is rendered as excessive to reflect the frenzy and chaos of the band's situation. In *Room*, the emergence of the gaze collapses the barrier between reality and the real for Jack. By contrast, *Green Room* exploits and renders the excess gaze by showing viewers too much information that coincides with the film's extreme violence, as well as The Ain't Rights' lack of organization to defeat their captors.

But this weakness does not eliminate the possibility of the captives becoming organized and vanquishing their captors. Here, *Room* and *Green Room* both use a fictional scenario in order to outwit and overcome their captors. Toward the end of *Green Room*, Amber and Pat sit in the green room trying to figure out how to escape. Pat tells Amber about a time when he played paintball and was teamed against ex-marines. The team that Pat was on was getting slaughtered by vets from the Iraq War. As Pat explains, "They knew real war and played real war." They knew the tactics such as hand-signaling and flanking. Pat's friend Rick got fed up and no longer cared about getting shot or losing the game. In the last match, Pat explains that Rick went to all-out war and wiped out the whole team until they were dead. Amber adds, "pretend dead." Pat says, "We can't play real war." Amber responds, "Let's *pretend*." That is, let's pretend to play real war. Here, Amber and Pat dress up the part of soldiers, painting their faces for an all-out attack on the Nazi skinheads. By enacting the scenario of soldiers ready for war, Amber and Pat are able to defeat the Nazi skinheads and escape the club. In *Room*, Joy plays on Old Nick's desire in order to trick him. In *Green Room*, Amber and Pat's performing a fiction within the fiction *organizes* them in order to overcome the Nazi skinheads. In both cases, survival depends on the captives using fictional scenarios to outwit their captors. Yet both films render the gaze differently in terms of excess and cinematic space.

The frantic style of *Green Room* has a social function in revealing an obscene underside of the American hardcore scene. The hardcore scene emerged out of the punk rock movement in the late 1970s, spawning bands such as Bad Brains, Minor Threat, Misfits, Agnostic Front, Cro-Mags, Circle Jerks, and Black Flag. Not unlike punk, hardcore is a reaction to the status quo and the hegemony of commercialized music. Yet hardcore's dark underside is that the very same music that connects its members also attracts Nazi skinheads, a faction within the scene. This is notable when Werm asks The Ain't Rights the name of the second-to-last song they played. Pat responds, "Toxic Evolution." Werm says that the song was "fucking hard." He shockingly adds that it was during their performance of "Toxic Evolution" that he killed Emily. Although Nazi skinheads share their love of hardcore music with members outside their group, they do not share the same values of racial harmony. Writing on the straight-edge hardcore community, Robert T. Wood explains, "Racist and non-racist factions of the American skinhead subculture . . . stylistically remained similar, yet each faction adopted different subcultural symbols. Racist skinheads marked their bodies, clothes, magazines and subcultural spaces with distinctly Nazi symbols such as the swastika and the death's head."[14] This is exactly what Amber recognizes before Pat is attacked during the negotiations with Darcy. Through the vent of the door of the green room, she sees that the bootlaces belonging to the people outside the door are red, which is a fashion symbol of the Nazi skinheads. Indeed, a song such as the Dead Kennedys' "Nazi Punks Fuck Off" is meant to preserve the integrity and values of the hardcore community in supporting inclusivity and racial harmony within the scene. Perhaps more importantly, the Nazi skinheads demonstrate that a subculture is never totalized in their vision or manifesto. There is always an opening within a subculture that can create a faction. This fissure can lead to a tension within a subculture, or what Woods calls a "subcultural schism."[15] The schism within a subculture can result in new recruits forming their own group, as in the case of the Nazi skinheads within the hardcore scene. Emily and Daniel attempt to leave the group because they no longer share the Nazi skinheads' values and nonracial harmony. As such, *Green Room* exposes this faction within the hardcore scene as "full frontal gore." The film's exploitation of excess demonstrates a disturbance that undercuts the functioning order of the hardcore subculture community. Here, the film's depiction of the excess of the gaze as a distorting presence is akin to the "Nazi" schism within the American hardcore scene. Yet this schism is not an exterior force that invades the subculture, but rather emerges from *within* the subculture itself.

Both *Room* and *Green Room* show two articulations of the gaze at work within a confined setting. In the case of *Room*, the gaze is rendered unknowable by allowing excess to manifest through the collision of fantasy and desire. In *Green Room*, the excess of the gaze is made knowable by overwhelming viewers with too much satisfaction in order to demonstrate the Nazi skinheads as a dark dimension within the hardcore scene. Together, *Room* and *Green Room* exemplify the fact that films that take place within a limited location can be shocking, suspenseful, and engaging.

2

Big Window, Big Other: Enjoyment and Spectatorship in Alfred Hitchcock's *Rope*

It goes without saying that Alfred Hitchcock was publicly lauded as the master of suspense who delivered the goods in a great number of films, such as *Strangers on a Train* (1951), *Rear Window* (1954), *Vertigo* (1958), *Psycho* (1960), and *The Birds* (1963), to name but a few. Yet Hitchcock was very much interested in experimental cinema. Peter Wollen explains that Hitchcock vacillated between seeing himself as a "100 per cent" commercial filmmaker of suspense cinema and "as a frustrated art-film director." For Wollen, "Hitchcock the public showman was in constant conflict with Hitchcock the private aesthete."[1] Hitchcock's interest in avant-garde art is evident in much of his work, such as the flashes of color and animation used during John "Scottie" Ferguson's (James Stewart) nightmare in *Vertigo,* and Salvador Dali's surrealistic painting of eyes on curtains during John Ballantyne's (Gregory Peck) dream sequence in *Spellbound* (1945).

Although Hitchcock made some of the greatest suspense thrillers ever put on screen, he was not completely satisfied working within the genre, a frustration he expressed to the French filmmaker François Truffaut. For Hitchcock, Truffaut had much more creative freedom in regard to genre and narrative form. Hitchcock wrote to Truffaut: "You are a free person to make whatever you want. I, on the other hand, can only make what is expected of me; that is, thriller, or a suspense story, and that I find hard to do."[2] This was not the first time Hitchcock expressed to Truffaut the limitations of the thriller genre and classic narrative form. In discussing *Jules and Jim* (1962), Hitchcock stated that Truffaut's film had more room for narrative and character experimentation, something that was harder to achieve in the suspense genre. As Hitchcock explained to Truffaut, "I'm often troubled by the dilemma of whether I should cling to what I call the rising curve of the story, or whether I shouldn't experiment more through a looser form of narrative."[3]

Hitchcock was well aware of the limitations of the thriller and horror genres, as well as the public's perception of him as the master of suspense. But that did not stop him from testing the barriers of these genres.

Indeed, the confined-space narrative of *Rope* is certainly one of Hitchcock's biggest and most challenging formal experimentations in all of his works. *Rope* is both Hitchcock's first color film and the first film he made after completing his seven-picture contract with the Hollywood producer David O. Selznick. The film is known widely for its experiment in long takes, as well as for its indirect representation of the murderers Brandon and Phillip as homosexuals.[4] Yet not much attention has been given to the significance of Brandon and Phillip's penthouse window and the cyclorama of Manhattan as part of Hitchcock "real-time" experiment. It is a film that not only exhibits Hitchcock's interest in avant-garde cinema, as Wollen points out, but his desire to transcend the barriers of the suspense genre that he would later express to Truffaut. At the same time, Hitchcock did not deviate from his bomb theory in terms of creating suspense for spectators in *Rope*. Even within *Rope*'s technical and formal experimentations, narrative immersion was still primary for Hitchcock.

A key way in which *Rope* sustains suspense within the film's confined space is the deployment of the gaze and its relationship to the authority of the big Other. The symbolic order is built on systems of language and networks of communication. It is the realm where meaning is produced and exchanged in everyday life. Embedded within the symbolic order is what Lacan terms the big Other. The big Other puts the symbolic order to work. The big Other is the communal network of social institutions, which entail the rules and unwritten rules of a given society.[5] Whereas the symbolic order is the realm of communication and signification, the manifestation of the real realizes an excess of reality—something that cannot be incorporated into the world of language. This collapse in the visual field is the encounter with the gaze. I argue that the primary function of the big penthouse window in *Rope* is to conceal the excess of the gaze (as a protected and contained space in the penthouse) in order to present a coherent reality to work in tandem with Brandon and Phillip's secret. But when their former professor Rupert Cadell (James Stewart) uncovers their secret and discovers David Kentley's (Dick Hogan) corpse hidden in the trunk, the window's containment of the gaze begins to collapse. The excess of the gaze is depicted in Hitchcock's stylistic uses of light, camerawork, and acting in the final act of the film to coincide with Brandon and Phillip's ensnarement with the authority of the big Other.

Containing the Excess of the Gaze

Rope tells the story of Brandon and Phillip, two college students who strangle and murder their friend David with a rope, and subsequently hide his body in a large Italian chest (*cassone*) in the dining room of their New York penthouse. That same evening Brandon and Phillip host a dinner party: the guests include David's fiancée, Janet (Joan Chandler), David's father, Mr. Kentley (Sir Cedric Hardwicke), and his sister, Mrs. Atwater (Constance Collier). To fulfill their maniacal plan of committing the perfect act of murder, Brandon and Phillip ghoulishly serve food off the chest while David's corpse is secretly concealed within it. Brandon and Phillip's former professor, Rupert, also attends the party. Rupert strongly believes in Friedrich Nietzsche's theory about the right of the superman, a notion that elevates superior beings, privileging them to commit acts of murder on those who are inferior. Ultimately, the superman thesis is the kernel that drives Brandon and Phillip to murder David. Yet it is Rupert who notices something awry, something that "sticks out" with Brandon and Phillip, eventually leading to his discovery of David's body inside the chest. It is Brandon and Phillip's surplus-knowledge that generates the suspense of Hitchcock's penthouse thriller.

Part of understanding Hitchcock's single-space narrative is exploring how German Expressionism shaped his film career. As David A. Cook points out, "this influence was to last throughout his [Hitchcock's] silent period and linger on considerably beyond it."[6] Hitchcock began as an art director and then made his first two films, *The Pleasure Garden* (1925) and *The Mountain Eagle* (1927), at Ufa (Universum Film Aktiengesellschaft) in Germany, so German filmmakers significantly influenced him in their emphasis on the visual. Hitchcock stated: "I've always believed that you can tell as much visually as you can with words. That's what I learned from the Germans."[7] Spawned out of a number of literary and artistic developments, the features of German Expressionism include stylized set design, exaggerated acting, and chiaroscuro photography. Hitchcock was particularly fascinated by the controlling style of German filmmakers in visually depicting haunting moods and atmospheric tension, and this can be traced in many of his films, in such scenes as Miriam's death (Laura Elliot) photographed through the reflection of her dropped glasses at the carnival in *Strangers on a Train* and Norman Bates's (Anthony Perkins) gothic home that hauntingly hovers above his motel operation in *Psycho*.

But German filmmakers also taught Hitchcock that set design can create impressions of reality as a sort of "trick of the eye." Hitchcock learned this specifically when observing F. W. Murnau set up an intricate shot of a railway station in *The Last Laugh* (1924). The scene involved both the use of a mock rail carriage and real passengers, carefully positioned and framed as a way to create forced perspective. Observing Murnau, Hitchcock learned that what is most important in blending the artificial and real components of a set is the illusion of reality that it creates for viewers. Murnau had supposedly told Hitchcock: "What you see on the set does not matter. All that matters is what you see on the screen."[8] We find this effect of forced perspective at work in Hitchcock's set design of the penthouse window and cyclorama of Manhattan in *Rope.* This forced perspective serves the film's correlation to a functional reality and Brandon and Phillip's concealment of their secret.

At a primary level, the penthouse window operates as a textual sign in order to create a "real-time" effect. As the narrative progresses, the skyline slowly darkens as the city lights subtly emerge to create the illusion of the passing of time. Hitchcock stated that he had designed an elaborate cyclorama of the city as "an exact miniature reproduction of nearly 35 miles of New York sky-line lighted by 8000 incandescent light bulbs and 200 neon signs requiring 150 transformers."[9] Steven Jacobs notes that Hitchcock devoted significant attention to the atmospheric shifts of the cityscape seen through the penthouse window, even calling in a Griffith Observatory meteorologist to authenticate the cumulus clouds that float above the city skyline.[10] Of course, these effects of the cyclorama were to support Hitchcock's "real-time" narrative. Moreover, they gave Hitchcock complete control of the elements in the background so that the passing of time appeared natural and unmediated, an effect he learned from Murnau (see figure 2.1).

A second level of the penthouse window is its social and architectural significance. The window's spectacular view of the New York City skyline clearly indicates Brandon and Phillip's wealth and privileged status. Penthouses, as Jacobs notes, were one of the most typical residences of the wealthy and rich. He states that "[the penthouse] drew its mystique from the verticality that was New York's special trademark."[11] Jacobs adds that Brandon and Phillip's penthouse can be seen as part of the skyscraper boom which "opened itself visually to the metropolis by means of great banks of windows."[12] Moreover, the penthouse window and its panoramic view indicate a new environment of glass properties and Modernist architecture. Anne Friedberg notes that the potential of glass is that it "performs a visual dematerialization, the material barriers of glass . . . isolate the other senses."[13] As such, the window is both transparent and a barrier, providing spectacular views while protecting observers from exterior elements such as cold, wind, and rain. Friedberg writes, "Plate glass performed this separation of the senses, in which it also contributes to the virtuality of experience."[14] The transparent barrier of the penthouse window not only helps to generate a "reality effect," but assists in subordinating the presence of the moving camera that concerned Hitchcock. As Hitchcock stated, "The audience must never be conscious of it [the camera]. If an audience became aware that the camera was performing miracles, the end itself will be defeated."[15] From this perspective,

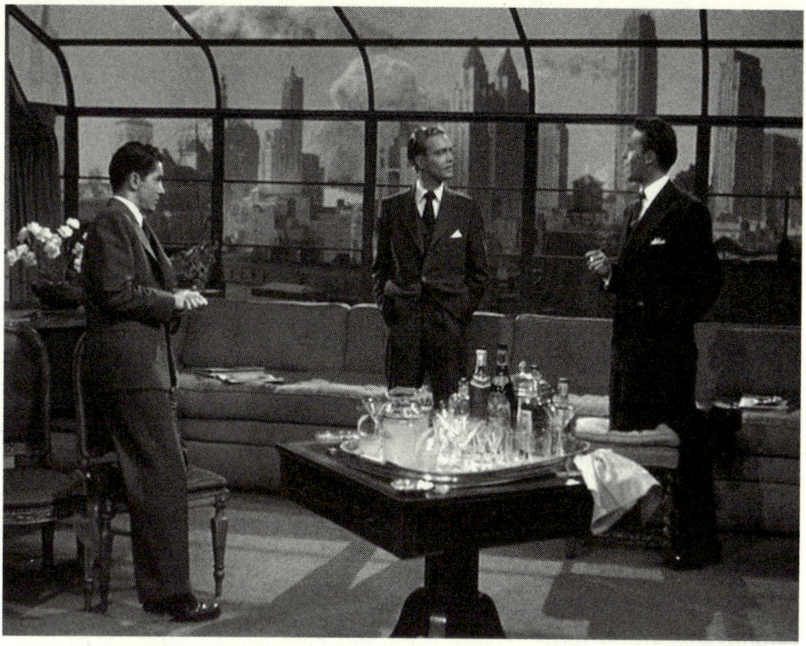

Figure 2.1. *Rope*. The large penthouse window and cityscape loom in the background.

the details of the cyclorama work in concert with Hitchcock's "real-time" narrative in order to follow Brandon and Phillip's command of space and concealment of the secret.

The transparency of the window is analogous to what Lacan describes as the logic of the big Other: the linguistic and communicative framework within everyday life. For Lacan, the big Other functions as a large network of language, providing the groundwork for the daily interaction of culture. The big Other supplies the subject with a world or a referent in order to generate meaning. In this regard, the view of Manhattan through the window is represented as a comprehensible reality displayed in the film's "real-time" narration. The window must sustain its transparent architectural effect (as a contained and protected space of the penthouse) to coincide with Brandon and Phillip's secret.

At the same time, the glass properties of windows have the potential to lose their transparent effect and cause the observer to become aware of his or her looking within the visual field. Consider L. B. "Jeff" Jefferies (James Stewart) in *Rear Window*, who exploits his rear window and telephoto lens to spy into neighboring apartments across the courtyard. Jeff takes advantage of the window's dematerializing effect for his own private enjoyment.[16] But in the last act of the film when Thorwald (Raymond Burr), the man who Jeff believes is a murderer, shockingly makes eye contact with him from across the courtyard, the window's transparent boundary collapses as Jeff becomes conscious of his own looking.[17] In this regard, windows can both evoke a sense of mastery in the field of vision, as well as transform into an apparatus of self-scrutiny where the observer's looking folds back upon itself. These structures of seeing within the visual field bring me to the window's third function: what Lacan calls the disrupting and self-scrutinizing effects of the gaze.

Lacan's premise of the gaze demonstrates the split subject (between conscious and the unconscious) within the field of visual perception. The gaze as a stain or distortion marks a point of failure in the visual field. It is a point where the subject's looking reaches the limits of the visible, where the space between object and subject collapses. The gaze lures the spectator into the picture—it entices the desire to look within the frame. For example, the viewer is drawn into Brandon and Phillip's devilish plan to throw a party with a hidden corpse in the room. It arouses the viewer's desire to see if Brandon and Phillip can pull off the perfect murder. To encounter the gaze realizes the observer's desire to look within the image. In other words, to encounter the gaze, one must already be involved or engaged within the visual field. Otherwise the gaze would have little or no effect.[18] Lacan's theory of the gaze demonstrates that the observer is not outside the picture as a transcendental spectator, but rather is included within the picture itself as a subject of desire.

This brings us back to the penthouse window's primary function in how Brandon and Phillip handle the plan during the dinner party. The primary role of the window is to provide the illusion of a coherent reality and forced perspective in order to coincide with Brandon and Phillip's secret of hiding the corpse. All the details in Brandon and Phillip's apartment must also provide the illusion of a bourgeois setting and smooth functioning of reality, such as the brightly lit setting of the dining room and the neatly displayed artwork on the walls—these elements must adhere to the plan in order to pull off the perfect murder.

These embellishments in the penthouse build the fantasy space of *Rope*. Fantasy is what allows the subject to know *how* to fantasize. Fantasy sets up the coordinates of desire. It is a framework which permits the subject to make meaning within the world. The appeal of cinematic fantasy is that we can experience events which are not permitted in everyday life. For example, we can root for Brandon and Phillip to get away with murder and succeed with the plan—something that is prohibited within the social order. As such, the primary function of the penthouse window in *Rope* is to provide the coordinates of fantasy and to diminish the disruption of the gaze. To call attention to the elements outside the window, however, can potentially jeopardize Brandon and Phillip's plan and destroy the fantasy space and forced perspective of the cyclorama. In other words, fantasy can reveal itself as a structuring force within the visual space, collapsing the distance between subject and object and displaying the excess of the gaze. As we shall see, this is precisely what Rupert achieves at the end of the film when he fires the gun out the window, calling attention to the Law after he discovers David's corpse and that Brandon and Phillip are indeed the murderers.

Exposing the Excess of the Gaze

Rope's one-location, "real-time" narrative can be traced to the *Kammerspielefilme* (chamber-play films) of the 1920s. Carl Mayer was the founder and practitioner of the *Kammerspielefilme,* which developed out of Max Reinhardt's conception of chamber theater: plays performed with limited characters in a small environment in front of a small audience. Reinhardt's idea of a small and intimate theater was for the audience to see subtle movements and facial expressions of the actors that might not be experienced in a large theater. Drawing upon Reinhardt's conception of chamber theater, Mayer's scripts contained only a few characters, generally had no intertitles, and relied on acting and mise-en-scène to communicate the narrative. The *Kammerspielefilme* differed from German Expressionist films in that they tended to counter expressionistic techniques, focusing rather on realistic and intimate psychological narratives of lower-middle-class milieus, such as the portrayal of the hotel doorman (Emil Jannings) in Murnau's *The Last Laugh.*

This is not to suggest that the *Kammerspielefilme* did not entail expressionistic elements. As David A. Cook notes, "the whole realistic cinema which grew out of the *Kammerspielefilme* can be seen as both an extension of and a reaction against the Expressionist cinema, in that it retained the morbid psychological themes of the earlier films but cast them in realistic form."[19] Hitchcock was always interested in stories that involved limited locations, which is evident in films such as *The Lady Vanishes* (1938), *Lifeboat* (1944), and *Rear Window.* Certainly *Rope*'s depiction of Brandon and Phillip as wealthy college students does not fit the lower-middle-class world of the *Kammerspielefilme.* But *Rope* does share a commonalty with the *Kammerspielefilme* in Hitchcock's emphasis on physical objects in the penthouse setting in relation to Brandon and Phillip's plan to commit the perfect act of murder.

Physical objects often have importance in the *Kammerspielefilme* and can take on additional meaning in relation to the lives and states of minds of the characters. Just as Reinhardt's concept of a chamber theater was for the audience to detect character subtleties, the same effect applies to physical objects in the space of chamber-play film. In *Rope*, for example, the viewer spends a long time in the penthouse, which in turn allows him or her to map and familiarize objects within that space. Changes to those objects have the potential to take on greater significance. This is attributed to Hitchcock's allowing us to participate in Brandon and Phillip's plan. Here, surplus-knowledge within the confined setting intensifies the mise-en-scène. As such, objects in the small and intimate setting of the chamber drama are more susceptible to becoming strange and uncanny rather than integrating into a coherent order of things.

Throughout the party, Rupert detects these small oddities that stick out within the confined space of the penthouse: food displayed on the trunk instead of the dining room table, and Brandon serving expensive champagne for no apparent reason. These small anomalies are produced by Brandon and Phillip's excessive enjoyment. Lacan argues that for the symbolic order to have a total, uninterrupted control of everyday life, it requires a renunciation of what he calls *jouissance*. The symbolic order functions on the sacrifice of enjoyment and will scrutinize those who enjoy excessively. Conversely, any surfacing of *jouissance* initiates a failure of the symbolic order—a failure that Lacan describes as an encounter with the real. Therefore, physical objects within *Rope* have the potential to lose their everyday textual significance, revealing an excess linked to the order of the real.

For example, during the party Phillip breaks his wine glass, cutting his hand when Mr. Atwater mistakes Kenneth for David. Hitchcock captures Phillip's anxiety by quickly tracking the camera into a close-up of his bloody hand, which holds the broken glass (see figure 2.2). Phillip slowly walks behind the guests and gently places the broken glass on the table near the liquor. Here, the quick movement of the camera and Phillip's protracted movement illustrate a momentary encounter of the real where time is portrayed as hindered and distorted. But more importantly, it demonstrates that physical objects are more vulnerable to losing their primary meaning within the chamber-space film. Like the primary function of the window, physical objects must maintain their everyday meaning and appear "natural" within the confined setting of the penthouse in order to coincide with Brandon and Phillip's secret.

In order for Brandon and Phillip to integrate into the reality of a dinner party and to fulfill their plan to commit the perfect act of murder, they must avoid any such encounters with the real. Brandon and Phillip's

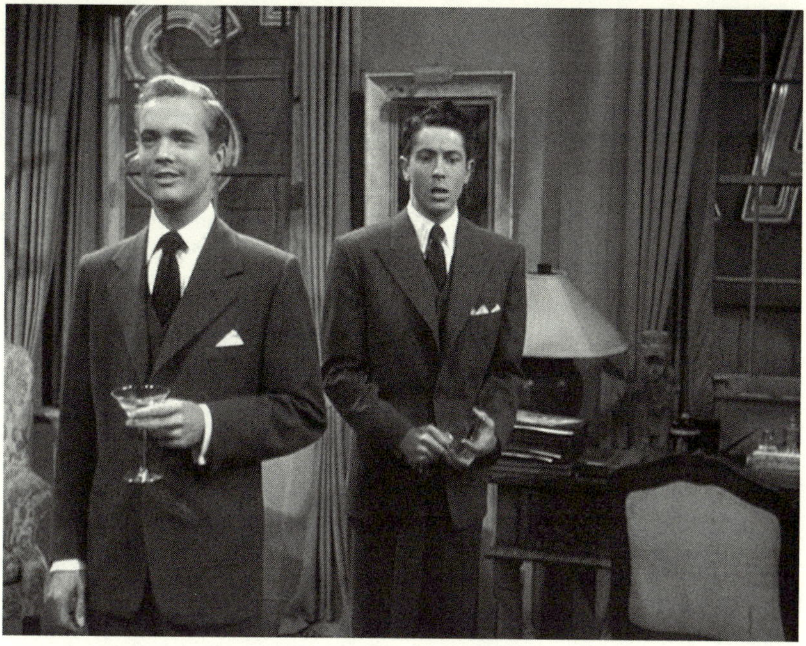

Figure 2.2. *Rope*. Phillip's encounter with the real.

inability to do so—specifically their inability to contain their obscene enjoyment—initiates an encounter with the real, which, in turn, piques Rupert's desire. This is especially evident when Brandon unexpectedly brings up Phillip's inability to strangle and kill a chicken at Shaw's farm in Connecticut. Phillip's emotional outburst in response to Brandon draws attention to himself, causing Rupert to become even more inquisitive. Later in the film, while Phillip plays the piano, Rupert inquires about his odd behavior pertaining to the incident at Shaw's farm in Connecticut. The sound of a police siren suddenly passes by as Phillip stops playing the piano and, startled, looks at the window. The sound of the passing siren coupled with Phillip's worried expression briefly disrupts the transparent effect of the window. Rupert's attempt to expose the secret is met when there are momentary encounters with the real, disrupting the protected fantasy space contained by the window.[20] This demonstrates that the window can have both pleasurable and monstrous effects in terms of looking. At the same time, these oddities within the fantasy space intensify the viewer's enjoyment of *Rope*. Phillip's emotional and physical breakdowns are welcomed encounters with the real, because they help to drive *Rope*'s suspense, as well as to sustain and even heighten the viewer's engagement with the narrative.

The Collapse of the Fantasy Frame

The big Other functions on the prohibition of enjoyment and scrutinizes those who enjoy excessively. Rupert takes on the aspect of the big Other, looking for what is hidden as the figure of the Law. Throughout the evening of the party, Rupert notices Brandon and Phillip's strange behavior due to their inability to conceal the secret: namely, what is in the room (the corpse) more than the room. Rupert's suspicions about Brandon and Phillip's odd behavior are confirmed by way of David's hat. As Rupert prepares to leave the penthouse, Mrs. Wilson (Edith Evanson), the nosey housekeeper, mistakenly hands him David's hat. Rupert puts on the hat, which does not fit on his head. Mrs. Wilson laughs, realizing she handed Rupert the wrong hat. Rupert looks at the initials D.K. on the hat with arrested attention. Brandon and Phillip's unawareness of the workings of the big Other reveals a large anomaly or stain in the visual space, something that clearly does not fit into the order of things. Like the skull in Hans Holbein's *The Ambassadors* painting, David's hat (as a stain within the picture) is a trap for Rupert to encounter the gaze and the real of his own desire.

At the same time, Rupert's discovery of David's hat is an encounter with the gaze for the spectator of the film. This is because the viewer has already been apprised of Brandon and Phillip's secret plan, which is now under threat by Rupert's new knowledge. The horror of Rupert finding David's hat demonstrates the viewer's investment in the narrative. Otherwise, this moment would have little impact upon the spectator. We should also note that Hitchcock frames Rupert so that only the viewer is privy to this moment. Just as the viewer is given access to David's death, he or she is also privy to Rupert's new knowledge pertaining to Brandon and Phillip's strange behavior. This intensifies the viewer's sense of spectatorship and suspense because he or she has information that is not known to Brandon and Phillip.

After Rupert discovers David's hat, he leaves with the rest of the guests. Brandon and Phillip believe they have succeeded in their plan. Just as they are ready to dispose of the body, Rupert calls and tells them that he left his cigarette case at the penthouse. Rupert returns and pretends to find his cigarette case. He asks Brandon and Phillip for a drink and begins to theorize about what may have happened to David. Rupert imagines how they would have killed David, suggesting that they would have strangled him with a rope. Hitchcock moves the camera close to Rupert's hand to reveal the rope Brandon and Phillip used to kill David. Phillip sees Rupert holding the rope and yells in horror: "He's got it. He knows!"

Without any warning, Phillip attempts to kill Rupert with a gun. Rupert goes for the gun as he struggles with Phillip. The gun fires at the floor as Rupert snatches the gun away from him. Brandon, however, remains relatively calm as he apologizes to Rupert, trying to convince him that Phillip is drunk and does not know what he is saying. Rupert says to Brandon that he does not want to "fence" anymore. This is because Rupert knows their secret and wants to open the chest. Brandon responds angrily: "Go ahead then. I hope you like what you see!" When Rupert opens the chest and with shock sees David's corpse, his suspicion of Brandon and Phillip is proven correct. But this discovery of knowledge comes with a price: namely, his encounter with the real of his own desire. This encounter can only occur with Rupert's investment in wanting to know Brandon and Phillip's secret.

To use an example from *Rear Window* again, consider when Jeff suspects his neighbor, Thorwald, of murdering his wife. When Jeff looks out his apartment window with his binoculars, he is looking for his own desire in Thorwald's apartment (wanting to know if he is indeed a murderer). But when Thorwald makes shocked eye contact with Jeff from across the courtyard during the denouement of the film, it is a horrifying experience because Jeff has encountered the real of his own desire. This effect is achieved because Jeff, like Rupert in probing Brandon and Phillip's behavior, is invested in the desire to know Thorwald's secret: did he kill his wife?

In the same manner, Brandon and Phillip's unusual behavior intrigues Rupert, causing him to search for the secret: what are they hiding from me? David's hat lures Rupert to return to the penthouse to further investigate David's disappearance, which leads him to encounter the real of his own desire. Here, we begin to see the full transformation of the penthouse window as an effect of the excess of the gaze, where the barrier between reality and the real begins to falter. When Rupert reveals the rope to Brandon and Phillip, the window fully transforms into an object of anxiety, demonstrating the disruptive effect of the gaze as an unknowable force. Hitchcock's "real-time" experiment of extreme long takes prevents him from using editing devices as a way to narratively depict character psychologically. For this reason, Hitchcock has to rely on elements of the mise-en-scène in order to visually show character emotions and narrative tension. Indeed, the window's metamorphosis emerges from the influence of German Expressionism on Hitchcock's work as a way to visualize the psychological tension in the film's final act.

The big Other resides in the realm of language, made up of networks of signifiers, providing the subject a referent in order to make meaning in the everyday world. The real disrupts this order, realizing a point of non-meaning within the big Other. German Expressionist cinema is characteristic of the real, in that it destabilizes an objective and coherent cinematic reality. Ian Roberts, for instance, notes that "the dream world of Expressionism, artificial worlds of light and shadow captured on celluloid, created a unique approach to mise-en-scène which enabled the German cinema industry to challenge, albeit briefly, the growing dominance of Hollywood."[21] Rather than reproducing an objective cinematic reality, German filmmakers attempted to depict forces of the invisible through abstract and subjective perspectives. Expressionist filmmakers wanted to show the "twilight of the soul," to represent and express dynamics of the strange and uncanny. As John D. Barlow puts it, German filmmakers saw the possibilities of cinema in representing "the mysterious, the strange, the fantastic, and the shadowy horrors of a soul in torment."[22] Lotte H. Eisner, in particular, points out that the set designs of German Expressionism "vibrate" psychological unrest, such as the slanted and oblique buildings and "twisting" back-alleys in Robert Wiene's *The Cabinet of Dr. Caligari* (1920). She explains that the "animation of the inorganic" can be traced to German novels "long before" the emergence of Expressionism. Eisner observes that "the Germans . . . have an eerie gift for animating objects. . . . We frequently find German-speaking authors attributing diabolical overtones" to objects, such as the description of streets in Gustav Meyrink's novel *Golem*, which "seem to have an insidious life of their own."[23] She notes: "In some mysterious way these streets contrive to abjure their life and feelings during the daytime, and lend themselves instead to their inhabitants, those enigmatic creatures who wander aimlessly around, feebly animated by an invisible magnetic current. But at night the houses reclaim their life with interest from these unreal inhabitants; they stiffen, and their sly faces fill with malevolence. The doors become gaping maws and shrieking gullets."[24] In the final act of *Rope*, the transformation of the penthouse window is characteristic of Eisner's description of the vivification of animate objects. The window, so to speak, becomes alive once Rupert exposes Brandon and Phillip's secret. The gradual change from day to night seen through the window visually transforms the penthouse into a state of unrest in order to visualize the film's narrative climax. This is most notable in the letters from a neon "Storage" sign outside the window that invades the space of the penthouse with red, green, and white pulsating light. Certainly the "Storage" sign is part of Hitchcock's description of *Rope*'s city lights as a "light organ." Hitchcock stated that "by the time the picture went from the setting of the sun in the first reel to the hour of total darkness in the final denouement, the man at the light organ had played a nocturnal Manhattan symphony in light."[25]

But it can be argued that the "Storage" sign and its flickering lights coincide with Rupert exposing Brandon and Phillip's secret. Hitchcock displays this by overpowering the right side of the frame as a lighting effect, visualizing the window's inability (as well as the space of the penthouse) to fit into a coherent reality. The metamorphosis of the window and city lights reflects a failure in the visual field caused by the gaze. More importantly, the atmospheric tension created through Hitchcock's complex lighting design emotionally depicts Brandon and Phillip's foiled plan to commit the perfect act of murder. Whereas the transparency of the window throughout the dinner party expresses an objective and transparent reality, the blinking of the lights of the "Storage" sign unravels the fabric of *Rope*'s contained and protected space as an effect of the excess of the gaze.

Furthermore, the excess of the gaze shows a darker side of these murderous characters, specifically Brandon, who appears to be proud of what he achieved, arguing that there is intellectual value and rationality in David's death. Brandon states to Rupert: "He [Phillip] and I lived what you and I talked." Here, the excess of the gaze allows us to see an obscene underside of power at work in Brandon and Phillip's commitment to the theory of the superman. Of course, Rupert is sickened by their act as he says to Brandon: "You were right too, if nothing else, a man should stand by his words. But you've given my words a meaning I never dreamed of. And you've tried to twist them into a cold logical excuse for your ugly murder." This suggests that Rupert's belief in the right of the superman is a fantasy. And as long as that right is not enacted on anyone, Rupert's fantasy continues. As such, the excess of the gaze permits us to see a dark dimension of Rupert's belief in the superman. David's death destroys Rupert's fantasy, causing him to feel extreme guilt and shame.[26] Yet Rupert thanks Brandon for these feelings as he states to him: "Tonight you made me ashamed of every concept I had of superior or inferior beings. And I thank you for that shame. . . . It's not what I am going to do, it's what society is going to do." Rupert then turns to society to correct this situation. He walks to the window, opens it, and fires the gun into the sky to call attention to the Law.

Finally, Hitchcock depicts the excess of the gaze in both the film's last camera movement and character performance after Rupert fires the gun out the window. After the call to the public, the camera slowly dollies back to the chest. The chattering of the public gradually increases. The juxtaposition of the movement of the camera against the amplified off-screen sound of the city creates a vertiginous and crippling effect on the film's fantasy space. Rupert's protracted and lethargic body movements, characteristic of German Expressionism, accommodate the hypnotic effect of the camera's movement as he moves from the window to the chest.

The enormous, utterly dominating penthouse window that is the centerpiece of the set for *Rope* thus carries many functions in the film. Its primary role is to sustain the illusion of a coherent reality in order to coincide with Brandon and Phillip's secret plan, as well as to support Hitchcock's "real-time" experiment. But when the window loses its transparent effect, when the gap between seeing and being seen breaks down, reality begins to falter. The window contains both a fantasy space and a failure in the visual field, as well being the locus of the set design, lighting experiments, and camera movements of German Expressionism and the *Kammerspielefilme* that so strongly influenced *Rope*. These functions of the penthouse window show that the viewer is not outside the picture in a transcendent perspective, but is included within it. Brandon and Phillip fail in their plan because of their ignorance of the public sphere and the necessity of sacrificing enjoyment. That is, they cannot conceal their surplus enjoyment, which inadvertently leads Rupert to the corpse. When Rupert discovers the corpse, he calls attention to the Law and thus publicly exposes Brandon and Phillip's obscene enjoyment. Brandon and Phillip, who privilege themselves as superior beings, attempt to close the gap between *jouissance* and the symbolic order. This is an impossible task because the social order functions on the shared sacrifice of enjoyment. This is precisely what Rupert states to Brandon: "By what right do you dare say that there is a superior few to which you belong? By what right did you dare decide that boy in there [David's corpse in the chest] was inferior and therefore can be killed? Did you think you were God, Brandon?" Or, in the words of Lacan: "The gods belong to the field of the real."[27]

3

Interior Confinement: Shattering and Disintegration in Ingmar Bergman's *The Passion of Anna*

The final act of *Rope* depicts the excess of the gaze in order to coincide with Rupert exposing Brandon and Phillip's secret: namely, David's dead body hidden inside the trunk. Rupert's uncovering of their secret collapses the fantasy frame, which provides the illusion of a functioning order within the confined setting of the penthouse. Hitchcock shatters the film's fantasy frame by deforming cinematic space through a panoply of exterior lights that flood the penthouse. Following the tenets of German Expressionism and the *Kammerspielefilme*, *Rope*'s symphony of lights physicalizes Brandon and Phillip's interior state: that is, what is in them (excess) more than them. More importantly, Hitchcock's deployment of the gaze as an unknowable force energizes the confined setting and "real-time" narrative of the penthouse as both shock and attraction. *Rope* elicits a highly active spectatorship by allowing us to secretly participate in Brandon and Phillip's failed attempt to pull off the perfect murder.

Ingmar Bergman's Faro island chamber drama, *The Passion of Anna*, offers another dimension of confinement cinema in relation to the gaze. The film focuses on the lone wolf and former geologist Andreas Winkleman (Max von Sydow), who lives on the small island of Faro, located off Sweden's southeastern coast. Andreas has sheltered himself from the world after a failed marriage. He has a past history of forgery and financial troubles. He has also been jailed for drunk driving and hitting an officer. Although most of the setting of *The Passion of Anna* takes place on Faro, the film is more concerned with intensities of psychological confinement. As Maria Bergom-Larsson puts it, "The island [of Faro] is not so much a geographical place, more a state of mind."[1] Andreas's self-imposed isolation is tested when he meets Anna Fromm (Liv Ullmann), a widow still mourning her husband and son, who both died tragically in a car accident. Whereas Andreas stifles the painful and violent memories of his past, Anna strives toward the truth and to be open about her past even when it causes her extreme distress. Andreas, however, knows that Anna has lied about her past and that she may have intentionally killed her family by causing the car crash. Upon meeting Anna, Andreas is introduced to her friends, Eva (Bibi Andersson) and Elis (Erland Josephson), a couple who live off the island. Andreas eventually forms a relationship with Anna. But instead of finding companionship, living with Anna on the island causes him extreme frustration, because he cannot get past her deceptions and lies; this leads to his return to solitude and, ultimately, to his disintegration. This is not to suggest that Andreas sees himself as completely removed from the social order. He does seek to communicate with others, such as in his friendship with Johan (Erik Hell), who, later in the film, commits suicide after being wrongly accused of animal cruelty by the island's residents. Andreas constructs a fantasy of solitude, a self-constructed prison that protects him from encountering the haunting memories of his failed marriage and legal problems. In the same way that Hitchcock shows us the film's fantasy space crumble at the end of *Rope* within the constricted setting of the penthouse, Bergman depicts Andreas's self-imposed confinement as an unattainable state of existence. This impossibility is visually displayed in the form of the gaze, a point of failure within the field of visual perception.

Bergman's deployment of the gaze not only unsettles cinematic space, but also embodies an "exterior" threat to Andreas's fantasy of isolation. Maria Bergom-Larsson explains that Bergman's films of the 1960s center on the theme of inner and outer violence: "the threatening society outside versus the private inner sphere."[2] The outer world is perceived as a force beyond one's control, whereas the inner violence is desire and frustration. At the same time, the outer world is not a clearly detectable, concrete world that threatens Andreas. Rather, as Bergom-Larsson summarizes, "Bergman's characters are incarcerated in a world in which they are unable to tell outer from inner, waging a despairing battle against an outer world which merely reflects their own inner conflicts."[3] This is most notable in Andreas's violent attack on Anna toward the end of the film. Andreas's pent-up frustration with Anna derives from her lies and deceptions. Andreas believes that she may have purposely crashed her car in order to kill her husband and son. Yet this information is not made explicitly clear to the viewer, which speaks not only to Anna and Andreas as unreliable narrators, but also to their inability to recognize their outer and inner worlds. But this accusation of Anna is not the only thing that unsettles Andreas. It is also Anna's attempt to be truthful and open (even though she may have lied about her past), something that Andreas struggles with internally due to his traumatic past. As Peter Harcourt puts it, "[Anna's] lies are not *just* lies. They represent as well an aspiration towards a truthfulness which, the film finally brings home to us, none of the characters can ever hope to attain."[4] As their relationship develops, Anna is both an inner and outer threat to Andreas's fantasy of self-confinement. Anna's desire to be truthful forces Andreas to face his traumatic past. At the end of the film, Andreas chooses to remain a lone wolf rather than continue his relationship with Anna.

Andreas's self-imprisonment offers us another instance of confinement cinema in which the encounter with the gaze emerges as an antagonistic and unknowable force that unsettles our spectatorship. *The Passion of Anna* is not only a cinema of confinement that physically depicts Andreas's solitude on the island, but also a portrayal of psychological imprisonment that prevents him from overcoming his haunting memories. Rather than coming to terms with the shame of his failed marriage and past legal issues, Andreas clings to his fantasy of solitude. Instead of moving toward what Lacan describes as "the act proper" by confronting his shame and abandoning his fantasy of solitude (in order to break free from his haunting past), Andreas turns to a violent "passage to act" in order to annihilate his guilt and shame, which thereby leads to his dissolution at the end of the film.[5] Not unlike Jack in *Room*, who sees the outer world as a threat to his fantasy space within the room, the outer sphere terrorizes Andreas's fantasy of being alone. Bergman depicts this threat as a shattering effect by allowing cinematic excess to emerge with disturbing results as the embodiment of the gaze. The encounter with the gaze realizes how our desire distorts the field of perception, as well as revealing a blind spot in our looking. Similar to that in *Rope*, the gaze in *The Passion of Anna* is kept at a distance in order to depict the illusion of Andreas's functioning reality that protects him from the menacing outer world. Roiling below the surface, however, is a domain of violence ready to erupt at any given moment to shatter and disintegrate Andreas's fantasy of self-confinement.

Bergman's Chamber-Play Films and Deconstruction

The Passion of Anna's island setting and small cast of characters are traits of a chamber-play film, a term Bergman borrowed from the playwright August Strindberg. Bergman identifies his chamber play films (such as *Through a Glass Darkly, Winter Light, The Silence,* and *Persona*) as having commonalities with the intimacy of chamber music: "music in which, with an extremely limited number of voices and figures, one explores the essence of a number of motifs." For Bergman, the chamber-play film entails a process of extrapolating backgrounds that are "put into a sort of fog. The rest is a distillation."[6] Bergman's chamber-play films closely follow the ideas of the German *Kammerspielefilme*, where the intricate mise-en-scène and limited setting play a vital role in the close examination of character and story. As such, *The Passion of Anna*'s confined location and limited characters provide viewers an up-close and in-depth account of Andreas. Bergman explores the motif of shattering and disintegration, both at the level of form and content. Like the intimate setting of the *Kammerspiele-filme*, Bergman articulates cinematic space as strange and unsettled as a means to intimately express Andreas's inner state, especially when he comes apart at the end of the film when he leaves Anna.

The Passion of Anna can also be seen as part of Bergman's "deconstruction" period, in which he and his cinematographer, Sven Nykvist, began to incorporate the experimental and avant-garde styles of French and Italian cinema. Beginning with *Persona*, Bergman became interested in the New Wave style of filmmaking, particularly the works of Jean-Luc Godard, who was known for employing alienation and distancing techniques. As Marc Gervais writes, *Persona* "exemplifies that Godard dictum that 'the adventure of contemporary cinema is the adventure of film language,' while adding its own pessimistic philosophical undertone. More than an example, really, it is a demonstration of this dictum in action."[7] For Gervais, *Persona* is a film about the "destruction of cinema, the destruction of the myth of Bergman's movies, and of Bergman himself as artist."[8] Bergman's stylistic change in the mid-1960s explored psychological themes of perception and identity by experimenting with the narrative conventions and the illusionary mechanisms of cinema. Bergman's experiment in film language in *The Passion of Anna* is most notable when he interrupts the narrative to show each of the main actors discussing the character he or she is portraying in the film. On first viewing the film, one finds the abrupt cuts to these interview segments to be a jarring experience. And, indeed, the film's unprompted interviews and loosening of causal relations are not entirely like the cinema of Godard in that Bergman is attempting to enact a wholesale evacuation of narrative immersion and character identification in exchange for critical distance and alienation. In writing about the projector breakdown scene at the midway point in *Persona*, Robin Wood observes, "What Bergman does here has nothing in common with the continual and delicate—at times near subliminal—play of distanciation devices with which Godard preserves the spectator's analytical detachment. Bergman, on the contrary, draws the spectator into the film, demanding total emotional involvement."[9] For Wood, the projector breakdown, as well as the pre-credit and credit sequences in *Persona*, "shock and disturb rather than detach."[10]

Whereas Godard constantly makes us critically aware of cinema's processes of mediation, Bergman's disruption of *Persona*'s fiction, according to Wood, is both formalistically and thematically "experienced both by the characters and by the artist, the 'formal' collapse as a means of communicating the sensation of the breakdown directly to the spectator."[11] If we find the interview sequences in *The Passion of Anna* unsettling to our viewership, this effect must be attributed to Bergman's enticing our desire to look into the film and to know more about Andreas and why he has chosen to isolate himself from the world. As such, the unprompted interviews are interruptions that briefly realize our desire to look into the film because Bergman allows narrative absorption rather than a wholesale evacuation of involving character identification, as is often the case in Godard's films. To read *The Passion of Anna* as Bergman playing with the processes of mediation to simply express deconstruction and critical distance misses the excessive dimension that makes up the film's chamber drama. Bergman's experiment with cinema's illusionary processes manifests the effects of the gaze in order to visually display the impossibility of Andreas's fantasy about being alone. Bergman shows the viewer this impossibility by exposing fantasy's excessive underside through the effect of the shattering and disintegration of cinematic space—most notably signaled in the film's foreboding opening sequence and Bergman's employment of the zoom shot.

Fantasy, Minimalism, and Expressionism

The missing object cause of desire (*objet petit a*) paradoxically fuels desire. As long as the object remains missing or lost, desire continues to desire. That is to say, the logic of desire functions on lack and absence, not mastery and plenitude. Fantasy, however, provides an escape route out of the dissatisfaction of desire. Fantasy stages the subject's relationship to its object cause of desire. Fantasy provides the coordinates and support of the subject's desire. As such, fantasy allows the subject to relate to *objet petit a*. At the same time, the framework of fantasy provides distance from the real. Therefore, getting too close to one's fantasy object can be traumatic, such as in Pyle's mental collapse in *Full Metal Jacket*, as noted in the introduction. Fantasy, in this regard, can have both consoling and harmful effects in visualizing the gaze in cinema. On the one hand, fantasy can create a scenario in which the subject imagines a relationship with the impossible object (*objet petit a*). Here the excess of the gaze is kept at a distance, demonstrating a blending of desire and fantasy, or what Todd

McGowan terms a "cinema of integration."[12] On the other hand, fantasy can depict a nightmarish form of reality by revealing its obscene underside. Here, the excess of the gaze is not normalized within the film's narrative space, but is deployed in order to create unsettling effects that shatter the spectator's control of his or her looking. To become a proper subject in the Lacanian sense, Andreas must traverse the fantasy and identify with his impossible object: namely, the haunting memories of his past marriage and legal troubles. For Andreas, however, the gaze must be kept hidden within his field of perception in order for his fantasy of living a life of solitude to properly function. At this level, fantasy supplies Andreas with a peaceful scenario of living life as a hermit. This is why Andreas has confined himself to the island as a lone wolf: to avoid the trauma of his past. At stake for Andreas is losing his fantasy of solitude on the island.

Bergman visually depicts Andreas's solitude through images of imprisonment and mummification, such as framing him walking along stone walls and standing next to the statues in Elis's home, but perhaps most notably in the film's use of claustrophobic close-ups set against a flattened background. Tightly framing Andreas not only speaks to Bergman's distilling effect of chamber-play cinema, but also alludes to Andreas's claustrophobia, which he confides to Eva during their one-night affair: "A geologist friend of mine used to make fun of me because I am scared of going into caves. . . . I get horrible claustrophobia. I always have."

At the same time, Bergman problematizes Andreas's fantasy of solitude, showing its impossibility by allowing its obscene underside to emerge in the form of the gaze. This obscene dimension of fantasy demonstrates that Andreas cannot escape his traumatic past. As such, Bergman builds an unstable space of confinement to reflect both Andreas's self-imposed imprisonment and his vulnerability to becoming destructive in the encounter with the real of his desire. By staging the gaze as the impossible object within the field of perception, Bergman shows the unattainability of Andreas's fantasy of solitude. Although Bergman draws upon the styles of French New Wave and Italian Neorealist filmmakers, he differs from these filmmakers in the way he deploys fantasy and desire in this regard. French New Wave and Italian Neorealist filmmakers often create what McGowan terms a "cinema of desire"[13] by keeping the gaze absent as a means of creating critical distance and diminishing emotional identification with the film's narrative. Certainly, *The Passion of Anna* has congruencies with films of desire, particularly its loosening of narrative causality. At the same time, Bergman permits us to form an identification with Andreas, since we are curious to see how he will respond to the film's unprompted events, such as Anna's first arrival at his home to use his phone, and Eva's random trip to the island to visit him. To experience the traumatic effects of the gaze, Bergman must allow for narrative immersion and character identification—even if the events are loosely ordered, or if character motivation is not always fully explained; otherwise, the emergence of the gaze would have little impact upon our spectatorship.

The chamber setting of Andreas's home intensifies the viewer's encounter with the gaze, as demonstrated in the film's opening sequence. The film begins with a wide shot of sheep grazing in a field. The bells hanging from the sheep are emphasized as they quickly walk off-screen while appearing to sense some sort of danger. It is revealed later that this danger is a person at large who is killing animals on the island. The image pans from orange-colored shingles to Andreas as he climbs to the roof of his home. The narrator, voiced by Bergman, introduces Andreas as he replaces the roof's shingles. Andreas looks off-screen and sees a sublime image of moving clouds as they forebodingly dim the sun. Andreas climbs down the ladder, leaving the bucket of mortar on top of the roof. As he walks away, the bucket falls off the roof, nearly hitting him as it crashes onto the ground. Andreas smiles as he grabs the bucket. The camera tracks with the bucket as he places it on top of the slanted doors to the basement. The bucket tumbles over as Andreas looks at it with concealed frustration.

The unnerving quietness of the opening sequence amplifies small details, such as the sheep bells hauntingly echoing in the distant landscape and the clouds creepily darkening the sun. When the bucket crashes to the ground, it disrupts the stillness of the sequence, calling conspicuous attention to itself. The crashing of the bucket suggests that something threatening is on the horizon that unsettles Andreas's peaceful setting. As Bergman states, "Something is foreboded [in the opening sequence], there's something menacing in the air. And then that nasty bucket which comes tumbling down from the roof, and won't stand up properly."[14] Bergman stages the tumbling bucket as an effect of shattering and disintegration to visually forebode Andreas's failure to reach a state of confinement and solitude. Indeed, the crashing of the bucket does not fit within the order of the moments' mise-en-scène. This transformation of the bucket is attributed to the gaze, turning a mundane object into something haunting. As such, the gaze not only exemplifies our involvement in the film's narrative, but also shows that our looking is positioned *within* the film—in short, the gaze captures our desire to look by presenting the bucket as an uncanny object that briefly thwarts our desire of looking.

The crashing of the bucket is one of many unexpected events that Andreas will encounter throughout the film. Andreas's concerned look at the bucket hints at something that threatens his fantasy of solitude. In order for Andreas to prevent fantasy's obscene underside from emerging, he must have complete control over his environment. The *New York Times*'s Vincent Canby makes a similar observation in his review of the film. Canby writes, "At one point, he [Andreas] stares off at the sun that hangs low and dim—with its edges made ragged by a telephoto lens—in the Scandinavian sky. Suddenly the sun disappears into the gray-blue haze, but it's as if Andreas had willed it invisible, much as he has tried to will himself invisible without taking the ultimate step."[15] Andreas's willing himself invisible is his fantasy to live a life of solitude, and "to wipe out his means, his expression," as Max von Sydow says later in the film during one of the four unprompted interview sequences. Fantasy sets up the coordinates of Andreas's reality. Reality and fantasy depend upon each other in this regard. If fantasy disappears, we are still not left with pure reality; rather, reality becomes a nightmare without fantasmatic support. The tumbling of the bucket briefly reveals the obscene underside of fantasy in the form of the gaze. The crashing bucket that barely misses Andreas's head demonstrates the power of the opening images of the film and how minimalism can amplify ordinary objects into an uncanny state. When the bucket does not stand upright, the film's mise-en-scène briefly becomes strange.

The opening sequence exhibits Bergman's creative use of minimalism in order to depict Andreas's vulnerability in constructing his self-imprisonment. But Bergman does allow for warm and expressionistic moments, such as when Eva surprises Andreas while her husband, Elis, is in Italy. Bergman constructs an expressionistic mise-en-scène in order to convey human intimacy between Eva and Andreas. Filmed with red tones to reflect the twilight hour, Andreas and Eva have dinner and share a number of passionate moments. At one point, Eva plays a romantic record and dances by herself in the red light. After dinner, Eva falls asleep. Andreas cleans the dishes as he whistles a bar from the song they had listened to. His expression and mood suggest comfort and content inspired by Eva's companionship. Later, when Eva awakens, she confronts him about how meaningless she feels. Andreas comforts her as they sleep together. Next morning, when Eva is about to leave, Andreas asks if they can meet again, even though he knows that forming a relationship with her is impossible. After Eva leaves, Andreas digests the silence of his home. Contrary to the expressive mise-en-scène of the previous night with Eva, the cold morning light fills the interior of his home, indicating Andreas's return to loneliness. Here, we have a reverse effect of excess in terms of expressionism and minimalism. In the opening sequence, the excess of the gaze manifests itself in the tumbling bucket.

This effect is achieved by Bergman's staging the excess of the bucket to burst through the scene's minimalism and quaintness. By contrast, Bergman creates an expressive mise-en-scène during Andreas's affair with Eva. When Eva departs, Bergman articulates Andreas's return to a cold and empty home. Maria Bergom-Larsson explains that the film's use of white light is "the victim's symbol, the mark of the naked and the innocent."[16] Indeed, the genuine connection between Andreas and Eva is elucidated by warm colors and soft lighting during their one-night affair. Now, Andreas's return to solitude unsettles him in the form of desire, captured by the hard, white morning light and the silence of his house. As Andreas stands alone in his home, he whistles a bar of the song from the record Eva had played the night before. The song now signals loneliness and isolation, rather than warmth and comfort. As such, Bergman's depiction of Andreas's home as cold and empty after Eva leaves calls into question Andreas's fantasy of being alone—a contradiction conveyed when Andreas lies on the bed and lets out a yell like an animal, gesturing to the film's horrific ending.

Zooming Too Close to Fantasy: Movement and Stasis

Bergman interrupts the narrative flow four times in the film, when the actors discuss their interpretation of the characters they are playing. As mentioned, Bergman became interested in modernist techniques to address cinema's illusionary processes—most notably enacted in *Persona,* when the filmstrip literally breaks apart at the halfway mark during the film. *The Passion of Anna* is also a film about the construction of fantasy. Bergman's experimentation in breaking the fourth wall not only addresses the film's illusionary and mediating processes, but underscores viewers' investment in the narrative. Otherwise, the jarring effect of breaking the film's fourth wall would have little impact on our spectatorship. We must understand how, similar to *Persona*'s investigation into identity and film form, *The Passion of Anna*'s exploration of cinema's illusionary forms coincides with the breakdown and collapse of Andreas's fantasy. Upon meeting Anna, Andreas's fantasy of self-confinement is called into question, a state of confusion captured in the film's creative use of the zoom shot and its correlation to movement and stasis.

Laura Mulvey explains that cinema is divided by two parts: cinema's mechanism (the projector) and the material (the film strip that moves through the projector). For Mulvey, cinema's division centers on "the fundamental and irreconcilable opposition between stillness and movement that reverberates across the aesthetics of cinema."[17] The still frame, according to Mulvey, is cinema's secret past, which the projector brings to life through movement. Cinema's forward movement (its mechanical process) merges with the narrative's linear movement. Metonymy is the linking or chaining of narrative events, unfolding and moving forward. For example, Andreas's meeting Anna ignites the narrative, which leads him to meet Eva and Elis and so forth; the end of the narrative, according to Mulvey, is characterized by stasis.[18] As Mulvey explains, "the metonymic structure of narrative, its causal links, changes to the register of metaphor. Death marks the end but also the point 'beyond narratability,'" for it "signifies total erasure, the nothing that lies beyond it."[19] As such, death hides the moving image's secret: the still frame. Drawing upon Peter Brooks's "Freud's Masterplot," Mulvey explains that narrative closure coalesces into two forms of stasis: death and marriage. This could be literally the hero killing the villain or the romantic union of two lovers at the end of the film.

Building upon the work of Garrett Stewart, Mulvey notes that the two metaphors of death and narrative ending can also occur at the site of the freeze frame. First, there is the metaphor that subordinates a film's secret: the still frame. Here, death stands in for the film's ending, giving the film added meaning, as in the freeze frame of George Roy Hill's *Butch Cassidy and the Sundance Kid* (1969). The freeze frame stands in for both characters' deaths, and the death of the narrative itself. The second metaphor is the freeze frame representing the film's mediation: namely, the single frame flickered over and over, leading into "infinity" and "an uncertain future."[20] An example of this is the famous ending of François Truffaut's *The 400 Blows* (1959), which freezes on Antoine (Jean-Pierre Léaud) at the lip of the ocean, inviting viewers to contemplate its meaning. In sum, the first metaphor refers to the film's narrative, and the second refers to film's materiality (the photogram or still frame repeating endlessly).

Mulvey further explains that stillness and infinity can have a dialectical relationship, as in the case of Michael Snow's experimental film *Wavelength* (1967), which executes a 45-minute zoom that slowly moves across a New York loft, halting on a picture of ocean waves. For Mulvey, *Wavelength*'s forward zoom shot characterizes the narrative's forward movement. As the zoom usurps the loft's space, Snow interjects flash frames as a means to check the zoom, which briefly manifests the film's hidden secret (the still frame). At the end of the film, when the zoom reaches the picture of the sea, the insertion of the flash frame gestures toward cinema's secret: the still frame that repeats endlessly as metaphor.

But we must consider how the excess of the gaze functions in relation to stasis and movement and narrative desire. Narrative films, as Todd McGowan explains, "do not create and sustain desire simply through delaying the revelation of the complete fabula or story."[21] They also function through the "absent object" of the gaze. As McGowan argues, "This object is necessarily absent—not simply an empirical absence introduced by the filmic narration—and it remains constitutively unknowable."[22] Certainly, narrative films withhold information and create narrative gaps in order to solicit the viewer's desire for knowledge. For instance, we do not know why Andreas's wife left him until later in the film. The enigma of Andreas's backstory is one component of the narrative that draws us into the film, eliciting our desire to know more about him. But there is another component at work in narrative movement: *objet petit a*—the object cause of desire that remains and must remain enigmatic. On one level, narrative desire involves the film's plotting of information that elicits our desire to know more. Our desire for knowledge, in this sense, fuels the forward movement of the story in the search for meaning. Certainly, the manner in which a film parcels out information can mediate the spectator's desire. Digital streaming services, for example, have shaped and intensified serialized television in the viewer's desire to keep watching. Consider the hyper-narrative television series *Breaking Bad* (2008–2013). At the end of almost every episode, the writers leave an unanswered piece of information, keeping us hooked so we tune in the following week for the next episode. Now, with digital streaming platforms, such as Netflix, Amazon Prime, and Hulu, we can continuously watch or "binge-watch" an entire season or series within a short period of time. As such, digital streaming platforms ignite our desire to know more in allowing for the immediate consumption of *Breaking Bad*.

A second level of narrative desire is the absence of *objet petit a* (the object cause of desire). Desire sustains its energy by not obtaining *objet petit a*. Objects can stand in for *objet petit a*. But *objet petit a* as the "lost object" can never be satisfied. Therefore, when Mulvey describes Snow's use of the flash frame to check the zoom in *Wavelength*, she does not account for a third component in the field of the perception: the gaze as a manifestation of *objet petit a* in the visual field of perception. Certainly, the still frame stands in as cinema's hidden secret, as Mulvey rightly points out. But this account of cinema's secret only entails the technological and material (the projector and celluloid) and the narrative (the freeze frame as metaphor). Mulvey does not consider the excess of the gaze in *Wavelength*'s exploration of movement and stillness. This is the death drive proper, the excess we can never get rid of, the piece of *jouissance* that perpetually sticks with the subject.[23] When the viewer sees the freeze frame at the close of *Wavelength*, the ending is not only metaphorical in its engagement with film's hidden secret (the still frame) and movement (the zoom and the ocean waves in the picture on the wall), but also reveals the gaze as a structuring and unknowable absence brought into the field of vision. Even the overpowering sound captures the disorienting effect of the gaze at the end of *Wavelength.* The film's distortion of sound follows what Michel Chion terms *rendu* in rendering cinematic reality. For Chion, *rendu* immediately penetrates the viewer at the level of the real, where the soundscape overpowers the image by providing audio details that are often undetectable. As Slavoj Žižek explains, "Chion refers above all to the contemporary sound techniques that enable us not only to reproduce exactly the 'original,' 'natural' sound but even to reinforce it and to render audible details that would be missed if we were to find ourselves in the 'reality' recorded by the film."[24] Here, the immediacy of sound does not so much accompany the still image of the ocean wave at the end of *Wavelength* as put the image in disarray in the form of the gaze.

A similar effect of the gaze occurs in *The Passion of Anna* through Bergman's use of the zoom and its correlation to Andreas's inability to surrender his fantasy as a lone wolf. *The Passion of Anna* employs only two zoom shots, but they serve a vital function in visualizing the excess of the gaze within the confined setting. The first zoom occurs when Andreas first meets Anna. The scene begins with an image of a pile of broken roof shingles, panning up to Andreas who hammers a nail into the wall, constructing his home of isolation. The image pans away from Andreas as Anna enters the frame, walking with a cane, limping past the shards of the broken shingles. Anna asks Andreas if she can use his phone. He lets Anna into his home and directs her to the phone. Curious about Anna, Andreas secretly closes the door (as if he has left the house), so he can eavesdrop on her conversation. Anna speaks to Elis about her deceased husband, who had deposited money into a fund for her and their son. Anna becomes upset, hearing that the transaction had not been made. As Anna becomes highly emotional, the image slowly zooms in on Andreas, ending in a close shot of him. Just as he hears Anna cry, he abruptly leaves.

The film's first zoom has two functions. First, it emotionally captures the desire of both Andreas and the viewer to know more about Anna's mysterious past. This is a typical technique of the zoom, which is to express the character's interiority, and to manifest emotions within the viewer in terms of character identification. In this sense, the forward movement of the zoom follows the fueling of narrative desire in wanting to learn Anna's mystery. On a secondary level, the zoom and its usurpation of space call into question Andreas's fantasy of solitude. For Andreas, his choice of self-confinement is to have no attachments to others. As Max von Sydow explains in the interview sequence that directly follows Andreas's encounter with Anna, Andreas is "trying to wipe out his means of expression. And this hiding place [Andreas's home] has become a prison." Andreas's concern for Anna not only shows his interest in her, which goes against the "means of expression" he is trying to erase, but also resurrects his traumatic past, since we later learn that Andreas also has financial problems. The zoom captures Andreas in a vulnerable state, manifesting the real of his desire. For this reason, he leaves the house, abandoning his eavesdropping on Anna. More importantly, Andreas has become curious about Anna, as when he finds the letter in her purse. Andreas reads the letter and learns it is from her husband, who no longer wants to live with Anna. Andreas stops reading and folds the letter. Like the zoom, Andreas's desire has been elicited by Anna's backstory. Here, Andreas decides to read the entire letter. The letter provides some backstory for both the viewer and Andreas. The letter strikingly parallels Andreas's past. Bergman places emphasis on the following passage: "I won't give in, because I know we'll run into new problems, which will result in a nervous breakdown and psychological and physical violence. Therefore, I ask you not to contact me." Certainly, the letter foreshadows the collapse of Andreas and Anna's relationship later in the film. But more so, it speaks directly to the real of Andreas's desire, which he attempts to avoid by not having a romantic attachment to the other. Bergman emphasizes this by repeating portions of the letter throughout the film.

Worth noting here is the scene in Francis Ford Coppola's *The Conversation* (1974) in which the sound and surveillance expert Harry Caul (Gene Hackman) checks into a hotel and books a room next door to Mark (Frederic Forrest) and Ann (Cindy Williams), a couple whom he has secretly recorded. Harry's recorded conversation of Mark and Ann's conversation suggests that their lives may be in danger. At the hotel, Harry inserts a special microphone into the bathroom wall and eavesdrops on Mark and Ann's conversation. Coppola frames Harry adjacent to the toilet and slowly zooms in on him as he hears an argument in the adjacent room. Just as the zoom begins to close in on Harry, he hears a man yell—possibly someone being murdered. Frightened, Harry removes the headphones. Similar to Andreas's eavesdropping on Anna, Harry encounters the real of his desire. Like Andreas, Harry lives alone and is haunted by his past. Harry's expertise in bugging and surveillance led to a murder in the past. For this reason, Harry tells his assistant, Stan (John Cazale), early in the film that he does not get involved with the subjects under investigation. Like Andreas, Harry wants no attachments to others. Yet the bugging of Mark and Ann's conversation haunts Harry, as he constantly replays the phrase: "He'd kill us if he got the chance." Not unlike Bergman replaying sections from Anna's letter, the repetition of the conversation functions as the death drive that Harry cannot disintegrate. As such, Harry's desire is caught, laying a trap for his encounter with the gaze as he becomes involved in knowing more about Mark and Ann. The zoom in the bathroom parallels the collapse of Harry's reality. Like Andreas, he escapes the zoom's grasp in order to avoid the traumatic effects of the real of his desire. The gaze is a visual manifestation of the real that disrupts our spectatorship. Of course, the gaze par excellence is when Harry breaks into the hotel room next door and investigates the bathroom.[25] He flushes the toilet and notices it is clogged. He flushes it again. This time the water turns to blood as it gushes out onto the floor. The blood not only shatters Harry's fantasy frame, but also demonstrates his implication in his desire to investigate his clients. In Andreas's first encounter with Anna and Harry's investigation into the murder in the hotel room, the zoom narratively immerses the viewer. At the same time, the zoom manifests past trauma for Andreas and Harry. In the case of Andreas, the zoom calls into question whether he can sustain his self-constructed space of confinement.

Andreas's Disintegration

Later in the film, we learn from the narrator that Andreas and Anna have been living together for over a year. Andreas now works for Elis, who offered to help him with his financial situation. But living with Anna has begun to chip away at him. In a pivotal scene, Andreas has a brief flashback of his ex-wife. Shot from Andreas's point of view, the flashback shows them about to have sex. His ex-wife then tells him that he has "cancer of the soul." Anna asks Andreas what he is doing. Bergman cuts to Andreas, who is distraught as he says, "Looking at photographs." Later, during a long sequence depicting Andreas and Anna framed against a black background, he says he is afraid of being humiliated again. Andreas cannot surrender his fantasy to live as a recluse, even as he forms a relationship with Anna. He says to her: "I'm outside that wall. I've shut myself out. . . . We can never leave. It's too late." For Andreas to move forward, he must renounce his fantasy of solitude and fully identify with his traumatic past. Here, the reference to photography and the claustrophobic framing of Andreas against a black background renders Andreas embalmed and mummified. That is to say, Andreas chooses stasis and self-imprisonment rather than Anna, a resolution that erupts into the film's final sequence.

The sequence begins with Anna and Andreas eating breakfast. All of their actions piggy-back off of each other: grabbing the pepper, chewing their food, buttering the toast—all of which seem mechanical and meaningless. Andreas becomes angered when Anna asks him what he is doing. Bergman cuts to Andreas chopping wood outside. Anna approaches Andreas, framed against the pile of chopped wood, evoking the pile of shingle shards seen when he first met her. She asks, "You realize that it's over?" Andreas responds, "You lied about your marriage. You lied about your divorce. I know the truth about you." Anna screams at him, telling him to go to hell. In a fit of rage, Andreas swings the ax at her. She moves out of the way as the ax impacts the fence. He slaps her, knocking her down. Anna slowly gets up as her red scarf lays on the ground, conjuring the blood from the slaughtered sheep seen earlier in the film. The image cuts to Anna leaning over the sink in the kitchen, while Andreas paces back and forth in the other room like a caged animal. Sirens are heard off-screen, catching Andreas's attention. Here, we see a series of images of a barn burning against the horrifying sounds of cows dying. The person at large killing animals on the island has set a cow barn on fire. At the site of the fire, Andreas looks at a badly burned horse still breathing. His neighbor tells Andreas: "The damn horse wouldn't die." In the same way that the dying horse clings to life, Andreas will not surrender his fantasy of living the life of a recluse. Anna arrives in her car to pick up Andreas. Bergman shock-cuts to a horse pulled hauntingly upwards over the sound of timpani, setting the stage for the film's final scene.

As Andreas and Anna drive along, he tells her that he wants his solitude back. He says that everything about her is lies, and he blames her for the car accident that killed her husband and son. As Anna accelerates, Bergman inserts a quick shot of the car driving over a puddle emphasized by the sound of timpani, creating uncertainty as if she might purposely crash the car and kill them both. Andreas grabs hold of the wheel and pulls the car over to the side of the road. Anna finally speaks, saying that she came back to apologize to him. At this point, Andreas can either stay with Anna or return to his life of solitude. He chooses the latter and exits the car. Framed in a wide shot, Andreas again paces back and forth like a caged animal as Anna drives away. The image slowly zooms in on him while the ticking of a clock is heard. As the zoom approaches closer to Andreas, his pacing becomes shorter, as if he is literally entrapped by the collapsing frame (see figures 3.1 and 3.2). At the same time, the grain of the film stock appears on screen. Just as the zoom completely isolates him, he

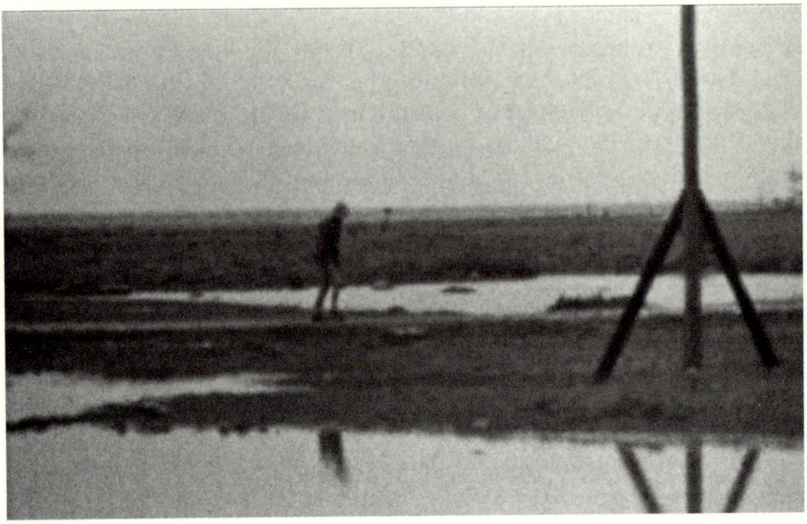

Figure 3.1. ***The Passion of Anna*****. The boundary between reality and the real begins to collapse.**

falls to the ground as the grain of the film literally disintegrates him. The sound of timpani is heard, evoking the dead horse. As the film ends, the narrator states: "This time they called him Andreas Winkleman."

Bergman's first use of the zoom shot shows the inception of Andreas's desire to know more about Anna. The first zoom challenges his fantasy of isolation, as Anna's arrival resurrects the trauma of his failed marriage and legal problems. The second zoom shot adds another level of complexity in reading Andreas's fantasy, as well as Bergman's experimentation with film form. Andreas's disintegration is reminiscent of the ending of Jean-Luc Godard's *Pierrot le Fou* (1965), where Ferdinand (Jean-Paul Belmondo) paints his face blue and commits suicide. After Ferdinand wraps dynamite around his head and kills himself, the last shot follows the plume of smoke and then pans into the sky until the screen is filled with blue, and finally white. Mulvey interprets this scene as an ending "that can only be given by cinema." As Mulvey notes, "The empty screen duplicates the still frame illuminated by the projector's beam, creating a return to the stasis of 'the end' that is derived from the cinema itself."[26] The ending of *The Passion of Anna* also ends with a white screen, which can also be interpreted as cinema's still frame. The ending not only deconstructs the film as a form of shattering and disintegration, but also follows the ending of the narrative itself. Similar to the zoom in *Wavelength*, which finds the picture of ocean waves on the wall across the loft,

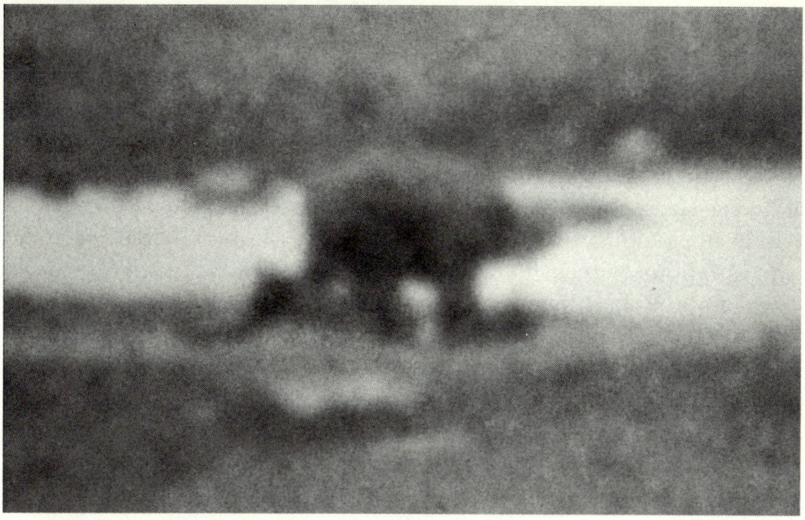

Figure 3.2. *The Passion of Anna*. Andreas disintegrates.

the zoom in *The Passion of Anna* finds its object: Andreas. Whereas the flash frame at the end of *Wavelength* reminds viewers of cinema's secret (the still frame), Bergman reminds viewers of *The Passion of Anna*'s subject: "This time they called him Andreas Winkleman." At the same time, the sound of the ticking clock during the zoom shot and the reference to Andreas's name gestures to the start of the film, suggesting a looping narrative that intimately connects to cinema's still frame flickering over and over into infinity.

Moreover, Andreas's appeal to return to a life of solitude demonstrates his inability to traverse the fantasy. This is emphasized during Andreas's speech, after Anna suggests that they should get away for a while and leave the island. He tells her, "Can one be sick with humiliation? Is this a disease we have to live with? We talk so much about freedom. Isn't freedom a poison for the humiliated? Or is it merely a drug the humiliated use in order to endure? I can't live like this. I've given up. . . . We can never leave. It's too late. Everything's too late." Andreas's concerns regarding freedom and humiliation certainly suggest that he has an awareness of the grip that fantasy can have upon us when we get too close to our object cause of desire. Fantasy provides a pathway out of the demands of symbolic authority. Fantasy allows us to imagine a better place—a beyond without antagonism and lack. To navigate the fantasy (at the end of psychoanalysis), however, is to accept that there is no beyond—that the infinite resides within the finite. Traversing the fantasy is the subject's movement from desire to the repetition of drive.[27] Desire allows us to imagine a solution to the questions it poses. This solution resides in the future—a beyond that fantasy can construct for us. Drive, however, finds enjoyment in the repetition itself. Drive does not seek a solution, but finds enjoyment in repeating loss. In order for Andreas to be truly free, he must come to terms with his past and fully identify with his symptom. Whereas Harry Caul in *The Conversation* wants to right the wrongs of his past by not handing in the tapes to the director (Robert Duvall), the man who hired him to record Mark and Ann's conversation, Andreas cannot overcome the haunting memories of his past and face the real of his desire. Andreas continues to cling to his fantasy of solitude in order to protect himself from his own shame. For Andreas, his self-imprisonment on the island is the beyond—a beyond that he has constructed to protect him from the haunting memories of his past marriage and legal problems. But his shame will always be with him, whether or not he resides on the island. To be truly free, Andreas must overcome his feelings of humiliation. By exposing the obscene underside of his fantasy, Bergman shows us that Andreas's self-imprisonment is an impossibility. After calling out Anna's lies, Andreas's recourse is to return to a reclusive existence. He forces Anna to confront the truth of her past, even as he cannot face his own past failures. This is not to suggest that Andreas cannot live a life of solitude, but can he live alone on the island and be at peace with his traumatic past? To confront his haunting past, in the Lacanian sense, would allow him proper distance from his impossible object cause of desire. To traverse the fantasy would allow him to break hold of his traumatic past. Instead, he over-identities with his fantasy of solitude, an alignment that literally destroys him. That is to say, Andreas gets too close to his fantasy. This is captured by the film's final use of the zoom and the film's disintegration into a white screen. Indeed, the white light of the screen is reminiscent of the morning light when Eva departs from Andreas after their affair, what Maria Bergom-Larsson describes as the "nakedness" of the victim.[28] It is a nakedness that can be described as reality without its fantasmatic screen. This nakedness is fantasy's obscene underside. Here, we can add a second level of meaning in Andreas's disintegration. The white screen not only has an ending that is "given by cinema" that Mulvey describes in *Pierrot le Fou,* but that is also given by fantasy. As explained, fantasy provides the coordinates of desire. Fantasy is the framework that allows one to have a relationship to the object cause of the desire. At the end of the film, Andreas gets too close to his fantasy, leaving viewers with a reality devoid of fantasmatic support. Not unlike the panoply of lights in the final act of *Rope* as Rupert exposes Brandon and Phillip's secret, or Jack's sensationalized experience when first encountering the outer world in *Room*, the collapse of the fantasy frame at the end of *The Passion of Anna* caves in on Andreas as he chooses to return to his existence of self-imprisonment. The crumbling of cinematic space is captured by the zoom, Andreas's creaturely movements, and the disintegration of the image into a white screen in the form of the gaze.[29] Viewers are not left with pure reality at the end of *The Passion of Anna*, but with a nightmarish depiction of reality deprived of its fantasmatic support.

4

It "Over-looks": Movement and Stillness in Stanley Kubrick's *The Shining*

The zoom that engulfs Andreas at the end of *The Passion of Anna* shares traits with the ending of Stanley Kubrick's *The Shining*, a haunted-hotel horror thriller adapted from Stephen King's 1977 novel. The film tells the story of Jack Torrance (Jack Nicholson), a writer and former schoolteacher, who is hired as a caretaker at a large hotel located in the mountains of Colorado called the Overlook. Jack, his wife Wendy (Shelley Duvall), and their son, Danny (Danny Lloyd), must live and manage the Overlook during the winter season when the hotel is closed. As Jack's writing goes nowhere, he becomes interested in the hotel's violent past, particularly the story of Charles Grady, a former Overlook caretaker who killed his wife and twin daughters with an ax. Jack discovers that the hotel is possessed by ghosts, which leads him toward madness that culminates in his attempts to kill his own family. The final image of *The Shining* is a forward traveling shot, ending on a black-and-white photograph from July 4, 1921, which presents a group of wealthy people in the Overlook's Gold Room dressed in black tie. Standing in front of the group, smiling, is Jack Torrance. Similar to *The Passion of Anna*, *The Shining* ends on a mysterious note, suggesting a circular narrative. In *The Passion of Anna*, the ticking of the clock and Bergman's voice-over, "This time they called him Andreas Winkleman," not only returns us to the film's opening scene, but also follows Laura Mulvey's description of the repetition of cinema's secret: the still image. Andreas is mummified by the zoom—rendering him creaturely as he gets too close to his fantasy object. In *The Shining*, the photograph not only embalms Jack, who happened to freeze to death in the Overlook's shrubbery maze while trying to kill Danny with an ax, but also suggests he has a secret and ghostly past. As the ghost of the former caretaker, Delbert Grady (Philip Stone) says to him in the Overlook's Gold Room bathroom: "You've always been the caretaker. I should know, sir. I've always been here." Jack even tells Wendy that he is having déjà vu: "When I came up here for my interview, it was as though I had been here before."

The ambiguity of the photograph not only contributes to *The Shining*'s uncanny atmosphere, but also speaks to the excess of the gaze that energizes the film's confined setting. Indeed, the mysterious photograph of Jack from 1921 follows Lacan's theory that the gaze is on the side of the object. Here, the photograph of Jack takes on a double meaning. The photograph literally speaks to the Overlook's mysterious and haunted past to which Jack is connected. At the same time, the gaze stands in for the blind spot within the field of representation which, as Lacan states, "photo-graphs" us the spectators.[1] The mysterious picture of Jack looking back at us realizes our desire to look within the film. Yet our encounter with the picture of Jack unsettles our spectatorship because we are left with no resolution to the question that the film's ending poses. Is Jack truly a ghost?[2] The photograph of Jack looking back at us speaks directly to Lacan's notion of the gaze. The photograph, as the embodiment of the gaze, sees us within the picture, because it signals how our desire distorts the visual field. If we felt disturbed by the ending of *The Shining*, it is because we have invested our desire to look into the film.

Perhaps more strikingly is the movement of the camera that finds the picture on the wall near the Overlook's Gold Room. Whose perspective is this attributed to? The same can be asked of the zoom that engulfs Andreas at the end of *The Passion of Anna*. In writing on the technique of suture, Slavoj Žižek explains, "one of the standard horror movie procedures is the 'resignification' of the objective into the subject shot."[3] An example of standard suturing is the shot/reverse shot technique. Take, for instance, a woman facing the front of a beach house. Ocean waves crash behind her while a man speaks off-screen. As Žižek notes, "the spectator is confronted with a shot, finds pleasure in it in an immediate, imaginary way, and is absorbed by it."[4] Our immersion into the image is then undone by realizing that we are only seeing a partial view. It is the "Absent-one," the "Other" that, as Žižek states, "manipulates images behind my back." It is the Absent-one who runs "the show."[5] The complementary reverse shot is the image of the ocean and the man behind the woman. The complementary shot embodies the place in which the Absent-one looks. The objectivity of the shot is now mapped onto the film's narrative space by a point of view. Reverse suturing, however, moves from objective *to subjective*; for example, the spectator sees an objective shot of a window, and suddenly a hand emerges off-frame and closes the curtain. The unoccupied space is now rendered with an observer.

But there is another reversal when, according to Žižek, "*there is no possible subject within the space of diegetic reality who can occupy the point of view of this shot.*"[6] This reversal undermines the technique of suture because "the tension remains unresolved."[7] The ultimate threat is a "free-floating gaze" that is *not* assigned to a specific subject, as captivatingly depicted in the traveling shot that locates the photograph of Jack. Here, the Overlook (like the photograph of Jack) carries a double meaning. On the one hand, the Overlook is the place of a free-floating gaze—an Absent-one or "Other" that does not occupy a point of view. On the other hand, it is our failure to notice: namely, a blind spot in the form of the gaze—a gaze that happens to *over-look* us. As such, the end of *The Shining* is one of many instances that manifest the film's exploration of the gaze in relation to the supernatural. From the very start of *The Shining*, Kubrick overwhelms and *disturbs* the viewer with excess information, as illustrated in the foreboding credit sequences of Jack driving to the Overlook (more on this later). From this perspective, the gaze is an unknowable force that lurks and haunts the visual field. It is an antagonistic power that makes its presence felt, but is not clearly identified as a spectral figure. The tension between showing too much and not identifying the force that follows Jack has to do with Kubrick's exploration of the supernatural and the Freudian uncanny. The way in which Kubrick articulates the film's narrative space and objects within the confined and haunted setting of the Overlook challenges us to question whether what we are experiencing is, in fact, the supernatural or the characters' imagination. Blurring the boundary between reality and the fantastic renders the setting of the Overlook a place of unreliability. As I argue, Danny uses his gift of telepathy, a special ability that allows him to see into the future and past to investigate and, ultimately, undermine the ghostly past of the Overlook Hotel as a place of "impossible subjectivity." Danny, from this perspective, operates as a supernatural detective. His ability "to shine" renders antagonistic and ghostly forces visible for the spectator, such as in his encounter with the Grady twins. Jack, too, operates as a detective into the Overlook's past. Whereas Danny's investigation of the Overlook is captured primarily by movement, Jack's exploration of the Overlook is depicted by stillness as he examines the hotel's archives (such as photographs and scrapbooks). As he says to Grady, "I saw your picture in the newspaper. You chopped your wife and daughters up into little pieces and you blew your brains out." At the same time, Jack's descent into madness renders him creaturely as he is mummified into a frozen archive at the end of the film. As such, examining the film's engagement with movement and stillness provides insights into the film's depiction of excess within the confined, haunted, and uncanny setting of the Overlook.

The Uncanny and Burnt Toast

It has been well documented that Kubrick and his screenwriter, Diane Johnson, read Freud's 1919 essay "The Uncanny" in adapting King's novel for the screen. For Freud, the uncanny manifests something "frightening which leads back to what is known of old and long familiar."[8] Through an analysis of E. T. A. Hoffman's story "The Sandman," Freud refutes Ernst Jentsch, who argues, in his 1906 essay "On the Psychology of the Uncanny," that the feelings of the uncanny are aroused by the new and unfamiliar. For Freud, the uncanny can only emerge through the old. Freud explains that the uncanny can manifest through a number of factors, including the castration complex, the return of the repressed, the double, the compulsion to repeat, the blurring of reality, the imaginary, and the animistic. Citing examples from literature, Freud specifically explains that fairy tales that channel the animistic have little impact in creating feelings of the uncanny: "Fairy tales quite frankly adopt the animistic standpoint of the omnipotence of thoughts and wishes, and yet I cannot think of any genuine fairy story which has anything uncanny about it."[9] This is because readers adjust their perception to accept the fairy tale's animistic universe. As Freud puts it, "In fairy tales . . . the world of reality is left behind from the very start, and the animistic system of belief is frankly adopted."[10] But in the case of the realist setting in literature, according to Freud, when the "writer pretends to move in the world of common reality," the uncanny has a greater chance to emerge.[11] Freud's notion of the uncanny in relation to the realist setting speaks directly to Kubrick's interest in depicting the supernatural within a natural setting in *The Shining*, challenging us to decipher what is reality and what is supernatural. As such, *The Shining* avoids many of the conventions of the horror genre, opting instead to depict a realist setting as demonstrated in the Overlook's elaborate production design, bright lighting, deep focus, and long-take cinematography. At the same time, these visual components render the space of the Overlook ominous and uncertain. Kubrick explained that he and the production designer, Roy Walker, devoted considerable research and time to photographing hotels: "We wanted the hotel to look authentic rather than like a traditionally spooky movie hotel. The hotel's labyrinthine layout and huge rooms, I believed, would alone provide an eerie enough atmosphere."[12] Kubrick's labyrinth aesthetic is reinforced by Ullman and Watson, who walk Jack and Wendy through the various sections of the Overlook early in the film. Kubrick films these sequences primarily using long and deep-focus tracking shots as we explore the spaces alongside Jack and Wendy. Yet, within these absorbing settings, an obscene underside of horror and supernatural is at work, such as when Danny witnesses the Grady twins in the Overlook's game room early in the film. Indeed, the scale and magnificence of the Colorado Lounge and the spectacular Art Deco design of the Gold Room—where Jack travels to the past and meets the ghost of the former caretaker, Grady—immerse viewers in the film's confined setting of the Overlook. At the same time, there is something more in the Overlook's space than space itself. Something sticks out within the Overlook's grand setting that infuses the film's constricted space with feelings of the uncanny. It is this excessive component that arouses our desire to look within the film, setting a trap for our encounter with the gaze.

Early in the film, Danny and the Overlook's head chef, Dick Hallorann (Scatman Crothers), converse about their gift of telepathy. Hallorann asks Danny how long he has been able to "shine." Danny replies that Tony (his imaginary friend who lives inside his mouth) does not allow him to talk about his power. Hallorann asks if Tony has ever told him about the Overlook. Danny imparts that he is not allowed to say. Danny then asks if there is something "bad" about the Overlook. Hallorann replies: "Well, you know Doc, when something happens it can leave a trace of itself behind, say like someone burns toast. Not things that anyone can notice, but things that people who shine can see." Hallorann's burnt toast example not only provides an olfactory explanation of the Overlook's bad past, but also offers a clue into Kubrick's depiction of the supernatural. This is particularly revealing in Kubrick's explanation to Michel Ciment: "As the supernatural events occurred you searched for an explanation, and the most likely one seemed to be that the strange things that were happening would finally be explained as the products of Jack's imagination. It's not until Grady, the ghost of the former caretaker who axed to death his family, slides open the bolt of the larder door, allowing Jack to escape, that you are left with no other explanation but the supernatural."[13] The evidence, or "proof," of the supernatural arrives late in the film, when Wendy knocks out Jack with a baseball bat and locks him in the kitchen's large food storage room. Grady is not Jack's imagination or a manifestation of cabin fever, but is revealed to be a supernatural entity that frees him from the larder, with the stipulation that he will murder his family. Kubrick states that this "kind of psychological misdirection [is] to forestall the realization that the supernatural events are actually happening [in the Overlook]."[14] Although Kubrick does not assign the Overlook's strange occurrences to the supernatural until the climax of the narrative, this forestalled information does manifest throughout the film as "traces of itself left behind." These traces are an excessive force that unsettles the confined setting of the Overlook.

The Unattributable Shot

One way in which Kubrick builds suspense and narrative tension without relying on traditions of horror's supernatural is by utilizing Joan Copjec's notion of the unattributable shot: a shot that cannot be connected to an observer. The unattributable shot, according to Copjec, "appears to be neutral or empty of subjectivity because . . . in contradistinction to the point-of-view shot, it is not filmed from a space that is proximate to, partially includes, or is spatially associated with a character, but from a space unaffiliated with any particular person."[15] The unattributable shot is not a reverse suturing of a subjective shot into an objective shot, but is what Žižek describes as "a place of *impossible* subjectivity."[16] For both Copjec and Žižek, the unaccounted bearer of the unattributable shot is the gaze—it is the excess that "spoils" the objectivity of the image. Yet the presence of the gaze affirms its "seal" of objectivity. Copjec specifically draws upon Jean-Paul Sartre's keyhole example in *Being and Nothingness* to explain the objectivity of the gaze of the Other. The scene Sartre paints is of a voyeur looking through a keyhole, which is, subsequently, disrupted by the sound of rustling branches and footsteps behind him that suddenly stop. Copjec explains that the voyeur's experience of the gaze "is neither an empty, transcendent *One* that unifies and guarantees existence, nor is it a *concrete community of others*, whose shared notion of reality acts as its own guarantee."[17] Rather, Sartre's keyhole example assures the subject that "some others exist." As Lacan similarly explains, "The gaze I encounter . . . is, not a seen gaze, but a gaze imagined by me in the field of the Other."[18] As such, one's encounter with the gaze provides evidence of objectivity. Yet this objectivity is also a failed or missed encounter with the gaze of the Other as a "surplus-object" that unsettles the unification of space. For Copjec, the gaze is felt through a sensible form, but it is not an object in the traditional sense: "The reference to a specific seer remains in suspense in the encounter with the Other's gaze."[19] The subject is aware that he is being seen, that the Other's gaze emerges aurally (footsteps and the rustling of leaves), but what is causing the noise is not to be seen. As Henry Krips explains, "the subject is brought to recognize that there is a hole, a lack, in the visual field" through his own scrutiny.[20] The distortion within the visual field of representation is the gaze when the voyeur becomes aware of his looking as a subject of desire.

Suture helps to explain the inapprehensibility of the gaze and the suspension of the seer. Suturing is an exchange in which the gaze of the Other and the subject would recognize each other. By contrast, the failed encounter with the gaze is the gaze of the Other seeing the subject, but there is "no there" of the gaze. In other words, there is no "Absent-one" as a bearer of the look to signify for the viewer.[21] As such, the "no there" of the gaze is the unattributable shot for Copjec. The unattributable shot make itself felt, but is not attached to a specific observer of the shot signified for the viewer. The inability to suture the excess linked to the gaze in *The Shining* is something that lingers like "burnt toast," as demonstrated in the opening aerial shots and rolling introductory credits.

Certainly, unattributable shots can be found in many movies. So what makes the aerial shots in *The Shining* different? How do these shots, which lack a point of view, create narrative tension? The composition of cinematic space typically corresponds to narrative causality. Classical narrative cinema builds shots that adhere to narrative action. Each shot and scene must push the narrative forward. Therefore, ambiguities will often be answered. For example, if we see a character framed far off to the right, we expect that something will fill in the extra space to the left. This is often the case in horror films, when the victim is being stalked. There are also shots that begin with an unattributed viewpoint, and are then suddenly filled with an observer, such as Hitchcock's famous omniscient shot of Bodega Bay in *The Birds* (1963), which turns out to be the birds' malicious point of view. As such, a gap opens in cinematic space, which is then filled with the bearer of the look.

But there are unattributable shots that are stressed in form, or have unusual emphasis and are not assigned to a point of view. These shots carry something that "sticks out," as in the opening images of the mountainous terrain in *The Shining*. The sublime aerial images are juxtaposed to Jack's yellow VW Beetle as he drives along the mountain to the Overlook for his interview (see figure 4.1). Indeed, Kubrick's expressive use of the unattributable shot captures the presence of the gaze that prowls its subject. The first image is a low aerial shot of Saint Mary Lake in Glacier National Park, as the image quickly approaches Wild Goose Island. The oddity of this opening image not only sets the uncertain tone of the film, but also establishes its connection to water as a form of rebirth, which may offer a clue to the mysterious photograph of Jack from 1921 in laying claim to the film's circular narrative. As the image moves past the lake, it tilts toward the mountains, dissolving into a very high omniscient shot of a yellow VW Beetle driving along the road. Kubrick's use of Wendy Carlos and Rachel Elkind's haunting synthesizer soundtrack, voices, and the wide-angle lens unsettles the enormous beauty of the mountains, expressing some sort of threat that follows or "overlooks" Jack. Like the clouds that dim the sun on the horizon in the opening of *The Passion of Anna*, the breadth of the wide-angle aerial photography resonates with something foreboding. At one point, the camera swoops alongside Jack's car as a note from the soundtrack loudly sustains itself. The image then

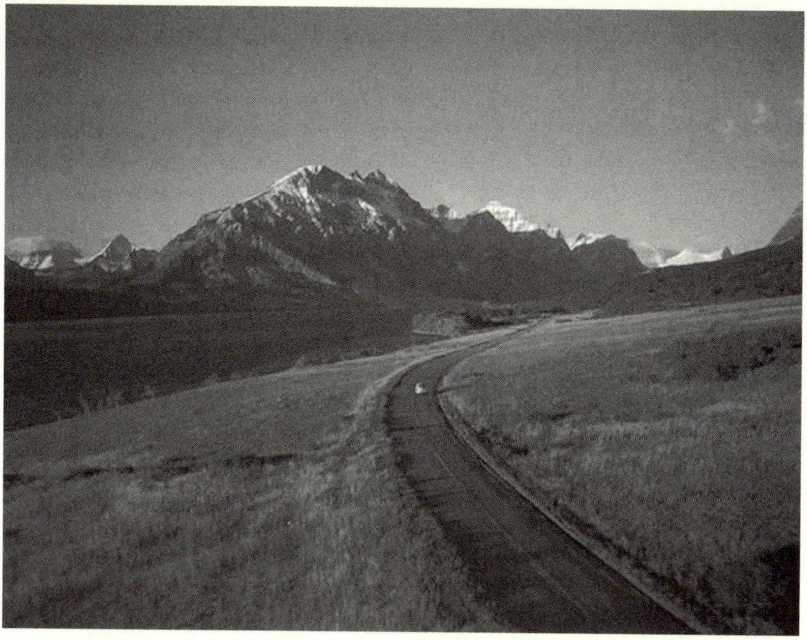

Figure 4.1 *The Shining*. The unattributable shot suggests something following Jack.

trails off the road, flying over the cliffs as we hear extra-diegetic dissonant sounds of a human voice. As such, the opening images of the film and haunting score are composed with unusual emphasis in order to evoke the notion that "some others exist"—that a gaze not identified with a specific observer lurks around Jack. The unsettling effect of the skulking aerial shots is reinforced by the film's blue rolling credits (often reserved for the end of a movie), suggesting, again, that *The Shining* is a circular narrative: the end is the beginning.[22]

The ethereal energy in the opening sequence carries over into the film's confined setting of the Overlook, particularly Danny traversing the corridors on his Big Wheel bike. Whereas the scope of the aerial images of the American frontier engulf Jack's VW Beetle, the wide-angle lens that captures Danny on his bicycle suggests something excessive that cannot be incorporated within the confined, maze-like setting of the Overlook. This is particularly enhanced by the loudness of Danny's wheels that roar throughout the Overlook's corridors. Not unlike the aerial images that follow behind Jack's vehicle, the mobile camera that trails behind Danny's Big Wheel suggest the presence of something that both visually and aurally prowls, as when Danny encounters the Grady twins in the west wing during the Saturday sequence.

While Jack types away in the Colorado Lounge, Wendy communicates with the Forest Service via radio about the downed phone lines from the snowstorm. After the Forest Service instructs Wendy to keep the radio on at all times, the image cuts to a long shot of Danny driving his Big Wheel down a green corridor. Whereas the earlier traveling shots of Danny positioned the camera in close proximity to his Big Wheel, the framing of the bike in the green corridor is kept at a far distance (see figure 4.2). Danny turns his bike and exits frame right, but the camera continues to creep forward within the empty space of the green corridor. The lingering movement of the camera and the ominous score draw unusual attention to themselves, suggesting something threatening. The emphasis on the lingering camera in the corridor is not only an anomaly that captures our desire, but also sets a trap for our encounter with the gaze. The image cuts to Danny as he pedals along the west wing corridor. He turns a corner and instantly stops as he sees the Grady twins holding hands, an encounter punctuated by a non-diegetic gong. The twins say in unison: "Hullo, Danny. Come and play with us. Come and play with us, Danny. For ever . . . and ever . . . and ever," as the image intercuts with a shot of the twins lying on the floor covered in blood. Danny's movement is thus met with a violent halt that triggers his shining. Danny covers his eyes, looking through his fingers until the vision of the Grady twins disappears. Danny lowers his hands and talks to Tony, saying that he is scared. Tony reminds him, saying: "Remember what Mr. Hallorann said. It's just like pictures in a book, Danny. It isn't real." Tony's words both comfort and challenge us, as Kubrick toys with the notion of what we are seeing: is it Danny's imagination or the supernatural? Indeed, the camera's stressed movement as Danny rides his Big Wheel in the green corridor after he exits the space sticks out, creating a sense of uncertainty that elicits our desire. It is this stain (the unusual emphasis on the empty space in the green corridor) that not only builds anxiety, but also sets up Danny's (and our) encounter with the gaze. The gaze realizes a blind spot in our looking, one that is further emphasized by the claustrophobic corridor in which Danny encounters the twins, and Kubrick positioning the camera behind Danny. These obstructions reveal that the logic of desire is not based on mastery but on absence, or what we cannot know. At the same time, the lingering camera movement within the corridor is a sensible form that cannot be attributed to a bearer of the look that unsettles the confined setting of the Overlook. This uncertainty captures the mystery of the Overlook—something in the space more than the space that cannot be apprehended. As such, the uncanny feelings of the Overlook's confined setting realizes our investment in the narrative as situated within the film and not as a transcendental spectator. As Copjec

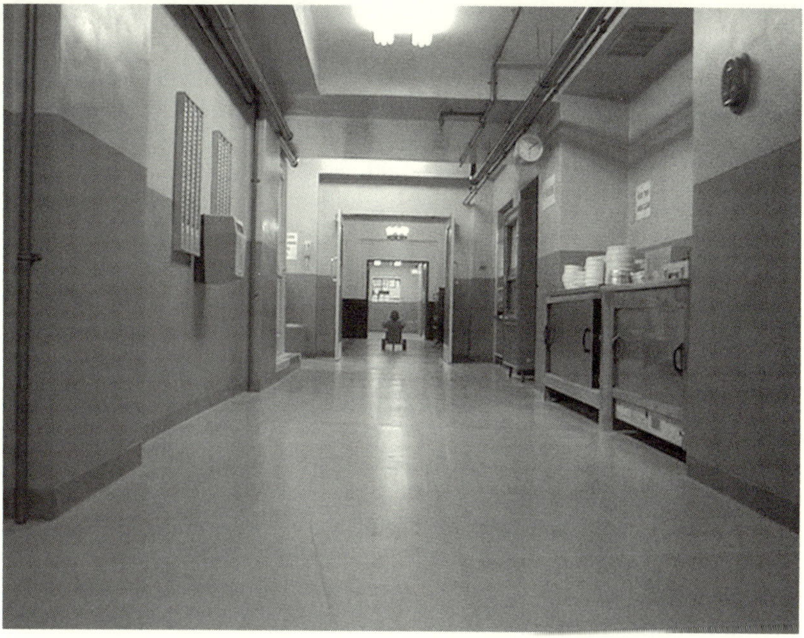

Figure 4.2. *The Shining*. The camera lingers far behind Danny to suggest something frighteningly unknowable.

states, "Point-of-view structure depends on there being no total view, no transcendental position from which an all would, if only in principle, come into view."[23] Kubrick's expressionistic movement of the Steadicam, wide-angle framing, and sinister soundtrack manifest the excess of the gaze. At the same time, the unattributable bearer of the look suggests the presence of others that exist in the Overlook. Danny's ability to manifest the past confirms what lurks in the corridors and may not just be his imagination. As I will explain in the final section of this chapter, exploring the reverse-angle shot offers a potential clue to uncovering the Overlook's ghostly dimension.

Television Screens

The mobile long take both energizes the confined setting of the Overlook and suggests a spectral presence that unhinges the film's confined space. But equally powerful is Kubrick's use of stillness, as demonstrated in Danny's encounter with the Grady twins in the Overlook corridor.

Stillness and movement are pitted against each other, not only to disturb our viewership, but also to explore the past and future of the Overlook, as demonstrated in both Jack's interview for the caretaker position and Danny's premonition early in the film.

Kubrick films Jack's interview with stillness, cutting between shot and reverse shot, between Jack and Stuart Ullman (Barry Nelson) and Bill Watson (Barry Dennen). At one point, Ullman tells Jack about a past event involving the former caretaker, Charles (or is it Delbert?) Grady, who killed his family with an ax and "stacked them neatly in one of the rooms in the west wing." The police believed it was a result of cabin fever, of being shut in for a long period of time. Jack ironically says: "Well, you can rest assured Mr. Ullman, that's not going to happen to me." Yet we sense uncertainty in Jack's reaction. We learn that he was once a violent drinker, but has now been sober for five months. After Jack's interview, the film cuts to an apartment complex in Boulder, Colorado. Danny brushes his teeth in a bathroom. The camera creeps toward him as Tony tells Danny that Jack got the job at the Overlook. This is confirmed when the image cuts to the phone ringing in the kitchen. Wendy answers as we learn that Jack has, in fact, been offered the job. After Danny finishes brushing his teeth, he continues to talk to Tony, a conversation that occurs in the mirror, an object often connected to the supernatural in *The Shining*. Danny asks Tony why he does not want to go to the hotel. Tony will not say. Danny begs him to tell him as the image zooms into his mirror image. The image cuts to a low and still shot of two red elevator doors at the Overlook hotel. The perfect symmetrical framing of the elevators and still camera are unsettled by a wave of blood slowly gushing out of the left side of the elevator door. As the blood flows toward the camera, Kubrick intermittently inserts two images of the Grady girls holding hands in a corridor, looking directly at the camera, and an image of Danny scared, with his mouth wide open, also looking directly at the camera. After the third insert shot, the blood reaches the camera, flowing upwards, filling the screen with darkness. Whereas Jack is tragically confronted with the Overlook's past of Grady murdering his family, Danny is horrifically and traumatically confronted with a future event. If we did not take Tony seriously when first meeting Danny and Wendy over lunch at the beginning of the film, the blood gushing out of the elevator certainly cements our investment within the film's narrative. Something is not "correct" about the Overlook hotel. Indeed, the past and future events manifest through movement and stillness. Ullman informing Jack of Charles Grady's murderous act and Danny seeing the Grady twins not only teleport us to the past and future, but establish *The Shining*'s suspense that carries over into the rest of the film. Additionally, these events provide us with surplus-knowledge pertaining to the Overlook, rendering the confined setting with uncertainty, or something that lingers like "burnt toast."

Perhaps most importantly, Danny's premonition of the blood gushing out of the elevator doors takes place in the bathroom, a recognized site for acts of violence in horror/thriller cinema. Two scenes worthy of note include the death of Marion (Janet Leigh) in *Psycho*,[24] and the blood emerging out of the toilet in *The Conversation*. After Marion's death in the shower, Norman mops up the mess to eliminate all traces of the crime. However, in *The Conversation*, Harry Caul encounters a bathroom devoid of any evidence of a murder. Yet, when he flushes the toilet, he notices that it is not working properly. Suddenly, blood gushes out of the toilet, as Harry steps back with disgust. Slavoj Žižek explains Harry's encounter in the hotel bathroom as a reference to a "preontological realm," a "netherworld" or void that is kept submerged by way of the drain. As Žižek observes, "What is 'Real' in the scene from *The Conversation* is thus not primarily the horrifying and disgusting stuff reemerging from the toilet sink, but rather that toilet's drain itself, the hole that serves as the passage to a different ontological order."[25] The drain not only flushes away "excrement" into a void, but can also return "things" back to us in the form of the gaze.[26] Not unlike the big window in Brandon and Phillip's penthouse in *Rope*, the drain functions as an empty fantasy screen that filters the real. When the fantasy screen crumbles, we encounter a nightmarish form of reality, as captured in the elevator sequence in *The Shining*. On the one hand, the elevator operates as something that physically carries people to the various levels of the Overlook. On the other hand, it serves as a passage of time in terms of the hotel's past and future, as depicted in the interview sequence and Danny's premonition. Additionally, the blood gushing out of the elevator door exhibits a supernatural force unleashed from within the void of the Overlook, an unknowable force that unsettles its confined spaces.

Indeed, the elevator becomes an animistic object, generating feelings of the uncanny that Freud posits as the return of the old. A notable film in this regard is Tobe Hooper's *Poltergeist* (1982), which tells the story of a Californian suburban family whose home is invaded and overtaken by malevolent ghosts that abduct the family's youngest daughter, Carol Anne Freeling (Heather O'Rourke). Early in the film, Carol Anne becomes fixated with the television set, which transmits static after the station signs off. In a well-known scene, the passing of a scary thunderstorm propels Carol Anne and her brother to sleep with their parents. As the family sleeps, the television plays the national anthem. The television signal signs off as flickering blue light floods the room with static and white noise. Carol Anne awakens and approaches the television, placing her hands against the screen. The hand of a ghost suddenly emerges from the television, followed by what appears to be an earthquake. A bolt of energy shoots out of the television and burns a hole in the wall above the bed. The family awakens shocked to see Carol Anne in front of the television frighteningly saying: "They're here." Not unlike the drain in the bathroom in *The Conversation*, the television (as a "haunted media," to use Jeffrey Sconce's term)[27] is a breakdown of the fantasmatic barrier that becomes a passageway into an unknown "netherworld." As such, the collapse of the television fantasy screen in *Poltergeist* is an encounter with the gaze, where unknown and evil forces from another dimension emerge and invade the Freelings' home. Here, the television's flickering blue light is not unlike the panoply of the city lights that flood the apartment through the windows in the climax of *Rope* as an embodiment of the gaze. In both cases, the barrier between reality and the real falters, as unknown entities invade the domestic space with disturbing results.

Televisions are also connected to the supernatural in *The Shining*. When Jack telephones Wendy to tell her that he was offered the job, a television can be seen in the background of the Overlook lobby. When the image cuts to Wendy on the phone, she stands in the living room with a television in the visual space behind her. Their conversation occurs at the same time as Danny's moment of shining in the bathroom, illustrating the presence of the lurking supernatural. Although the television behind Jack is turned off, its uncanny presence speaks to the film's exploration of the paranormal. Writing on Raymond Williams's notion of "planned flow" in television, Jeffrey Sconce explains, "TV is a world that is always there, at least in unrealized form, even when the set is turned off."[28] Even when we turn off the television, the live flow of television never stops. Television continues to show up in *The Shining*, such as when Danny explains to Jack that he learned about the Donner Party on television as they drive to the Overlook. As many have observed, the crammed shot of Jack, Wendy, and Danny in the VW Beetle alludes to Jack's mental collapse due to cabin fever. At the same time, the tight composition of the three in Jack's VW is reminiscent of television's squared-frame screen. Indeed, the Torrance family on display is not the wholesome family typically depicted in shows such as *Father Knows Best* (1954–60) or *The Donna Reed Show* (1958–66)—sitcoms often nostalgically interpreted as representing the innocence of the 1950s. Perhaps the most striking connection between the television and the supernatural is Danny's use of telepathy to contact Hallorann for help after being attacked in room 237. Hallorann, who happens to be watching TV in Miami, receives Danny's message as they both "tune in" to "watch" Jack "live" as he enters room 237 and encounters the shape-shifting ghost who attacked Danny.

When Jack encounters the ghost in the bathroom of room 237,

he too encounters the "netherworld" of the Overlook. A young woman emerges naked out of the bathtub, approaches Jack, and begins to kiss him. The image cuts to a reverse shot of Jack in the bathroom mirror, which shockingly reveals that the woman is now covered in grotesque scars. When Jack looks directly at the woman, she is now an old woman. Jack slowly backs away as she laughs, approaching him with outstretched arms. The image cuts to a dead corpse slowly rising out of the bathtub. Both the shape-shifting ghost and the corpse in the bathtub not only unsettle Jack's sexual desire, but are also "things" from the spectral dimension of the Overlook that unsettle the confined space. Here, the post-effect of the gaze has captured not only Jack's creaturely movements out of room 237, but also the harsh laughter and repulsive outstretched arms of the ghost that suggest bodily *jouissance.* The mummified movement of the shape-shifting ghost correlates to what Lacan terms the "sinthome." Whereas the subject's symptom can be analyzed and interpreted, the sinthome withstands meaning. The sinthome, as Žižek explains, is "the kernel of enjoyment that simultaneously attracts and repels us."[29] Certainly, the strange laugh of the old woman and her creaturely extended arms portend Jack's freezing to death in the maze at the end of the film, captured in his animal-like noises, and raising his ax in the air—all signifiers that lack meaning but remain intimately connected to the Overlook's supernatural dimension.[30]

The Reverse Shot

The reverse shot plays an important role in unleashing the Overlook's apparitions. During his talk with Hallorann early in the film, Danny asks: "what is in room 237"? Danny bluntly says to Hallorann, "You're scared of room 237. Aren't you?" Hallorann forcefully instructs Danny to stay out of room 237. Later in the film, while riding his Big Wheel, Danny stops at room 237. He tries to open the door, but it is locked. Kubrick quickly inserts an image of the Grady twins, reminding him not to further his investigation. During the Wednesday sequence, Danny plays with his toys on the maze-designed carpet, not far from room 237. A yellow tennis ball, the same ball Jack throws against the wall in the Colorado lounge earlier in the film, rolls into Danny's circle of toys. The image cuts to a reverse shot that reveals an empty hallway and then cuts back to a front shot of Danny as he stands and looks down the empty hallway. He shouts: "Mom." Here, Kubrick's use of the wide-angle lens engulfs Danny within the space of the corridor, suggesting an unknowable presence at work.

The image cuts to a reverse angle, still revealing an empty hallway, and then returns to a front shot of Danny slowly walking down the hallway. As he approaches room 237, the image shows Danny's point of view as he sees the door mysteriously open ajar. Indeed, the reverse shot carries extra meaning. As explained, suturing replaces the position of the "Absent-one," the diegetic space behind the subject, with an observer. What cannot be sutured, however, is the "impossible subjectivity" assigned to the gaze. Kubrick emphasizes this impossibility by including Danny's body within the filmic space when cutting to the reverse shot of the empty hallway rather than to Danny's point-of-view perspective. As such, the ball rolling into the frame follows Copjec's premise of the unattributable shot in that "some others exist." But we are not granted a bearer of the look when cutting to the space from which the ball came, demonstrating Kubrick's depiction of the supernatural as leaving "a trace of itself behind."

More significantly, the reverse shot not only suggests the presence of the Overlook's "netherworld," but also operates as a key that unlocks doors to the Overlook's ghostly dimension—such as Jack's encounter with Lloyd the Bartender (Joe Turkel) in the Gold Room. Having been blamed by Wendy for hurting Danny, who was attacked in room 237, Jack enters the Gold Room and sits at an empty bar. In a medium-close shot, Jack covers his face with frustration and says: "God, I'd give anything for a drink. My goddam soul, just a glass of beer." Jack uncovers his face, smiles, and says: "Hi, Lloyd. A little slow tonight, isn't it?" The reverse-angle shot shows Lloyd standing behind the bar, which is now filled with liquor bottles. Lloyd appears through the reverse perspective, demonstrating that ghosts are connected to mirrors and doubling in *The Shining*.[31] Yet we are not entirely sure if Lloyd is a product of Jack's imagination or is truly a ghost. Wendy finds Jack at the empty bar to tell him about the woman in room 237. After his horrific encounter with the ghost in room 237, Jack meets Wendy at their living quarters. He lies, saying that he "didn't see one goddam thing." He strikingly suggests that Danny hurt himself. Wendy emotionally reacts by saying that they need to leave the Overlook, an urgent assertion that upsets Jack, who forcefully responds: "It is so fucking typical of you to create a problem like this when I finally have a chance to accomplish something. When I'm really into my work. I could really write my own ticket if I went back to Boulder now, couldn't I? Shoveling out driveways, work in a car wash, any of that appeal to you? Wendy, I have let you fuck up my life so far, but I'm not going to let you fuck this up." Jack storms out of the room and heads back to the Gold Room. He hears music from the 1920s and enters the Gold Room, which is now filled with people of the past, signaled by the elaborate Art Deco design of the setting. Jack buys another drink from

Lloyd, but this time drinks are on the house. Notably, Jack did not have money to pay for his drink when he first encountered Lloyd. Now he has money, calling into question what is real and what is supernatural. Moreover, the economic and class concerns that Jack expresses to Wendy proffer another clue to the mysterious photograph from 1921 at the end of the film. As Roger Luckhurst notes: "This is not the photograph of a janitor but one of those jet-set-before-the-jet-set playboys. This is Jack the celebrity, an F. Scott Fitzgerald in his pomp, not the later Fitzgerald, a struggling alcoholic."[32] As Jack leaves the bar, a waiter, Grady, spills a drink on him. Grady escorts Jack into the red bathroom to clean his jacket. Not knowing that the waiter is Grady, Jack asks him what they call him. The waiter answers: "Delbert Grady, Sir." The image cuts to a reverse angle of Jack and Grady. Jack realizes Grady was the Overlook's past caretaker who killed his family and himself. Jack tries to get Grady to admit that he was the caretaker. But Grady denies it. Jack explains that he saw his picture in the paper and read the article. The image cuts to a reverse angle, holding for a moment, and then back to the two-shot of Jack and Grady, creating a mirroring effect. Grady says to Jack: "You've always been the caretaker. I should know, Sir. I've always been here." He explains that Danny has a special talent which he plans to use against Jack's will. Jack blames Danny's willfulness on Wendy. Grady suggests that maybe "they need a good talking to. . . . Perhaps a bit more." Not unlike Danny's encounter with the open door in room 237, or Lloyd the bartender's first appearance, the reverse angle opens a door into the Overlook's ghostly past. Through the use of the reverse shot, Delbert Grady becomes Charles Grady, the caretaker who killed his family in 1970. Like Tony, Grady is a supernatural messenger who informs Jack of Danny's talent, which poses a threat "against Jack's will." Indeed, Kubrick offers a twist on the suturing effect in the use of the reverse shot in relation to the supernatural. The Absent-one is sutured for the viewer by cutting between shot and reverse shot in the bathroom. At the same time, Kubrick subverts the suturing effect by using the shot/reverse-shot technique to open a portal into the Overlook's haunted realm. In this sense, the Absent-one allocates and signifies a bearer of the look through the use of the reverse shot. Paradoxically, the occupied space of the Absent-one is filled in with a subject (Charles Grady) who is indeed *absent.* Kubrick explained to Michel Ciment why he depicted the apparitions as physically real rather than as see-through ghosts: "From the more convincing accounts I have read of people who have reported seeing ghosts, they were invariably described as being as solid and as real as someone actually standing in the room."[33] This explanation certainly follows Freud's claim that there is a stronger possibility of the uncanny emerging within a realist setting.

Instead of showing Grady, the Grady twins, or Lloyd the bartender magically appearing as ghosts in a cliché form, Kubrick employs the reverse angle and mirrors, as well as staging ghosts as real people in order to produce the effect of the uncanny.

In the climax of the film, Jack chases Danny through the Overlook's shrubbery maze during a blizzard. Mirroring his movement on his Big Wheel bike, the camera lurks behind Danny. Jack shouts: "I'm right behind you, Danny," as he follows Danny's footsteps in the snow. Danny realizes that in order to survive he must trick Jack. Danny stops and slowly steps backwards into his own footprints in the snow in order to create a trail that ends nowhere. Once Jack encounters the end of the trail, Danny quickly sneaks off and follows his tracks back to the entrance of the maze. While Danny is working on his escape plan, Wendy (who has been encountering ghosts in the Overlook) is traveling down a red corridor, an area we have not seen in the film. She suddenly stops as she sees two elevator doors. Suddenly, blood gushes out of the left elevator door. It is the premonition Danny had seen at the start of the film, suggesting that this future event (by way of Tony) was his mother's perspective. Wendy's encounter with the elevators occurs in an unidentified area of the Overlook, thus demonstrating a sort of déjà vu effect upon the viewer. On the one hand, we are familiar with the Overlook elevators by way of Danny's premonition. Yet something is rediscovered when Wendy travels down the red corridor, an uncharted space in the film. We have and have not been here before, as we experience something old within the new, demonstrating what Freud attributes to the uncanny.

By moving backwards in his snow prints, Danny outwits his father and escapes the maze. Danny reunites with his mother outside the maze, and they leave the Overlook. Meanwhile, Jack stumbles along the maze, lost and freezing as he hears Wendy and Danny drive away. Kubrick abruptly cuts to Jack frozen to death in the maze. The still image is both hilarious and frightening. Moreover, the still image mummifies Jack, an image that mirrors the black-and-white photograph of Jack from July 4, 1921, in the Gold Room revealed at the end of the film. Kubrick's surprise by way of the photograph is not unlike horror films' trick finales. As explained in the introduction, both *Alien* and *Carrie* draw on the trick ending that the "horror" is not over, though in the case of *Carrie*, it was all in Emily's mind. Nevertheless, these endings offer a shocking surprise as an embodiment of the gaze. Here, Kubrick's surprise ending follows a convention of horror cinema, denying narrative closure.[34] As the camera reaches the photograph, we are unsure whom we should be focusing on. After two dissolves, which bring us closer and closer to the figure in the photograph, we see that the person is Jack dressed in black tie, looking directly at us as he stands with a group of wealthy people from the past. Jack's smile in the photograph is not unlike his laugh and smile when first meeting Lloyd the bartender early in the film. This raises a question: are the photographs on the wall in the Overlook ghosts acting as Poe's purloined letter—hidden in plain sight?

Many factors that Freud argues produce feelings of the uncanny are at work in *The Shining*, particularly the compulsion to repeat, as when Wendy discovers Jack's manuscript that endlessly reads: "All work and no play makes Jack a dull boy." Certainly, the ending of the film on the photograph of Jack from 1921 suggests a circular narrative. At least, according to Roger Luckhurst, the elusive meaning of the photograph invites and challenges us to review and decode the film again and again.[35] As depicted in the documentary *Room 237* (Rodney Ascher, 2012), fans and academic scholars have taken up Kubrick's challenge in numerous interpretations of, and debates about, the film's ambiguous meanings. Perhaps the need for repeated viewings of *The Shining* speaks directly to the death drive and the monotony of never finding the solutions to the questions posed by the film. Here, the feelings of the uncanny are intimately connected to the film's exploration of excess within the confined setting of the Overlook. Just as Jack finds that Danny's snow footprints abruptly end in the maze, we are forced to tarry with the film's uncanny and unexplained ending. Like the opening images that hauntingly track Jack across the mountains, the film leaves us with uncertainty. At the same time, it is the antagonism that captures our desire of looking. Desire manifests from absence and lack, which enables us to encounter the shocking impact of the gaze. But, unlike most Hollywood films, *The Shining* does not offer a solution to the question it poses at the end of the film.

Finally, the photograph from 1921 not only suggests the Overlook's ghostly dimension, but closely follows Laura Mulvey's description of cinema's secret: the still frame, cinema's index of light and space. As Mulvey observes, "Although the projector reconciles the opposition and the still frames come to life, this underlying stillness provides cinema with a secret, with a hidden past that might or might not find its way to the surface."[36] For Mulvey, digital playback devices now allow one to conjure cinema's still image as a "ghostly presence" by delaying and halting the flow of images.[37] Indeed, Danny's ability to shine operates like a "haunted" playback device (by way of Tony) in investigating and resurrecting the Overlook's ghostly past—to detect and explore the "traces of itself left behind." But at the end of the film, Danny and Tony are long gone and cannot teleport us to the past to find the answers to all of the questions the film raises, particularly the mysterious photo of Jack from 1921. As such, we, too, are left inside a maze with no trail or map to find our way out.

5

"It's Just a Show"? Paranoia and Provocation in Oliver Stone's *Talk Radio*

So far, we have examined the different ways in which the gaze impacts the confinement of cinematic space, and how it elicits our spectatorship as a mode of shock and attraction. The encounter with the gaze illustrates how our desire distorts the visual field of perception. Desire does not function on the mastery of looking. Rather, desire is triggered by what we cannot see and know. It is absence and lack that draw us into a film's story world. Through cinematic fantasy, the gaze reveals itself as a force that both entices and unsettles our spectatorship. *The Shining*'s embodiment of the gaze demonstrated how excess energizes the confined spaces of the Overlook hotel as a spectral presence. At the same time, the film challenges our formal expectations of the horror genre by Kubrick's uses of a natural setting, hard lighting, and long-take cinematography. These components create the conditions to evoke Freud's notion of the uncanny as a return of the old, the familiar within the unfamiliar.

Just as the gaze reveals *objet petit a* within the field of perception, sound, too, functions as a partial drive.[1] It is what Lacan calls the invocatory drive. The invocatory drive reveals how our desire to hear shapes the aural field, such as the disembodied voice. Michel Chion terms the presence of the bodiless voice in cinema as *acousmêtre*: "when we cannot yet connect it [the voice] to a face."[2] To hear a voice that is separate from the owner of the voice's body manifests our desire to hear. The exploration of sound and voice in cinema can have a tremendous impact upon spectatorship, particularly within the confined setting of Oliver Stone's *Talk Radio*.

Stone's body of work in the 1980s was recognized for its political and social commentary and leftist vision in examining recent U.S. history and culture. Films such as *Salvador* (1986), *Platoon* (1986), *Wall Street* (1987), and *Born on the Fourth of July* (1989) polemically and critically interrogated social issues, such as America's foreign policies, financial greed, the Vietnam War, and post-Vietnam experience. But little scholarly attention has been given to *Talk Radio* (1988) and its dark examination of American shock jock and political talk radio. Stone's films are often excessive in order to visualize the mechanisms of ideology and symbolic authority, whether they are exploring the issue of wealth and greed in *Wall Street*, or the conspiracy theories debated in *JFK* (1991). Stone applies this same approach to the confined setting of *Talk Radio*, by rendering the disembodied voice as an unknowable force in order to unearth an obscene underside to the participatory form of talk radio and media economics in the late 1980s.

The emergence of the American talk radio format in the 1970s and 1980s reinvigorated the medium and directly engaged audience participation. Talk radio shows such as *The Bob Grant Show* and *The Larry King Show* offered listeners a platform to voice their opinions and concerns about social issues, especially those who increasingly felt disconnected from the mainstream media. As Susan J. Douglas explains, "NPR [National Public Radio] and political talk radio both tapped into the sense of loss of public life in the 1980s and beyond, the isolation that came from overwork and the privatization of American life, and the huge gap people felt between themselves and those who run the country."[3] Along these lines, controversial shock jocks such as Howard Stern, Don Imus, and Rush Limbaugh helped boost radio's listenership, as well as to give voice to those who felt detached from the mainstream media. Both shock jock broadcasting and the participatory democracy of political talk radio are points of concern in Stone's *Talk Radio.* Made during a short window of time between *Platoon* and *Born on the Fourth of July*, *Talk Radio* tells the story of provocative talk show host Barry Champlain (Eric Bogosian), who is gunned down by a disturbed listener/caller of his show *Night Talk.* Adapted from Eric Bogosian's one-man play and based, in part, upon Stephen Singular's *Talked to Death: The Life and Death of Alan Berg*, the film takes place over the four days leading up to Barry's murder. Stone's adaptation of Bogosian's play intensifies the drama, adds more settings and events—including a basketball game Barry attends as a guest celebrity speaker—and creates a more complex character—presenting his backstory as a men's clothing salesman, his rise as a shock jock media celebrity, and a divorce from his wife, Ellen (Ellen Greene). But the majority of the film occurs at Dallas's radio station, WGAB, a deranged and deranging space that plays a crucial part in the narrative. Here, Stone makes up for the disembodied voice by creating a cinema of excess where the gaze is made knowable within the confined setting.

According to Stone, Bogosian's play was technically challenging to adapt to the screen. As Stone stated, "It was a bit of an exercise to stretch myself and to try new ways of shooting, working with a small cast: severe discipline, six people and a limited set, like a submarine film or an elevator film. How to deal with a limited amount of space was challenging to me after having worked with large canvases. It was like doing a chamber piece."[4] Stone's visual transformation of Bogosian's one-man play is evident in Barry's frenetic performance, the film's complex camera movements, and its creative set design. Indeed, Stone enhances the visual interest and narrative drama of Bogosian's play in order to create what the film critic David Denby describes as "one of the most complete expressions of paranoia ever put on film."[5] On the one hand, the film sustains narrative suspense by not revealing the faces that belong to the callers. On the other hand, Stone visualizes the disturbance in the separation of voice and body by exposing cinematic excess in order to visualize a space of paranoia where Barry is constantly under threat by the public.

But another component of *Talk Radio* makes it more than simply a filmed stage play. The suspense, paranoia, and visual energy of *Talk Radio* are attributed to Barry's obscene enjoyment as a shock jock. As Barry states in his last radio show before he is murdered: "*Night Talk* still has a purpose, a standard to which it must rise, and I will not let you down on that score. This show is about saying what's got to be said. That's what we're gonna do tonight. Tonight, anything goes. I wanna hear you. I want you to tell me what you really think. No holds barred." In *Rope*, Brandon and Phillip's goal is to contain their excessive enjoyment during the dinner party in order to prevent the big Other from recognizing David's body in the trunk. By contrast, Barry not only exposes the obscene enjoyment ("no holds barred") he derives from unfiltered speaking on controversial topics, but also invites his listeners to do the same. For Barry, radio also plays a compensatory role, one involving far more familiar, benign exchanges; as he says: "Talk Radio, it's the last neighborhood in town. People don't talk to each other anymore."

At the same time, Barry's "no holds barred" ethos on sensitive topics has resulted in death threats from some of his extreme participant audience members, particularly Chet (Earl Hindman), a neo-Nazi who often calls to express his frustration with Barry's views on controversial issues, such as race and religion, as well as to voice his own racist remarks aimed at Barry's ethnicity as a Jewish American. As such, Barry's refusal to "soften his show" has a political and ethical dimension. Politically, the very definition of the social order—in this case, the symbolic identities of America and the right to free speech—become sites of tension between Barry and his callers. Ethically, Barry stubbornly refuses to tone down his comments or soften his show regardless of the death threats he receives. The film's confined spaces intensify this strife, because viewers cannot visually access racist and bigoted callers such as Chet; rather, they are spatially and exclusively restricted to Barry's perspective and what arguably creates *Talk Radio*'s spectatorship of paranoia.

Visualizing Barry's Enjoyment

Jacques Lacan's concept of the symbolic order is the realm of culture, the place of language, the signifiers and networks of everyday life. The symbolic provides languages and systems in order for one to generate meaning and make sense of everyday experiences. The symbolic not only sustains one's identity, but provides identities that one can pursue. For example, taking up the identity of an American has symbolic currency that one can adopt, such as freedom and democracy. Of course, the definition of American identity in the 1980s is a central topic and concern of Barry's talk show. Barry's abrasive and carnival barker style follows the macho and over-the-top antics associated with the shock jock talk radio format that emerged in the 1980s. As Susan J. Douglas explains, "Talk radio is as much—maybe even more—about gender politics at the end of the century as it is about party politics."[6] For Douglas, talk radio is not only about "rudeness" and "the amplification of right wing politics," but also about restoring masculine entitlement.[7] Here the historical moment is crucial. The Reagan administration's platform ran on the philosophy of restoring America to traditional values of religion and family, and part of Reagan's doctrine in reclaiming America's greatness was exemplified by a particular masculine figure: the rugged individual who was embodied in popular forms of entertainment, particularly in the Hollywood action film genre. As Daniel Marcus summarizes, "The Reagan era had seen a series of hyper-masculine heroes, particularly in spectacular action films, who responded to feminist and international challenges to masculine American prerogatives with macho attitudes, steroidal physiques and hyperbolic firepower."[8] Films such as *Rambo: First Blood Part II* (George P. Cosmatos, 1982), *Commando* (Mark L. Lester, 1985), and *Die Hard* follow the strong male of Reagan conservatism in late Cold War America. As Stone portrays, these features of the masculine figure were no less a part of talk radio discourse, as when Barry states that people would rather watch television than have sex with their loved ones. Even Barry's provocative remarks on the excessive consumption of suntan lotion by white Americans—at $165 million—portrayed in a flashback sequence when he is a guest on *Talk of the Town* calculatedly seeks to ridicule masculine anxieties. As he explains, "white Americans" spend vast sums of money on suntan lotion because they "feel sexually inferior" to black men. Barry's show's theme song "Bad to the Bone" also underscores the macho persona associated with shock jock radio.

The symbolic order functions as a large network of language, providing the groundwork for the daily interaction of culture. For Lacan, the basis that holds the social order together is the prohibition of enjoyment, which is enacted by the authority of the big Other. It is important to stress that Lacan's sense of the term "enjoyment" (or what he terms *jouissance*) is not the same as pleasure. One engaging in mere pleasure poses no threat to the big Other. Enjoyment, however, disrupts the functioning of the social order. As Todd McGowan explains, "the prohibition of enjoyment . . . provides the foundation on which all the structures of society necessarily rest. . . . Without prohibition, enjoyment would constantly threaten the stability and security of the social order."[9] Indeed, a subject who fully embraces enjoyment draws attention to the very excess that the big Other attempts to regulate. To indulge in enjoyment demonstrates the subject's detachment from societal rules and public laws that constitute the network of the big Other. Further, Barry invites attention to his obscene enjoyment by speaking openly and unabashedly on controversial topics, such as race, religion, gender, and sexuality—even if he risks receiving death threats from his listeners/callers. This tension between Barry and his callers produces an unsettling and paranoid space within the already-confining setting of WGAB. As Michel Chion explains, "For when the voice is not localized, it tends to suffuse the whole filmic space, and to take on terrifying powers."[10]

Talk Radio's spectatorship of paranoia involves viewers identifying with Barry's obscene enjoyment, which is initiated in the film's opening credit sequence via an aerial image of Dallas while a radio announcer states that a tornado watch is in effect. The image cuts to a tall building and pans down as Barry's vintage Chevy pulls into WGAB's parking lot. As Barry exits his vehicle, a parked car reveals a suspicious-looking man sitting in the driver's seat smoking a cigarette, watching Barry walk toward the studio. Over a close shot of a cigarette being lit, viewers hear Barry discuss a number of problems facing America—drugs, crime, and television consumption. During Barry's monologue, viewers are introduced to his engineer Stu (John C. McGinely), Barry's producer Laura (Leslie Hope), and WGAB station manager Dan (Alec Baldwin), who is talking to Chuck (John Pankow) from Metro Wave, a media conglomerate interested in picking up Barry's show for national syndication. The sequence ends with a full shot of Barry at the console as his voice is finally embodied. Indeed, the opening of *Talk Radio* is similar to *Rope* in that viewers are initially positioned from the perspective of the big Other.

During the opening credit sequence in *Rope,* Hitchcock aligns viewers outside of Brandon and Phillip's penthouse. Once the credits end, the camera moves through the penthouse window as viewers see Brandon and Phillip choking David. *Rope*'s suspense functions on viewers knowing Brandon and Phillip's secret. Viewers' investment in *Rope* is to see whether or not Brandon and Phillip can successfully conceal the perfect murder during the dinner party. A similar transformation occurs during *Talk Radio*'s credit sequence. Viewers are aligned from the listener's perspective. Once Barry's voice is embodied, viewers are positioned from his perspective until his death at the end of the film.

Confining the film's primary setting to the radio studio is, in part, what generates *Talk Radio*'s spectatorship of uncertainty. Barry's unfiltered talk on controversial issues angers and offends many of his callers, placing him under constant surveillance. Not unlike a celebrity, Barry's listeners know what he looks like, thus intensifying his public scrutiny. But this visual access only goes one way. Barry's brazenness in speaking out about sensitive topics ultimately stirs discomfort because the film's viewers have no visual information regarding the show's callers. They are disembodied, angry voices, unrecognizable threats, a condition that Stone establishes via the mysterious man in the station's parking lot at the beginning of the film. From the start of the film, a cloud of doom hangs over Barry. Confining viewers within the limited space of WGAB elevates this danger.

Stone visually establishes Barry's vulnerability by creating tension between foreground and background planes, as exemplified by the large window near Barry's console that looks out upon the cityscape (see figure 5.1). At the end of the credit sequence, Stone connects Barry to the show's listeners by focus-pulling from the window's view of the city skyline to Barry's microphone. This lens operation establishes two visual planes of action: the city as a looming presence that monitors Barry at his console in the foreground. The spectacular cityscape transforms into a haunting presence that in fact surveils Barry, precisely because viewers lack visual information regarding the show's callers. This menace is illustrated when Barry receives a package, possibly a bomb from Chet. As Barry examines the package, Chet calls to ask if he received the package. While Dan is concerned and wants to call the bomb squad, Barry tells Laura to tell Dan "My mail is my business." In the midst of talking to another caller, Barry slowly opens the package, which contains a dead rat, a swastika flag, and a message that frighteningly reads: "I know where you live. I know what you look like. Your [*sic*] dead." On a primary level, WGAB's window view of the cityscape represents a beautiful perspective of Dallas. On another level, the view of the city connotes a dark reversal

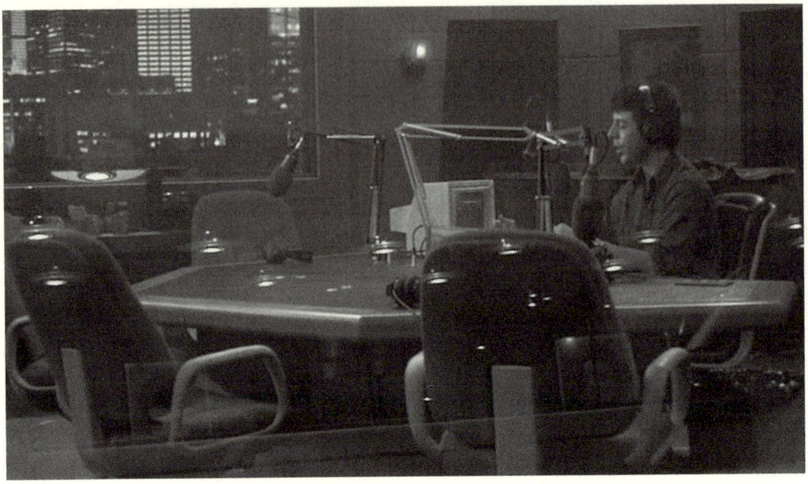

Figure 5.1. *Talk Radio*. The city looms as a figure of surveillance.

in which Barry is under surveillance by a looming, amorphous public eye. Because Barry stubbornly refuses to shy away from racist and dangerous callers, the confined setting of WGAB transforms into a space of deep uncertainty.

Walking in Circles and Haunted Media

The visual tension between foreground and background is even more prominent when Barry is invited to speak during halftime at a local basketball game. The scene begins with the camera tracking Barry and Laura from behind as they walk through a corridor leading into a packed house. Stone keeps the camera tight on Barry and Laura while the crowd stays in the background softly out of focus. Similar to the background of the city that functions as an impending threat at WGAB, viewers are unsure if any individual in the massive crowd embodies a voice of Barry's callers. As Barry talks with Laura, a fan (Bill Johnson) approaches him for his autograph. While Barry signs the fan's autograph, a woman (Anna Levine) suspiciously follows Barry in the background. Moments later, she approaches Barry and tells him how much she despises him. As Barry talks to the woman, the fan who asked Barry for his autograph now recedes into the background, watching them (see figure 5.2). Who is this man? Is it Chet? Again, narrative tension is fueled by viewers' lack of

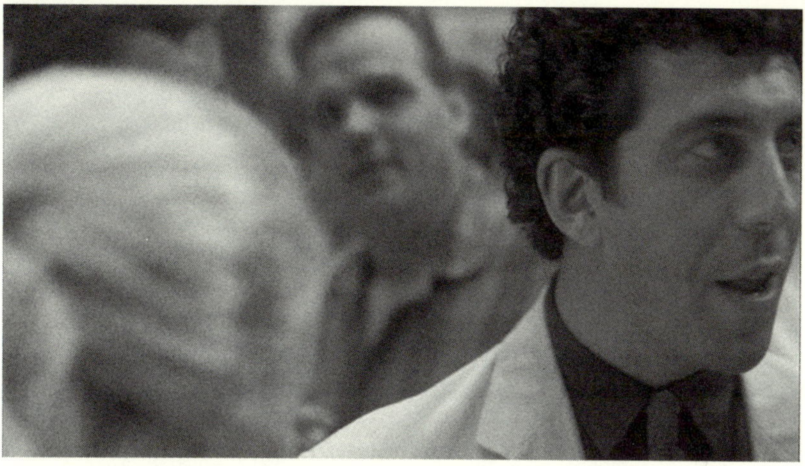

Figure 5.2. ***Talk Radio*****. Fan or threatening figure? Barry under surveillance.**

visual information. After the woman argues with Barry, she throws her drink on him, subtly demonstrating his vulnerability in the public sphere. The scene climaxes when Barry is introduced at the podium, as the crowd becomes rowdy. Barry tries to speak, but is drowned out by boos and shouting from the crowd. The importance of the basketball sequence is not only that it grants listeners the opportunity to meet Barry, but also lies in the juxtaposition between the confined setting of WGAB and the sea of surveilling eyes at the basketball game, which underscores that Barry has many enemies as well as fans. Moreover, the scene illustrates the importance of foreground and background planes that establish *Talk Radio*'s mise-en-scène of paranoia. Although the basketball space far exceeds the small space of WGAB, Stone still effectively confines Barry through tight framing and predominantly keeping the background plane in soft focus. The close framing and soft-focus background of the crowd at the basketball game prevent viewers from obtaining visual mastery, thereby reflecting Barry's public vulnerability due to his perverse, aggressive enjoyment as a shock jock.

But it is not only Barry's enjoyment and showmanship that Stone interrogates in talk radio and public discourse. Stone's visual examination of talk radio's dark side can be traced back to the supernatural and horror discourse of wireless radio in the early twentieth century. Early radio was often described in magical, supernatural, and spiritual terms. "The ether," as it was called in the early days of radio, referred to the spectrum of airwaves that carried sound across time and space. Susan J. Douglas explains that the disembodied voice of radio functioned as a

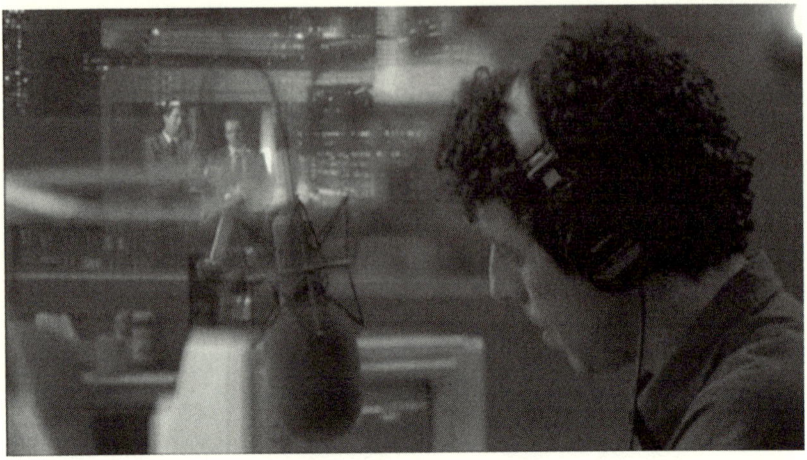

Figure 5.3. *Talk Radio*. Dan (*left*) and Chuck (*right*) observe Barry like ghostly figures.

spiritual contact, "a telepathic contact across space and time, a reassurance that we weren't alone in the void."[11] For Douglas, radio's "spiritual longing" was not so much a religious experience as it was there to "reel in distant voices out of that incomprehensible dimension called the spectrum and effortlessly bring them straight to us, linking us, through the air, to unseen others."[12] Broadcast radio connected listeners to distant voices, presenting a new technology that bridged a yearning for community and solidarity during the emergence of modernity just as everyday life was becoming increasingly fragmented.[13] Stone questions talk radio's community-building aspect by injecting aspects of horror into the film's mise-en-scène. After all, Stone is no stranger to the conventions of the horror genre, having written and directed *Seizure* (1974) and *The Hand* (1981). In *Talk Radio*, Stone depicts radio as ghostly and nightmarish—a medium that is fraught with sinister qualities and is blatantly contrary to the work of projecting community and the hopes of solidarity associated with early radio.[14] Consider Stone's frequent use of characters' reflections framed in the windows at WGAB, such as Dan and Chuck eerily watching Barry at his console like prying ghosts (see figure 5.3).

As Don Kunz observes, "Barry seems to be under intense scrutiny. His antagonists' images literally cast shadows over him."[15] Furthermore, Stone conjures a number of images that associate talk radio with traits of the horror genre. For example, when talking to the racist Chet, Barry refers to a white racist book called *The Order* as "an idiotic book written for people with bubblegum brains who never got out of the fourth grade, watching reruns of *The Blob*." Of course, Irvin S. Yeaworth Jr.'s

The Blob (1958) and other alien invasion movies of the 1950s have been interpreted as metaphors for communist infiltration.[16] These movies, as Barry suggests, fuel the fear of social impotence and the threat of the stranger. Another film worthy of note in this regard is Don Siegel's *Invasion of the Body Snatchers* (1956), in which humans and aliens are indistinguishable from one another.[17] In his final diatribe toward the end of the film, Barry demands: "Who the hell are you anyways, you audience?" The disorienting blurring of human, alien, audience, and mass culture speaks to the film's paranoia, particularly the basketball game sequence where a mob of eyes probe Barry as he circles the basketball court. As Kunz explains, *Talk Radio*'s circle motif contributes to the film's "paranoid atmosphere."[18] Here, Barry's circling of the court mirrors the constant movement of the camera at WGAB. Both are designed to underscore anxiety, uncertainty, and predator/prey thematics within the film's confined setting. Not unlike watching the human/alien confusion in *Invasion of the Body Snatchers*, viewers are unable to visually distinguish between Barry's fans and his enemies at the basketball court.

"Take It or Leave It"

Just before Barry announces to his listeners that his show will be going national, he states: "I've had these offers before and I've been asked in the past if I could ever soften my touch, go a little easier, and my answer has always been the same: 'Take it or leave it.'" Barry's refusal to "soften his touch" has an ethical dimension because he will neither adhere to the standards and practices of broadcasting, nor will he allow anyone to tell him how to run his show. His refusal demonstrates the intimate connection between ethical action and enjoyment. Whereas the big Other functions on the prohibition of enjoyment, the subject's ethical activity displays enjoyment that exceeds the social order. Drawing on Kantian ethics, McGowan explains that ethical action "derives not from obedience to the demands of the social order, but from adherence to and embrace of the enjoyment that exceeds that order."[19] The ethical subject follows his or her duty for the sake of duty, regardless of whether it profits or hurts others. As such, loyalty to duty refuses "external influences." For McGowan, a subject who performs duty for the sake of duty displays an "ethics of excess." For example, McGowan explains that the films of Michael Mann employ "cinematic fantasy in order to make ethical subjectivity visible for us."[20] Although many of Mann's characters are criminals, they nevertheless perform ethical action in their devotion to duty for the sake of duty. In *Heat* (1995), criminal Neil McCauley's (Robert De Niro) motto is: "Don't let yourself get attached to anything you are not willing to walk out on in 30 seconds flat if you feel the heat around the corner." McCauley's loyalty to duty for the sake of duty demonstrates that he will abandon everything (including his love interest) to avoid the law. As McGowan explains, Mann's heroes "sustain a pure devotion to the duty that they have given themselves, and the films depict this purity as a possibility for us as spectators."[21] Like McCauley, Barry's pure devotion to his duty of "no holds barred" talk is not influenced by the standards and practices of broadcasting. Consider again the flashback sequence when Barry is invited as a guest speaker on *Talk of the Town,* hosted by Jeff Fisher. Jeff's shtick is haranguing his callers and then hanging up on them, saying: "You're history." Jeff and Barry discuss fantasy love affairs on the air. Barry jokingly says that he would sleep with Marie Osmond. A listener calls and angrily tells Jeff and Barry that they are a "couple of liberal pinkos." As Jeff is about to hang up on the caller, Barry stops him and says: "It's true, sir, indeed, Jeff Fisher and I are lovers." Barry then says to the caller that white Americans spend $165 million a year on suntan lotion because they secretly want to be black, a race that makes them "feel sexually inferior." Jeff regains control of his show as they cut to a commercial break. He scolds Barry: "When I say 'cut,' you stop talking." Jeff explains that he does not want to lose his license, and—unlike Barry—refuses to violate the standards and practices of broadcasting. Barry continues to delve deep into controversial and taboo topics regardless of broadcasting's standards and practices, thus illustrating his loyalty to unapologetically speaking on controversial issues. Like Mann, Stone visually displays the excess of ethical action through expressive cinematic form, such as the camera that circles the studio during Barry's rant on suntan lotion. Indeed, Barry's pure devotion to "no holds barred" talk unearths an underside of political talk radio that the standards and practices of broadcasting attempt to regulate and neutralize. As such, ethical action (duty done for the sake of duty) discloses the excess or obscene enjoyment that the social order prohibits.

Of course, Barry's ethical action in not toning down his comments on controversial topics violates the standards and practices of broadcasting. Yet Barry's devotion to unfiltered talk has monetary value for WGAB, a factor made expressly clear when, after his incident with Jeff on *Talk of the Town,* Barry is offered a job to host his own talk show. But incorporating Barry's obscene enjoyment into talk radio's format does not prevent him from continuing his ethical action to speak unfiltered on sensitive topics. This is precisely Dan's concern in losing the deal with

Metro Wave, namely, that Barry's abrasive style may be too much for a national audience. A subject engaged in ethical action forsakes pathological motives for the sake of his or her duty. An ethical action, for example, could involve one sacrificing a love interest in order to stay loyal to one's duty. Of course, ethical action can also be harmful to others. During a flashback sequence, Barry tells his wife, Ellen, that Dan is giving him the 10:00 A.M. slot and is hiring a producer for his show. Barry wants Ellen to be the producer. But Ellen does not want to take on the role of producer because she believes it may create tension between them and destroy their marriage. Unlike Barry, Ellen will not risk destroying their marriage for the show. Barry's response to Ellen is: "Fuck our marriage. Come on. This is important. I need you." What is most important to Barry is the show and not his marriage, demonstrating his commitment to his duty for the sake of duty. As such, Barry's ethical action results in the end of his marriage.

At the same time, it is not always clear whether Barry simply enjoys being a celebrity shock jock, or if he most likes confronting his listeners by discussing controversial topics unfiltered. These components (celebrity and radio provocateur/performer) are called into question when he spontaneously invites Kent (Michael Wincott), a frequent caller of the show, to the station as a guest. Early in the film, Kent pranks Barry on the air and tells him that his girlfriend overdosed on drugs. When Kent calls again, he begs Barry to meet him. Dan confronts Barry about inviting Kent to the station, stressing that there is too much riding on the deal with Metro Wave. But Barry does not sway from his duty, asserting: "This is my show. I put who I want on my show. If I wanna have Charlie Manson on my show, I'll put him on my show." Dan warns Barry about the number of threatening packages and envelopes that the station receives: "Think about that, Barry. The time it takes to sit down and write that on paper, put it in an envelope, lick it, send it to the station. . . . These people are dead serious. All I'm suggesting is that you simply pull it back, just for a little bit." Dan underscores that being a shock jock is just a job: "You can come in here and start predicting Armageddon if you want to, Barry. But it's still a job. . . . Do you think you are changing the world, Barry? . . . You hang up on people, that's your job." For Dan, Barry's show is simply labor and economics—the very reason he hired Barry when he first saw him on *Talk of the Town.* Now that *Night Talk* is about to be picked up nationally by Metro Wave, Dan asks Barry to tone it down and play it safe. Barry, on the other hand, sticks to his duty, even if it involves inviting a guest he knows nothing about, or risking unraveling the deal with Metro Wave, as well as risking his own life.

Generation X Ruins the Show

In the scene right before Kent arrives at the station, the visual tension between the foreground and background planes again underscores the tension between Barry and the uncertainty of his callers. Here, Stone repeats a similar long-take/focus-pull technique seen at the end of the film's opening credit sequence. Shot in one long take, this sequence shows Barry trying to help a caller named John (Bill DeAcutis), who may or may not be a rapist. Stone frames Barry close to his microphone with the panorama of Dallas out of focus in the background. As John hangs up on Barry, the image slowly focus-pulls as the city view of Dallas comes into the plane. Barry says: "Another lost soul goes into the Dallas night." The camera slowly pans left to reveal Kent's and Laura's reflection in the window. Kent's reflection appears like a ghost transported from the Dallas cityscape, further illustrating the film's horror dimension. Kent is young, wears sunglasses, has long hair, and holds a can of Pepsi in one hand and a cigarette in the other (see figure 5.4). The camera pans back to Barry, finishing the long take. As noted, Stone's articulation of foreground and background planes builds narrative tension within the chamber-space setting. Again, this tension is in part generated by viewers' lack of visual information regarding the show's callers. And although one caller (Kent) is now fully embodied, there is something uncertain about him, because his intentions in wanting to meet Barry are not made clear.

On air, Barry introduces Kent as a way "to get an inside look at the future of America." Kent is caffeine fidgety and has difficulty containing his laughter. He asks Barry if the microphone is on. Barry tells him that he is sitting in front of a live microphone and that "when you speak, thousands of people hear your voice. It penetrates their minds." Kent screams into the microphone like a rock star. Barry tells Kent that they are discussing America and asks if he has any thoughts on the subject. Kent talks about how lots of rock stars have girlfriends who are models. He says to Barry, "Look at you, man. You're a big guy, famous star and all. I mean, you got that fine babe [Laura] right over there." Kent proceeds to speak about revolution and how they are going to design two-way television sets in the future so people will be able to see one another. He adds that there is no way Big Brother is going to stop the revolution. In turn, Barry calls Kent an idiot and hopes that he does not represent the future of America. Kent laughs uncontrollably, saying how funny Barry is. Barry firmly informs Kent that they discuss serious subjects on *Night Talk,* sharply asking Kent: "Does any of that bother you?" Kent responds, "No." Barry asks why not. Kent replies, because "it's just a show. . . . It's your show."

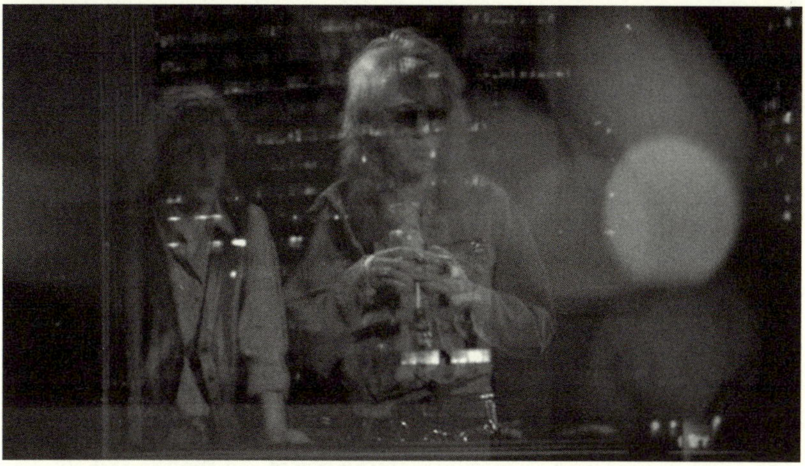

Figure 5.4. *Talk Radio*. Kent (*right*) appears in a ghostlike form.

Susan Mackey-Kallis interprets Barry as the "disillusioned messiah" who realizes that "his real audience is—not enlightened striving intellectuals with hearts, but rather mind-numbed drug crazed 'Generation X-ers.'"[22] Further, Mackey-Kallis identifies Kent as one who "has been completely destroyed by the excesses of his generation."[23] It is not so much the fact that Kent lacks knowledge about political and social matters facing America, or that he is an excessive consuming and "drug crazed" Generation X-er, which unnerves Barry. Rather, what frightens Barry is that Kent clearly sees that *Night Talk* is nothing more than entertainment. Kent identifies with Barry's over-the-top antics and haranguing his callers. He enjoys Barry's duty to speak unfiltered regardless of the consequences. That is, Ken identifies with Barry's excess rather than with his words, a response that upsets Barry because he hopes to impact and enlighten his listeners. As Barry tells Kent, using a sexual metaphor: "When you speak, you penetrate their minds." It is not that Kent has been destroyed by the excesses of his generation, but rather that Kent is excess itself, which is why Wincott plays Kent with exaggerated acting. If Barry's duty of unabashed talk exceeds what is permitted by the big Other, then Kent must top Barry's enjoyment by overplaying the role of the MTV television-watching, drug-consuming Generation X-er. Kent reveals that in the end "Night Talk" may not really change the thoughts of its listeners, an accusation that causes Barry to question his duty.

Shortly after Kent's brutal assertion, Barry takes a call from Julia, who has been listening to the show for five years and praises the show. Barry asks her what it is about the show that she likes so much. Julia cannot express why. Barry yells: "You've been listening to this show for five years. You don't know why you listen to it?" The next caller, Ralph, tells Barry that we are "the kind of people that feel too much." Ralph speaks about people who watch television and see tragedy and disaster that add up to nothing, and serve only to generate revenue for networks and advertisers. Kent interrupts and tells Ralph that he is a wimp and should kill himself. Dan instructs Laura to remove Kent from the studio. As Kent is escorted out of the console area, he digs into his jacket and retrieves a camera. He takes two pictures of Barry. Stone films this moment in slow motion to give the impression that Kent is about to pull out a gun and kill Barry. The overexposure of the camera's flash slowly illuminates Barry as if he is being assassinated, which in a sense he has been, having been intellectually murdered by Kent's presence. Kent has revealed that Barry may be nothing more than a performer, a celebrity who entertains mass audiences, rather than an intellectual figure who can change and educate the minds of his listeners.

Fearing that Barry may be losing control of the show, Ellen, who is visiting from out of town, attempts to rescue him, pretending to be a caller called Cheryl Ann. Dan asks Ellen why she wants to call Barry. Ellen says that he is all alone. Dan tells Ellen: "It's Barry's show. Let Barry do Barry's show." Nevertheless, she calls him to talk about how she still has feelings for her ex-husband. Barry figures out that it is Ellen. Perhaps one of the film's most powerful demonstrations of Barry's commitment to duty for the sake of duty takes place when he tells Ellen: "You blew it. . . . Your ex doesn't want you. He's got women all over the place. He doesn't need you. He's not some suburban zombie like your husband. He's out there having fun. . . . So why don't you stick with Mr. America there, go out and buy yourself a heavy-duty vibrator, and knock yourself out. We reap what we sow." Now having lost Ellen, Barry goes into a diatribe about himself and his frightened listeners. In one of the most kinetic moments of the film, the camera circles around the studio as Barry admits that he revels in his success and high ratings, denounces the system and then embraces it. He declares that he doesn't care about the world and despises his listeners because they have "no brains, no power, no future. No hope." Barry adds that he "makes his case every night and says what he believes in." In a desperate, vulnerable plea, he asks if anyone out there understands what he is saying. Stone then shows a quick montage of Barry taking a number of calls which demonstrate that his work is nothing but a job, as Dan expressed earlier. Toward the end of the show, Barry does not speak for sixty seconds. The moment of dead air is extremely discomforting, painfully drawing attention to itself. Ironically, it is within this uncomfortable moment of silence that Barry fully realizes that his "no holds barred" talk has little influence to change things. Here, Barry finally admits: "I guess we're stuck together." Afterwards, Chuck from Metro Wave tells Barry how great his show was, ironically asserting: "I'm gonna talk to the lawyers, and we'll get started on this deal right away." Dan also tells Barry that he did a great job and did not destroy the deal with Metro Wave. Barry asks Dan: "What if I don't come in tomorrow night?" Dan says, "You'll come in tomorrow, Barry. You always do." At the end of the film, viewers are not sure if Barry will return to radio. Then he is killed in the parking lot of WGAB by one of his listeners.

The Fisher King and the Dark Underside of Fame

Barry's rants attract listeners who have been impacted by the economic and political alienation of America in the 1980s. As Barry forcefully states: "This country is rotten to the core and somebody better do something about it. Take your hand out of that bowl of Fritos, throw away your *National Enquirer*, and pick up that phone. . . . . Open your mouth and tell me what we're going to do about the mess this country is in." At the same time, his diatribes reveal that he may be more concerned with performance and male ego than public discourse and a rationale to address the concerns of Americans. A film notable in this regard is Terry Gilliam's *The Fisher King* (1991). Similarly to Barry's antics, Jack Lucas (Jeff Bridges) enjoys giving his listeners unabashed straight talk. Like Stone's glass cage setting of WGAB in *Talk Radio,* Gilliam visually depicts Jack's studio in a highly stylized manner, particularly through the use of shadows and confined spaces. Gilliam often frames Jack from above in the console area, using a wide-angle lens, while shadows of black bars on the walls depict his self-entrapment. But whereas Kent's appearance on Barry's show forces him to question whether—and to what extent—words have an impact on his listeners, Gilliam depicts a nightmarish form of talk radio when a frequent caller, Edwin (Christian Clemenson), literally reenacts one of Jack's diatribes. Edwin, who has had bad luck with women, asks Jack for dating advice. Jack blabs on about a yuppie woman whom Edwin met at an upscale restaurant called Babbitts in Manhattan, declaring, "They only mate with their own kind. It's yuppie inbreeding." Jack further stresses that yuppies are "retarded," do not feel love, and only "negotiate love moments." According to Jack, yuppies are evil—horrified by banality and "everything America stands for." Certainly naming the restaurant "Babbitts" alludes to Sinclair Lewis's 1922 novel and its theme of middle-class conformity. Here, Jack emphasizes to Edwin that yuppies must be stopped. Edwin takes Jack's words literally and shoots and kills a woman at Babbitts. When Jacks learns that his words have played a part in Edwin's murderous act, he leaves radio. Three years later, Jack is working at a video store, forming a hot-and-cold relationship with the store's owner, Anne (Mercedes Ruehl). Now a video clerk, Jack cannot get past the dullness and predictability of everyday people; as he states to Anne: "I hate desperate people." Jack denounces mass entertainment while watching a television sitcom, the same show Jack was supposed to star in before he left radio. He frustratedly tells Anne, "It is important to think. It separates us from lentils and people that read books like *Love Song*." That same night, Jack, drunk out of his mind, attempts suicide by tying cinder blocks to his feet and jumping into the river. But he is saved by Parry (Robin Williams), a homeless man whom we later learn is the husband of the woman Edwin had killed. Ultimately, *The Fisher King* is about Parry's mental illness and homelessness. But it is also about Jack's transformation, whereby he takes on the righteous role of helping Parry overcome the trauma of his wife's death. Whereas Stone interrogates Barry's performance and his duty to take unfiltered talk to its extreme, Gilliam explores Jack's metamorphosis from duty to reincorporation into the big Other as a subject of desire. When Jack leaves Anne to return to radio at the end of the second act of that film, he learns that Parry has been attacked and is in a coma. Jack knows that he must retrieve the Holy Grail in order to awaken Parry and restore him to sanity.

Part of Jack's change involves surrendering the macho persona of a shock jock celebrity. Jack's abrasive style assimilates the hyper-masculine, over-the-top antics associated with the shock jock talk radio format. Consider when Jack says to Parry at the hospital: "Everything's been going great. . . . I'm going to have my own cable talk show. . . . I've got an incredible, incredibly fucking gorgeous girlfriend. I'm living an incredible fucking life." Jack's articulation of his job in sexual terms is similar to that of *Talk Radio* when Barry indirectly tells Ellen on the air: "You blew it. . . . Your ex doesn't want you. He's got women all over the place. He doesn't need you. He's not some suburban zombie like your husband. He's out there having fun." But whereas Barry sacrifices his marriage to Ellen in order to sustain his duty for the sake of duty, Jack gives up his duty by committing to Anne. At the end of the film, he returns to the video store to tell her that he loves her. Anne slaps Jack in the face and then makes love to him, while a cascade of porno VHS cases falls on top of them. Jack's journey begins with entrapment—visually manifested in the cage space at his radio console—and concludes with his awakening in the mass entertainment space of a video store. By contrast, Barry's ethical commitment to spouting raw talk, his selfishness, and his ego result in loneliness. He loses Ellen and questions whether his job as a shock jock has any value for talk radio. The price Barry pays for sticking to his duty is unhappiness.[24]

Talk Radio's exploration of public discourse, performance, and celebrity is a point of interrogation for Stone in examining American broadcast radio and mass culture. He would continue to explore these themes in *Natural Born Killers,* targeting exploitative media such as trash TV. Indeed, Kent, as the figure of the MTV caffeine-fueled Generation X-er, is not that far removed from Stone's hyper-kinetic depiction of Mickey and Mallory in *Natural Born Killers.* Stone asks viewers not to identify with Kent, but rather to take notice of his excesses in relation to shock jock radio.[25] For Kent, Barry's over-the-top on-air rants are no different than the exploits of trash TV. Kent forces Barry into self-examination, questioning whether he is a voice of reason or simply a performer/celebrity carnival barker for mass entertainment.

Talk Radio is a film about media economics and the investigation of mass entertainment and political talk. Above all, it is a film about the potential grotesquerie of performance, celebrity, and fame. Dan, Chuck, Kent, and the listeners of *Night Talk* do not see Barry as an agent of change, but as a perpetuator of crass culture. It is Barry's form, not his words, that have economic value. As Dan states to Barry: "Your job is to hang up on people," not to evoke productive dialogue. Barry's commitment is to a format that values sensationalism and entertainment, rather than to supply information and rationality as a form of public service. This is where Stone locates the nightmare of talk radio, by unearthing its obscene underside through expressive cinematography and Barry's ethical action of "no holds barred" talk radio. Both Barry's enjoyment and the film's confinement of space not only help to generate the film's suspense, but also force viewers to confront the underside of America that Barry is not afraid to talk about—albeit within the confines of WGAB. At the end of the film, after Barry has been gunned down in the parking lot, an overexposed light sizzles upon him as the camera pans from his body and up to WGAB's radio tower in the night sky. Susan Mackey-Kallis reads the radio tower as an image of a crucifix, through which Barry's death takes on Christlike symbolism.[26] But Barry's death can also be interpreted as being sucked into radio's spiritual ether ("another soul goes into the Dallas night"). Here, the aerial shots of Dallas during the film's ending credits not only depict the faceless world of radio listeners.[27] The aerial images also suggest that Barry literally becomes part of the spectrum, traveling through space and time as each caller ironically talks about Barry's contribution to talk radio.

6

Voices, Telephones, and Confined Spaces: *Phone Booth* and *Locke*

In May 2000, Pacific Bell removed what has been referred to as the "Mojave phone booth." Captured in a short documentary called *Mojave Mirage* (Derek Roberto and Kaarina Cleverley Roberto, 2003), the phone booth was built for volcanic cinder miners working in the desert in the 1960s. In the late 1990s, the phone booth became a popular site of attraction, with websites devoted to the oddity of its location. Covered with markings, graffiti, and bumper stickers, the Mojave phone booth elicited constant visitors to answer calls from all over the world. Certainly one of the curiosities of the Mojave phone booth was its location within an uncontactable place, especially in the age of cell phones and satellite communication. Indeed, the Mojave phone booth's curious location closely follows the public's fascination with fantastic tales about communication technologies, which can be traced back to the telegraph and early wireless radio.[1] As one of the visitors in the documentary points out, a phone booth within the vastness of the desert is something out of *The Twilight Zone.*

The Mojave phone booth's social attraction illustrates the power of telecommunication in relation to spaces, places, and the bodies that anchor distant voices. The telephone, historically, has played an important role in building narrative tension and suspense in cinema. As Michel Chion explains, the telephone is a favorite device in suspense cinema, noting that it "serves in separation and disjunction; the voice travels through space, bodies stay where they are."[2] For Chion, the disembodied caller creates narrative suspense in viewers' desire to locate the face that belongs to the voice. As explained in the chapter on *Talk Radio,* Chion terms the presence of the bodiless voice as *acousmêtre*: "when we cannot yet connect it [the voice] to a face."[3] The disembodied callers demonstrate how the subject's desire distorts the aural field. It is what Lacan terms the invocatory drive: *objet a* within the aural field. Just as the excess of the gaze energizes the confined space, the voice can produce a similar effect in intensifying our spectatorship. In *Talk Radio,* for example, Barry's hostile callers create a paranoid atmosphere because the bodies that belong to these callers are unknown to the viewer. The basketball sequence, in particular, builds a disjunction between voice and body as we speculate whether Barry's unstable callers are present in the crowd. Introducing the caller's voice before we see the caller himself not only illustrates the powerful effects of the *acousmêtre* as a narrative device, but also shows how it formally shapes cinematic space. Stone's excessive cinematic style correlates to Barry's ethical activity and perverse enjoyment. Barry's pure devotion to duty is to speak candidly on controversial topics regardless of the numerous death threats he receives.

As explained, *Rope, The Passion of Anna, The Shining,* and *Talk Radio* render space unstable within the confined setting by exposing cinematic excess. I have attributed this effect to Jacques Lacan's notion of the gaze: the manifestation of *objet petit a* in the field of vision. The gaze exhibits a distortion within the visual plane as the scopic drive, revealing an excess that realizes what is in the space more than the space. As explored in *Talk Radio,* the voice as the invocatory drive contributes to a similar effect of the gaze within the confined setting. Whereas our encounter with the gaze realizes how our desire to look distorts the visual field, the disembodied voice realizes how our desire to hear shapes the aural field. What follows is an examination of voice, telecommunication, and confined spaces and their relationship to cinematic excess in Joel Schumacher's *Phone Booth* and Steven Knight's *Locke.* In *Phone Booth,* an unnamed Caller (Kiefer Sutherland) embodies sinister qualities assigned to the *acousmêtre* as omnipotence and authority in holding Stu (Colin Farrell) hostage in a phone booth. At the same time, the use of split-screen photography, mobile screens, and an oversaturation of images makes cinematic excess visible within the film's confined setting. As such, *Phone Booth* demonstrates the gaze as a knowable and distorting presence within the field of vision and hearing. In *Locke,* cinematic excess is linked to voice diction as a mode of melodrama. Ivan Locke's (Tom Hardy) calm and logical voice is pitted against the emotional voices of the disembodied callers as they react to his spontaneous decision to drive to London to support Bethan (Olivia Colman), a woman with whom he had a one-night affair. Bethan is about to give birth to his child, and Ivan drops everything to be with her. Ultimately, Ivan's motivation to drive to London is to avoid making the same mistakes as his father. In both films, excess unsettles space within the confined setting. In *Phone Booth,* the oversaturation of visual information and the disembodied voice of the Caller destabilize any sense of ordered space. At the same time, the excess of the image and the voice are intimately connected to the film's exploration of screen culture and news media sensationalism. In *Locke,* excess is depicted not only in Ivan's ethical decision to be with Bethan, but also in how he derives surplus-enjoyment from organizing the last details for Birmingham's biggest concrete pour by way of his car phone. Ivan's pure devotion to his plan costs him his job and destroys his family. Yet, in both films, the confined space is where Stu and Ivan confess their lies and infidelity. Together, these films provide a glimpse into the development of telecommunication devices and their imagination within the confined setting. Moreover, both films speak to their current social moments, exploring how digital communication is reshaping our relationship to work, family, and community.

Phone Booth Fantasy

The phone booth conjures up a number of meanings linked to popular media. In television and cinema, phone booths are often associated with time and teleportation, as in *Doctor Who*'s TARDIS (Time And Relative Dimension in Space), a design based on a London telephone police box. Consider the ending of *Get Smart*'s (1965–70) credit sequence, in which agent Maxwell Smart (Don Adams) enters a phone booth strangely housed inside an office building. Max dials a number as a trap door below him opens, transporting him somewhere within the building, a location not revealed to the viewer. Or, in *Bill & Ted's Excellent Adventure* (Stephen Herek, 1989), a time machine is disguised as a phone booth that Bill (Alex Winter) and Ted (Keanu Reeves) use in their hilarious travels to learn about three historical figures for their oral high-school report in San Dimas, California. Perhaps the most iconic image is Clark Kent using phone booths to transform into Superman.

Before the 1950s, most phone booths were wooden structures located in hotels, railroad stations, and banks. J. M. Hayward explains that the demand for the outdoor booth arose due to "the popularity of telephones along highways, parkways and turnpikes."[4] The new aluminum phone booths served an important purpose because they were "a great convenience and a necessity in time of emergency."[5] As Hayward notes, the design of the aluminum outdoor phone booth was engineered for "weathering, for economy of manufacture, installation and maintenance, and for attractiveness of appearance."[6] The glass design of the phone booth allows for private conversation to occur within a public setting. The phone booth's windows operate as barrier and transparency at once. Certainly, one is reminded of the scene in Alfred Hitchcock's *The Birds* when Melanie (Tippi Hedren) finds temporary refuge in a phone booth as the birds attack the town of Bodega Bay. It is interesting to note that in the 1960s, *Phone Booth*'s screenwriter, Larry Cohen, initially pitched the concept of a film taking place entirely in a phone booth to Hitchcock. Since Hitchcock had made a number of films that take place in one location, it is no surprise that he was drawn to Cohen's concept. But Cohen and Hitchcock could not design a plot that would sustain a feature-length film.[7] It would take almost thirty years before Cohen's idea would come to fruition.

Phone Booth takes place in contemporary New York City. The story follows Stuart "Stu" Shepard, a media publicist who makes his living using media gossip as a form of leverage to promote his clients. Stu is cheating on his wife, Kelly (Radha Mitchell), and uses a phone booth to talk to his mistress, Pam (Katie Holmes). We learn from the film's narrator that this is the last standing phone booth in New York City, and it is scheduled for removal the following day. As the narrator explains, this phone booth is the "last vestige of privacy." For Stu, the phone booth provides anonymity because his calls to Pam cannot be traced. After one of Stu's conversations with Pam, a man holding a pizza approaches the phone booth. Confused, Stu rudely turns the delivery man away. After Stu finishes his call with Pam, the phone rings. Curious, Stu answers it and learns that an unnamed Caller warns him not to leave the phone booth or he will shoot him. We later learn that the Caller is a sniper who has already killed two people in New York City. Having bugged the phone booth, the Caller has obtained knowledge of Stu's life and his affair with Pam. Tethered to the phone booth, Stu is forced by the Caller to prevent pedestrians from entering the booth or risk being shot. A group of prostitutes who need to use the phone bang on the windows, shouting obscenities at Stu. At one point, their pimp, Leon (John Enos III), smashes the phone booth with a baseball bat and pressures Stu to leave. The Caller asks Stu if he wants him to stop Leon. Stu says "yes." The Caller shoots and kills Leon. When the police arrive, the prostitutes blame Stu for Leon's death. Headed by Capt. Ed Ramey (Forest Whitaker), a standoff ensues because Stu cannot leave the phone booth. Soon, Stu's situation turns into a media spectacle. With all eyes watching—including the Caller—Stu has to covertly convey to Ramey that he is being targeted by an unseen sniper.

Similar to the Mojave phone booth, *Phone Booth*'s depiction of the last remaining phone booth in New York City has surreal qualities. The phone booth is attractive because it no longer fits within the new technological landscape of cellular phones. Whereas *Mojave Mirage* explores the communal dimension of the desert phone, *Phone Booth* conveys a sinister quality that is connected to mobile communication and the voice of the Caller as the *acousmêtre*. For Stu to stay alive, he must stay on the phone and obey the Caller's demands. Except for point-of-view shots of the

Caller's gun crosshairs, viewers have no visual access to his whereabouts. Both *Mojave Mirage* and *Phone Booth* demonstrate two sides of fantasy. As portrayed in the documentary, the Mojave phone booth evokes a peaceful fantasy scenario, a vast environment to which people from all over the world travel to connect with each other. In *Phone Booth,* a nightmarish and obscene underside of the phone booth is depicted, as the Caller uses the confined space as a form of power and torture to extract a confession from Stu. As such, Schumacher exploits cinematic excess to both visually and *audibly* depict this obscene dimension of communication.

Recording the Voice

Part of the Caller's power is attributed to the film's sound perspective in recording Sutherland's voice. Sound in cinema is often subordinate to the moving image. In examining the evolution of sound technology, John Belton explains that "sound achieves authenticity only as a consequence of its submission to tests imposed upon it by other senses—primarily by sight."[8] For Belton, sound "lacks 'objectivity' (thus authenticity) not only because it is invisible but because it is an attribute and is thus incomplete in itself."[9] It is when the source of the sound is synched to the image that sound has achieved its fidelity (faithfulness to its source), such as synching dialogue to the actor's lips. One practice of sound mixing and recording, as Belton explains, is the removal of a noise "that interferes with the transmission of meaningful sound."[10] Just as filmmakers avoid intrusive camera bumps or unnecessary camera shakes, the art of sound mixing involves diminishing the presence of noise or distortion. Although it is hard to achieve the perfect sound, *Phone Booth* shows a dark dimension to the Caller in recording Sutherland's voice with little noise. The Caller's voice lacks reverb, presenting an up-close and personal connection with viewers. The flattened effect not only eliminates noise, but also prevents little or no scale to the Caller's environment. Background noises, for instance, are not audible when the Caller speaks due to the flattening perspective of his voice. As such, when the Caller is talking to Stu, no other sounds vie for the viewer's attention. The mixing of this voice eliminates any sense of mediation or noise in order to stress the Caller's immediate and powerful presence as the *acousmêtre.* At the same time, the flat recording of the Caller's voice not only draws attention to itself as a haunting presence, but also uncomfortably realizes how our desire to hear shapes the aural field as the invocatory drive.

Although the Caller forces Stu to obey his commands, he also operates as a listener, taking on aspects of what Chion calls commentator-*acousmêtre*: "he who never shows himself but who has no personal stake in the image."[11] This entails a performative dimension in which Stu has to make up excuses and enact scenarios on the spot, such as telling Ramey that he cannot leave the booth because "he is busy." Stu's improvisation often causes the Caller to laugh while adding comments such as "Good one, Stu," or "I didn't know you had it in you." But there is a dark side to the Caller as commentator-*acousmêtre*. At one point, Ramey tries to talk Stu out of the phone booth, speaking about his own intimacy issues. He reveals to Stu that he is divorced. The Caller instructs Stu to ask Ramey if it was because "he couldn't satisfy his wife." He forces Stu to ask Ramey if he "masturbates on those lonely nights." Indeed, the Caller's uncomfortable demands demonstrate the power attributed to the *acousmêtre* as both the disembodied voice and listener. The flattened and "noiseless" recording of the Caller's voice builds narrative tension. His voice sounds too perfect, creating a sense of imbalance and uncertainty. It is as if we are inside his head, which is demonstrated in the Caller's frequent "thinking out loud" commentaries to Ramey, such as "get this man a seat on Oprah," or "this guy is really getting on my nerves."

At the same time, the flat mixing of the Caller's voice not only problematizes his location, but also emphasizes his unreliability as a source of knowledge. For instance, the Caller connects Leon's dead body in the street to his experience in the Vietnam War. At one point, he emotionally explains to Stu that his mother did not love him. Of course, the Caller tells Stu that these are all lies. But Stu's sudden empathy for the Caller shows his naivete. As spectators, we are not fooled by the Caller. These are cliché motivations employed in cinema, illustrating *Phone Booth*'s self-reflexivity. We only know that the Caller has targeted certain people whom he deems immoral and that he has technical skills to keep himself untraceable. As such, the flat and raw recording of the Caller's voice underscores the power he commands over Stu. As Chion explains, "*the acousmêtre is all-seeing*, its word is like the word of God: 'No creature can hide from it.' The one who is not in the visual field is in the best position to see everything that's happening."[12] The dry recording of the Caller's voice contributes to the film's narrative tension. Here, *Phone Booth*'s creative use of the split-screen format not only demonstrates the all-seeing disembodied voice, but also shows how new technologies inform the film's design in presenting simultaneous information in unsettling narrative space as an embodiment of the excess of the gaze.

Obey: Screen, Screens, and More Screens

Tom Gunning explains that the new technology of the telephone had an intimate relationship with the development of narrative cinema, as shown in D. W. Griffith's *The Lonedale Operator* (1911). The phone's collapsing of time and space, according to Gunning, "could support and interrelate with new narrative devices such as the suspenseful parallel editing."[13] Similarly, digital and satellite communication have informed new forms of narrative, as in the increasing use of multiscreens and the presentation of simultaneous information. It is what Marsha Kinder terms "database narrative": "narratives whose structure exposes or thematizes the dual processes of selection and combination that lie at the heart of all stories and that are crucial to language."[14] A tenet of classic narrative is presenting visual information that emphasizes unity and linear order with a beginning, middle, and end. Even when the narration digresses or departs from its forward flow, it must continue its effort to motivate, such as a flashback to depict a character's memory. Databases, however, do not adhere to the logic of narrative, nor do they have beginnings, middles, or endings. Instead, databases invite users/viewers to organize and narrate a constellation of items, for example, scrolling through a list of apps on an Internet-ready television, or exploring the bonus features of a DVD. Whereas continuity editing synthesizes and subordinates narrative time to a linear and chronological order, database narratives manifest their structure to underscore the processes of selection and combination. Database narratives elicit a highly interactive spectatorship by inviting viewers to organize, compare, explore, and navigate their disparate pieces, acts that can lead to multiple outcomes of meaning.

Although the narrative structure of *Phone Booth* unfolds linearly, the multiple-screen display of visual information closely adheres to a database aesthetic. Whereas the telephone enhanced the parallel editing techniques of the silent and classical periods of cinema, the split-screen format allows Schumacher to create narrative tension, not only in the separation of voice and body, but also to present multiple planes of action that unfold simultaneously for the viewer (see figure 6.1). Here, Schumacher's use of the split-screen format follows the film's exploitation of excess as a knowable presence within the confined setting by showing us too much information. For example, when the Caller first calls Pam, he puts Stu on mute. Although Stu and the Caller do not have visual access to Pam, viewers see Stu and Pam's reaction to the Caller's phone call unfold at the same time. The characters' shared reaction allows viewers to experience simultaneous information. Moreover, the split-screen format permits simultaneous information to be circulated without the

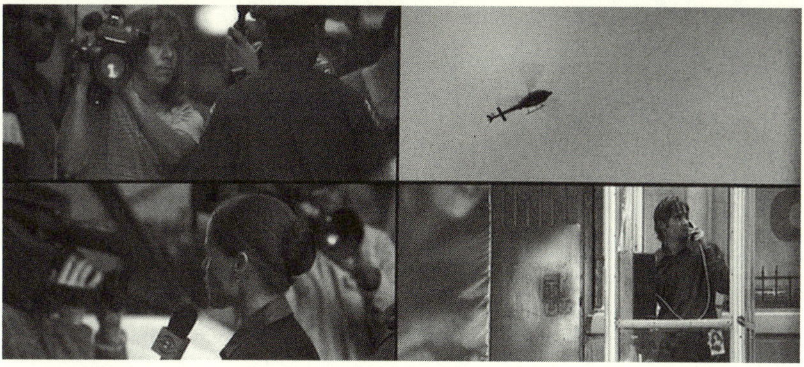

Figure 6.1. ***Phone Booth.*** **Simultaneous information renders the gaze as a distorting presence.**

Caller's knowledge, such as when Stu covertly dials Kelly while talking to the Caller. Kelly's image appears in a split screen as she answers her cell phone. Hearing Stu's conversation with the Caller, she now knows that he is being held hostage by a sniper. Kelly brings her phone to Ramey, which significantly changes the narrative.

At the same time, the film's excess of information not only speaks to film's investigation of the screen culture, but also addresses the imprisonment of both spectators and Stu and the Caller. In writing about the body and the screen, Lev Manovich explains that the cinema spectator remains immobile while ready to receive the mobility of the moving image.[15] Classical cinema situates the audience with the best viewpoint, but the body of the spectator remains seated. Stu and the Caller are characteristic of cinema's immobile spectator because they must remain tethered to their designated spaces. Stu cannot move from the phone booth or risk his life, nor can the Caller leave his "all-seeing" position or risk being captured by the police. Although viewers remain tethered to their seats in watching *Phone Booth,* the use of the split-screen format closely reflects the film's saturation of mobile screens, creating a highly interactive spectatorship. Indeed, there is already a battle of images de picted in New York City, as signs and advertisements compete for viewers' attention. Yet the Caller uses these public screens to his advantage, particularly when the news media covers Stu's standoff with the police. The Caller latches onto the televisions displayed in an electronics store across from the phone booth. The TV screens are another set of eyes for the Caller. This becomes problematic for Stu when the news media interviews Kelly. The Caller sees Kelly on the television screens across from the phone booth and uses this visual information to his advantage, targeting her with his gun. This ultimately forces Stu to make an uncomfortable decision. Knowing the Caller has identified Kelly as his wife, Stu must publicly admit his lies to her and to the public itself.

Notably, behind the phone booth are Shepard Fairey's stickers of his street art campaign of the professional wrestler, Andre the Giant (OBEY Giant) (see figure 6.2). These stickers would become part of Fairey's well-known OBEY logo, which derived from John Carpenter's film *They Live* (1988). For Fairey, these stickers were designed to provoke people to question and observe their relationship to their surroundings. Here, the OBEY Giant stickers contribute to the film's self-reflexivity, as we are reminded of the Caller saying to Stu: "You see people come in and out of this phone booth. The same ones every day. You make up names for them. You imagine their stories. But eventually, you get tired of imagining and follow one of them." Two people that the Caller follows are a German porn king and a corrupt executive, whom he will eventually kill. Of course, we should not equate Fairey's OBEY Giant stickers with the Caller's motivation for killing these two men. Rather, it is what the Caller says to Stu in relation to his media and image-saturated environment: "Life has given you more than your fair share, Stu. But it appears you don't appreciate it. Look, look, listen, appearances can be deceiving." At one point the Caller says to Stu that he has gotten himself into this situation because of the "sin of spin" and "avoidance and deception." Indeed, the Caller's ability to see things that otherwise go unnoticed in the city frighteningly connects to *They Live*, taking on an extraterrestrial dimension. In *They Live*, aliens conceal their appearances, blending in with the people of Los Angeles. Yet the aliens, or "ghouls," as they are referred to in the credits, are manipulating people to spend money, breed, and accept their subordinate positions.[16] John Nada (Roddy Piper) discovers special sunglasses that allow him to see the hidden messages (such as obey, consume, and conform), as well as the aliens posing as humans. The Caller takes on a similar role by figuratively forcing Stu to "put on the glasses" and not only see his surroundings, but also look within himself, as the Caller states: "I'm trying to help you, Stu, but you won't help yourself." In one of the film's emotionally charged moments, Stu redeems himself, telling the police, news media, and crowds of strangers that he has never done anything for anybody and that he lies to people and his friends. His gold watch is a fake and underneath his Italian clothes, he "still feels like the Bronx." He confides in Pam and Kelly that he has been "dressing up as something I'm not for so long, I'm afraid you won't like what's underneath." For Stu, this moment of pathos not only demonstrates the confessional mode under which the phone booth operates, but also its connection to *They Live* in exposing Stu's lies. Moreover, by showing us

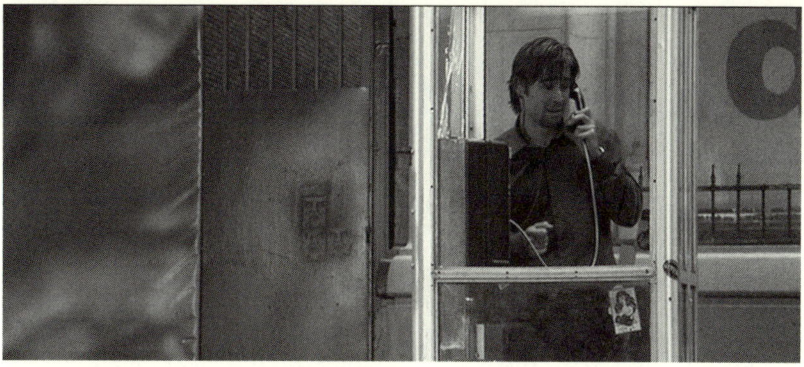

Figure 6.2. *Phone Booth.* OBEY Giant stickers loom in the background.

too much information as a cinema of excess, Schumacher, in a sense, is forcing the viewer to put on the glasses. As such, the film's exposure of excess explicates not only a dark dimension of the news media and celebrity gossip culture, but also the concern with mobile communication emerging at the turn of the millennium.

Excess is certainly not new territory for Schumacher. Schumacher, who started out as a fashion designer, is known for his highly visual style and production design, as seen in the expressionistic and classic horror film atmospheres of *The Lost Boys* (1986) and *Flatliners* (1990). As explained previously, excess is made visual by the deployment of fantasy within the confined setting. In *Rope*, the mise-en-scène becomes unstable once Brandon and Phillip's secret is revealed. Hitchcock times the revelation of the secret as the city lights emerge, flooding the penthouse with an orchestration of lights. The neutral lighting evokes a tableau of German Expressionism as Rupert exposes Brandon and Phillip's secret. The revelation of the secret is intimately connected to the film's exploration of excess, whereby the gaze is produced with disturbing results. But in the case of *Phone Booth*, the film's design begins and ends with oversaturation—what Todd McGowan terms a "cinema of fantasy."[17] The gaze is made knowable within the visual field as a distorting presence, demonstrated in the frenetic editing, the over-the-top performances, the use of the split-screen format, and the inundation of images. Yet there is a social factor at work in connection to the film's depiction of excess: the gaze as a knowable force corresponds to Stu's admission of his lies not only to Pam and Kelly, but also to the public itself, as captured by the news media. Here, we are reminded of the Caller's concerns about deception and the "sin of spin." The film's excess is intimately connected to an obscene enjoyment that ideology attempts to neutralize and regulate.

The Caller's sadistic act exposes ideology's obscene underside by taking on the role of a vigilante in his execution of those he deems immoral and corrupt.

Falling Down and a Ringing Phone Must Be Answered

After the police trace the location of the Caller, they arrive at the apartment and discover that a man's throat has been slit. The police assume that the Caller committed suicide. As they cart the man's body away, Stu and Kelly request to see the body. The police lift the sheet, revealing the pizza delivery man. Stu believes that the pizza delivery man was the Caller because of their previous altercation. But this moment is a knowing-wink to the audience, because it is assumed that viewers know that the voice of the Caller belongs to the actor Kiefer Sutherland. This ironic moment is what Chion calls the already visualized *acousmêtre*: "the one temporarily absent from the picture, is more familiar and reassuring—even though in the dark regions of the acousmatic field, which surrounds the visual field, this kind can acquire by contagion some of the power of the complete acousmêtre."[18] Of course, one does not need to know that Sutherland is the Caller in order to enjoy the film. But this moment of the already visualized *acousmêtre* has a self-reflexive dimension. There is a strong connection between Sutherland and Schumacher as an actor-and-director team in the films *The Lost Boys* and *Flatliners.* Those who are familiar with Sutherland's work, particularly the television series *24* (2001–2014), would most likely recognize his voice from the very start of the film. Stu's confirmation of the delivery man as the Caller affirms the film's self-reflexivity. It addresses the film's exploration of celebrity spectacle, whereby Stu, who makes his living on media gossip, is the target of attack.

During the last scene, Stu relaxes in the ambulance after being given a sedative. From his perspective, a male voice is heard off-screen saying "nice shoes." A man wearing glasses appears from the corner of the ambulance door. The man is blurry and out of focus as Stu realizes that he has identified the wrong man as the Caller. The clue for the viewers is knowing what Sutherland looks like as the already visualized *acousmêtre.* This moment for Stu is his encounter with the gaze, as he realizes that this man is, indeed, the Caller. Here, voice and body are finally embodied as the Caller walks away holding a gun case. The embodiment of the voice is emphasized by the slow-motion photography, an excessive aesthetic that emphasizes the gaze as a distorting presence. The irony is that Stu, who had been tethered to the phone booth, is immobilized as the tranquilizer takes its effect upon him, and therefore cannot call for help.

The Caller looks strikingly like the character William Foster, aka D-Fens (Michael Douglas) from Schumacher's *Falling Down* (1993), which continues *Phone Booth*'s self-reflexivity. Arguably, *Falling Down* can be read as a companion film to *Phone Booth* in their exploration of change and progress. Although *Falling Down* is not a limited location film in terms of space, it does share a feature with *Phone Booth* in its compression of time (approximately eight hours). *Falling Down* is set in Los Angeles and follows Foster, a divorced, laid-off missile engineer who wants to go home to be with his daughter on her birthday. In an homage to Federico Fellini's opening dream sequence in *8½* (1963), Foster mentally collapses during a traffic jam when his car's air conditioner breaks down. He abandons his vehicle and begins his journey on foot across Los Angeles, transforming into a vigilante. As such, Foster is prone to violence, as demonstrated by his anger over the high price of a can of Coke charged by a Korean store owner and his altercation with gang members over territory. Of course, Foster's psychological breakdown and racist dimension should not be solely equated with the Caller's sniper attacks. Both the Caller and Foster, however, do share concerns with change and progress. *Falling Down* takes place shortly after the Cold War, when highly educated engineers such as Foster are no longer needed or are "not economically viable." Dressed in 1960s attire, Foster is a fish out of water as he traverses the urban geography of Los Angeles, interacting with different people along the way. He reflects on the Cold War era of defending America from the Soviet Union. Similarly, the Caller takes on a defensive role as a vigilante. Like Foster, the Caller sports old brow-line glasses, a conspicuous look in his contemporary period. Like the phone booth itself, the Caller no longer fits in this changing world. But whereas Foster is shot and killed by police Sgt. Prendergast (Robert Duvall) in Venice Beach, the Caller outsmarts both the police and Stu, leaving the film with an ambiguous ending. Indeed, both films speak to their current moment in terms of space and telecommunication. Whereas Foster frequently stops to use pay phones to call his wife, the Caller is fixed within one location. *Falling Down*'s narrative tension relies on parallel editing, moving back and forth primarily as a cat-and-mouse narrative between Foster and Sgt. Prendergast, who maps Foster's movement through Los Angeles's diverse neighborhoods. By contrast, *Phone Booth* relies on the split-screen format as a means of depicting multiple spaces while Stu and the Caller remained fixed within their locations. Yet both films depict the gaze as a distorting presence within the field of visual perception that overwhelms the viewers. Schumacher's treatment of the excess of the gaze as a knowable force within the field of perception shows us that Foster and the Caller are angry men who no longer fit in current social reality.

At the end of the film, the Caller repeats the aphorism delivered during his first exchange with Stu: "Isn't it funny? You hear a phone ring and it could be anybody. But a ringing phone has to be answered, doesn't it?" The Caller's question addresses a formal aspect of answering a ringing phone. It is not so much about the content as it is about the ritual that a ringing phone has to be answered. Certainly, this is what Louis Althusser means by interpellation: how the structures of ideology hail or construct the subject.[19] But perhaps the Caller's mocking effort to compel Stu's agreement that a ringing phone must be answered shows us two sides of fantasy. The appeal of the Mojave phone booth is not only its strange location, but also how this technology of modernity, once thought of as alienating, can suddenly bring people together. The people represented in the documentary express excitement in answering the desert phone's calls. In *Phone Booth,* however, a ringing phone from a landline seems to be the oddity within the crowd of people and the surge of mobile communication devices. Yet, the fact that the ringing phone must be answered is what the Caller knows so well in hatching his sadistic plan. Here, a dark and sinister side of telecommunication emerges in the emerging cell phone era. In both cases, a ringing phone elicits our desire because we seek to know who the caller is.[20]

Locke and the Road Movie

Whereas *Phone Booth* explores the sadistic and sinister effects of the disembodied voice, the separation of voice and body in Steven Knight's real-time thriller *Locke* offers new insights, not only in its employment of dramatic effects of the *acousmêtre,* but also in its augmentation of the European road movie in its uses of communication technology. The story follows Ivan Locke, an architectural foreman who is preparing for one of London's largest concrete pours. Ivan unexpectedly learns that Bethan, a woman with whom he had a one-night affair, is about to give birth, and he is the father. Ivan spontaneously decides to drive to London to be with her, a decision that involves abandoning the concrete pour and canceling his plans to watch an important soccer game with his sons, Eddie (Tom Holland) and Sean (Bill Milner), and his wife, Katrina (Ruth Wilson). Using his BMW's communication technologies, Ivan juggles a number of calls, including confiding in Katrina about the affair, and guiding his less-experienced deputy, Donal (Andrew Scott), in managing the various moving parts in preparation for the concrete pour.

Although *Locke* takes place entirely in Ivan's vehicle, the film abides by many themes of the road movie narrative. David Laderman explains that the road movie seeks the unfamiliar in traversing space into the unknown. For Laderman, road movies often entail a rebellious component that "celebrates subversion as a literal venturing outside of society."[21] Many American road movies involve outlaws, such as *Gun Crazy* (Joseph H. Lewis, 1950), *Bonnie and Clyde* (Arthur Penn, 1967), and *Natural Born Killers.* Of course, American road movies are emblematic of the road's powerful attraction and the political currency it entails, such as *Sullivan's Travels* (Preston Sturges, 1941), *Easy Rider* (Dennis Hopper, 1969), and *On the Road* (Walter Salles, 2010). As Laderman notes, the propelling force of the road film is not only movement, but also a "journey as means of cultural critique."[22] By contrast, European road movies, as Laderman explains, "tend toward the quest more than the flight, and imbue the quest with navigations of national identity and community—navigations that often take on sophisticated philosophical and political dimensions."[23] Consider the theme of national identity associated with the soccer match Ivan is supposed to watch with his family, a ritual that involves cooking sausages, wearing the team's shirt, and drinking special beer. At one point during Ivan's journey, he has to convince Donal to get "the Albanian" to help with the rebars in preparation for the concrete pour, only to discover that "the Albanian" is watching the soccer match. Ivan then asks Donal to call his son to help with the rebars, only to learn he is in Germany digging missile silos. Ivan tells Donal to call Stefan (a Polish concrete farmer) and his road gang. Donal, however, is concerned about hiring a road gang, which Ivan acknowledges, stating: "They are slumming it for cash. But Stefan is the best concrete farmer I know." As Laderman explains, "With smaller countries sharing more national borders, the European road movie explores different national identities in intimate topographical proximity."[24] Although we never see Ivan traversing these spaces, his phone conversations exhibit the close continental borders of a European road film.

Locke, like many European road movies, such as *La Strada* (Federico Fellini, 1954), *Wild Strawberries* (Ingmar Bergman, 1957), and *Alice in the Cities* (Wim Wenders, 1974), is more concerned with self-reflection and introspection, as opposed to the outlaws or criminals on the run so often depicted in the American road film. Aesthetically, the film is permeated with reflections of streetlights and the lights of passing cars that reflect across Ivan's vehicle. Indeed, *Locke* is not only about a physical journey, it also tracks an existential quest. Here, *Locke* shares a common trait with film noir in its engagement with questions of fate. Ivan's journey is to be with Bethan, but it is also to prove that he will not commit the sins of his father. Conversations with the ghost of his father unfold when Ivan is speaking to his rearview mirror, one of the aesthetics that Knight employs within the film's confined space.

As much as *Locke* is about Ivan trying not to make the same mistakes as his father, it is also a film about how digital communication technologies have changed our relationship to labor and the automobile. It is well known that the risk of an accident greatly increases when driving distracted. Just as the aluminum outdoor phone booth met a demand due to the growing number of vehicles on the road in the 1950s, today's car companies have responded to the rising number of car crashes caused by distracted driving by developing new anti-distraction technologies such as Bluetooth and hands-free texting. The goal is to reduce the cognitive load for drivers, diminishing the risk of distraction. Indeed, *Locke* is a film about hyper-attention and multitasking, and speaks to our current cultural moment of mobile communication devices. Yet the film's confined location and real-time depiction of events command deep attention from its viewers. The film's one-location experiment challenges viewers to ride along with Ivan to London while he juggles a number of phone calls. Whereas both American and European road movies involve detours and roadside attractions—picking up strangers, stopping at diners, and filling up at gas stations—*Locke* employs none of these components. *Locke* takes place entirely within the vehicle as a real-time film of confinement. Whereas *Phone Booth* provides an early account of cell phone usage, *Locke* adds another dimension to the road movie, allowing one to be mobile yet interact with other characters through automobile communication technologies.

Locke is more than simply a filmed one-man play. It employs a dimension of cinematic excess. Here, *Locke* shares features with *Talk Radio* in relation to subjectivity and ethical action. Knight show us how excess grounds our subjectivity by experiencing Ivan's commitment to duty for the sake of duty. Like Barry, Ivan will not deviate from his plan to be with Bethan, even if it costs him his marriage and his job. Following the ethical dimension explored in *Talk Radio*, *Locke* renders space uncertain in Ivan's commitment to duty for the sake of duty. But, unlike Barry's over-the-top performance in *Talk Radio*, Hardy's low-key, minimalist performance and calm voice embody his precision and logical thinking as he juggles a number of phone calls. At the same time, he has to manage his family's emotions in their learning of his affair. Here, anti-distraction technologies add a new dimension to ethical action and cinematic excess. Barry's ethical action is to speak unabashedly on controversial topics, even if it risks his marriage or losing the deal with Metro Wave. In *Talk Radio*, Oliver Stone illustrates how Barry's duty for the sake of duty exceeds the social order's prohibition of enjoyment. Ethical action for both Barry and Ivan is extreme because they enjoy a pure devotion to their duty. In the case of *Locke*, anti-distraction technologies allow Ivan to operate ethically at two levels simultaneously: one that involves his drive to London, and the other to make sure that all elements are ready for the concrete pour to occur, which can be described as an ethic of multitasking. Ivan cannot detach from his work duties even though he has been fired. Ivan's pleasure in working, in particular, can be traced to voice diction as a mode of melodrama.

The Ethics of Voice and Diction

The relationship between desire and fantasy can generate different effects of the gaze within the confined setting. The power of cinema lies in its ability to depict events and situations in ways that are harder or even impossible to experience in the everyday world. The pathway toward having what we want is through fantasy; fantasy sets the coordinates for desire, allowing one to relate to his or her impossible object, or what Lacan terms *objet petit a*—the object cause of desire. This visual manifestation of *objet petit a* is the gaze. Rather than depicting the gaze as a traumatic force that interrupts our spectatorship, *Phone Booth* deploys the gaze as a knowable presence within the field of perception. This is often the case with visually excessive filmmakers such as Schumacher, who employs frantic editing, over-saturation of images, and split-screen displays of information in *Phone Booth.* Schumacher overwhelms viewers with simultaneous information in a form of database aesthetic as a means to reflect Stu's frantic situation. At the same time, the film's excess reveals a dark underside pertaining to media technologies in the age of cell phones and satellite communication technologies.

By contrast, films that evoke desire emphasize what we cannot have. These films are about lack and dissatisfaction. Of course, films that employ desire can be challenging, because they withhold satisfaction. This does not mean they are not pleasurable to watch. But they do demand more from viewers. *Locke* certainly bears similarity to a film that emphasizes desire. For one, the film never embodies the callers with whom Ivan communicates. Second, the film lacks narrative closure. This is partially attributed to the film's experiment with confining the narrative solely within the space of Ivan's vehicle.

At the same time, *Locke* entails a dimension of fantasy not only in Ivan's incommensurate pleasure in multitasking with various callers to prepare for the concrete pour, but also in the expressive and excessive diction of his callers. Ivan's interlocutors lack what Chion terms "de-acousmatization," whereby the "end point of de-acousmatization [is] the *mouth* from which the voice issues."[25] As Chion explains, "*embodying the voice* is a sort of symbolic act, dooming the fate of acousmêtre to the fate of ordinary mortals."[26] Because viewers do not see Ivan's callers, the callers are assigned certain powers. Part of *Locke*'s narrative tension pertaining to the *acousmêtre*'s power is voice diction and the callers' reactions to Ivan's decision to drive to London. In this regard, *Locke* and *Talk Radio* both share and differ in dramatizing the disembodied caller. In *Talk Radio,* Barry refuses to tone down his comments, even as he continues to receive death threats from his more extreme listeners. Barry's ethical action to enjoy creates a paranoid and unsettled space. In the case of Ivan, his disembodied callers do not so much create a space of paranoia as evoke emotional violence through voice and inflection in their reactions to Ivan's affair and his decision to abandon the concrete pour. Writing on the modes of melodrama, Thomas Elsaesser explains that the importance of expressive diction is creating "emotional resonance." For Elsaesser, "sound, whether musical or verbal, acts first of all to give the illusion of depth to the moving image, and by helping to create the third dimension of the spectacle, dialogue becomes a scenic element, along with more directly visual means of the mise-en-scène."[27] It is not only words that give emotional punch, but the sound and orchestration of the voice itself as an aesthetic effect. Elsaesser's reading of the voice and melodrama closely follows Roland Barthes's "grain of the voice": when sound becomes the "material" of the body. As Barthes explains: "[The] grain of the voice, which is an erotic mixture of timbre and language, and can therefore also be, along with diction, the substance of art: the art of guiding one's body. . . . The language lined with flesh [is] a text where we can hear the grain of the throat, the patina of consonants, the voluptuousness of vowels, a whole carnal stereophony: the articulation of the body, of the tongue, not that of meaning, of language."[28] For Barthes, the grain of the voice is not a search for meaning, but the pleasure in the emotion of the performer. From a psychoanalytical standpoint, the emotional responses of the callers are uncomfortable to listen to. They realize how our desire to hear shapes the aural field. In *Locke,* voice diction stands in for the disembodied callers in order to give expressive means and narrative tension within the confined setting of Ivan's vehicle. For example, Donal reacts emotionally to Ivan's leaving him in charge of the concrete pour. Bethan's voice becomes highly emotional in preparing for the task. Probably the most expressive voice comes in Gareth's reaction to Ivan's decision to abandon the concrete pour: "Oh! Sweet monkey Jesus! This is not happening." Later, Gareth tells Ivan that he vomited because of this shocking news, connecting the body to the voice as a mode of melodrama.

Ivan's enunciation, however, characterizes his devotion to duty in his minimal expression. Even in the midst of his crisis, Ivan continues to be specific, calm, and logical, which is captured by his voice diction. When Ivan confides in Katrina about his affair, he repeatedly tells her that he wants to discuss a "practical next step." Or, when Gareth calls Ivan to tell him that Chicago fired him, he explains that he spoke about Ivan working for ten years, "working for Park without a foot wrong." Ivan corrects him by saying he worked for Park for nine years. When Ivan first informs Donal of his decision to abandon the dump in order to drive to London, Donal becomes upset, saying, "Ivan, at 5:45 a.m. tomorrow morning, three hundred and fifty metric tons of wet concrete is being delivered to the site. We have two hundred trucks from all over the fucking country descending on us." Ivan calmly replies by correcting Donal, stating: "Three hundred and fifty-five metric tons, two hundred and eighteen trucks." Of course, Donal thinks Ivan's decision to leave him in charge of the concrete pour is a joke. But Ivan replies that he has no choice, demonstrating his pure devotion to his duty to drive to London. Yet when Ivan is truly private, he unleashes his pent-up frustrations, shouting "Fuck" when he learns that he has the phone number Donal needs for the sign-offs for the road closures. It is only when Ivan is not on the phone that his voice emotionally modulates, particularly his conversation with his father in the rearview mirror. Certainly, these conversations speak directly to the film's noir aspect of fatalism. At one point Ivan says to his dad: "You think this is all fate, don't you dad? Your dirty fucking fingerprints all over me. It was bound to happen because of the little seeds you planted. Well, let me educate you. Let me teach you something. Even no matter what the situation is, you can make it good. Like with plaster and brick." This is precisely what Ivan is attempting to achieve with his callers—to make good out of a dire situation. Ivan's managing Katrina's emotional meltdown is no different than his orchestrating the moving parts of the concrete pour. Yet, as he attempts to quell his callers' feelings, he cannot escape that fact that he has inherited the past sins of his father. These dimensions of the *acousmêtre*'s powers derive not only from voice diction, but also from their relationship to Ivan's calm and logical expression. Not unlike the flat and dry recording of the Caller's voice in *Phone Booth,* Ivan's monotone diction closely relates to the perfect sound. Ivan's minimalist reaction to his callers closely mirrors his ethical action in not deviating from his plan to be with Bethan. These competing voices shake up and disturb *Locke*'s confined setting, drawing attention to the film's excessive dimension.

At the same time, Hardy's minimalist performance has more in common with desire than with fantasy. For one, the film refuses to visually present the callers. At the same time, the disembodied callers represent a certain power, which is expressed in voice diction. Secondly, the film lacks narrative closure: viewers never see Ivan getting to Bethan. Ivan makes it to London, receives the calls from Bethan, and says he is on his way. But we never see Ivan arrive at the hospital. The final image is of Ivan driving away. The film's open ending leaves viewers speculating about whether Ivan actually arrives at his destination. In certain ways, the disembodied voice mirrors the unrepresented places in the film, such as Ivan's home, the hospital, or Donal at work. These details certainly position *Locke* as a film of desire. Yet Ivan's excessive enjoyment with work makes *Locke* a film about fantasy. Through fantasy, *Locke* shows us that excess constitutes our subjectivity. Entry into the symbolic order requires the renunciation of enjoyment. The regulation of enjoyment grounds the functioning of the symbolic. Our participation within the symbolic also leaves us with a piece of enjoyment (surplus-enjoyment) that sticks with us as the privileged "lost object" (*objet petit a*). The perpetual absence of the *objet petit a* sustains the engine of our desire. Ivan's ethical action is to carry out all the steps in preparation for the concrete pour, whether he loses or profits. We cringe at Ivan's ethical action, because he gives up everything to commit to the plan. We cannot turn our eyes away or close our ears as he juggles multiple calls during his journey to London. Yet we root for Ivan to make sure all points are checked off in preparation for the concrete pour. Even though Ivan succeeds in preparing for London's biggest concrete pour, he fails to fix his domestic situation. These components intensify the film's constrained-setting narrative.

Indeed, excess shapes the dynamics of space within the confined setting. *Locke* is not simply a filmed play, but involves an obscene enjoyment assigned to Ivan's refusal to relinquish his plan to be with Bethan and his determination not to commit the same sins as his father. Knight's attention to visual details, such as the emphasis on the kaleidoscope of lights that reflect and slither off of Ivan's vehicle as it drives along in the night, are some of the ways in which space is energized within the film's constrictions. Similar to *Phone Booth*, the film hardly employs long takes, but instead relies on fast editing and a variety of camera angles on Ivan as he traverses the highway. Knight will often cut to Ivan's car as it moves along the highway. But these shots are not Ivan passing by the camera, but the camera positioned onto the vehicle to give the viewer a sense of movement. But this movement lacks direction—as if Ivan is driving out of time. This is reflected in *Locke*'s film noir tone and its exploration of fate and memory production. Even Ivan's name entails these dimensions, where his fate is "locked."

At the end of the film, Ivan continues to drive, leaving viewers to speculate whether he will truly meet Bethan. Ivan's ethical action closely follows Lacan's notion of the drive—where enjoyment is found in its movement and not in obtaining its goal by repeating loss. For Lacan, drive circles endlessly around *objet petit a,* whereas desire seeks to obtain the *objet petit a,* but always fails to achieve it. The drive is literally and connotatively rendered in *Locke* in both the physical and the mental travel to London. Ivan's enjoyment is not in reaching his goal, but in the drive itself and his obscene enjoyment and devotion to work, a commitment enhanced by his vehicle's communication technologies and his logical voice diction.

Locke demonstrates how digital communication devices not only augment our understanding of the road movie in terms of time and space, but also involve a dimension of power in our inability to embody his callers. The *acousmêtre* creates suspense not only because viewers do not see the callers, but also by the diction of the callers' reactions to Ivan's affair and his spontaneous decision to abandon the concrete pour. In the case of *Phone Booth,* the disembodied caller takes on powerful effects not only in viewers' inability to localize the Caller, but also in how the film imagines digital communication in the use of multi-screen imaging and mobile screens. Yet both films explore Ivan's and Stu's infidelity through confined spaces. At one point, Stu explains to the Caller why he cheated on his wife, using the metaphor of home and hotel: "Look, I don't want to hurt Kelly. She's always there for me. . . . Kind of like having a beautiful home. With everything you ever dreamed of. But you still need that vacation now and then. Some nice hotel room with a great view." Similarly, Ivan explains his affair to Katrina using the analysis of painting: "She [Bethan] isn't what you would call an oil painting." Ivan attempts to use logic and reason for his bad decision, as if he can manage his infidelity like the concrete pour: "I want to talk about a practical next step." What connects Stu and Ivan is that their confessions take place within a confined setting. Both the phone booth and Ivan's car are confessional spaces. In *Phone Booth,* the Caller frequently reminds Stu of his sins: "Your sins have caught up to you," "Redeem yourself," and "I know your crimes, tell them." In *Locke,* Ivan not only confesses to his wife about his affair within his vehicle, but also his conversation with the ghost of his father functions as a mode of confession, explaining that everything will work out—the concrete pour and the birth of his baby.

Ivan adds that Katrina "will be ok. In the morning she will be ok. That is how it can be. That is my prayer. . . . The Lockes were a long line of shit but I straightened the name out." Certainly, the film's ambiguous ending suggests that Ivan may have saved the concrete pour from turning into a disaster, but whether Katrina will ever forgive him remains unknowable. In both films, telecommunication devices and *acousmêtre* render the confined spaces unsettled and antagonistic.

7

Captive, Captor, and Aliens: *10 Cloverfield Lane*

In *Phone Booth,* the Caller threatens to kill Kelly if Stu does not publicly admit his lies. Stu must adhere to the Caller's demands and face the consequences of his infidelity. In certain ways, the Caller's actions have a close correlation to the torture narrative. Terrorizing Stu and Kelly is key to procuring the truth. By holding Stu hostage and threatening to murder Kelly, the Caller forces Stu to confess his lies. Indeed, the phone booth acts as a space of confession—a terrain of torture. Here, it is worth adding that the Caller, played by Kiefer Sutherland, happens to play Jack Bauer of *24,* who is known for tracking down terrorists and using torture to extract information.

Spy thrillers often resort to the biopolitics of torture as a reliable method to extract the truth. Biopolitics suggests that truth can be rendered by inflicting pain on the subject's body. Although *Phone Booth* is not a spy or mission narrative, it shares motifs in that both envision accessing truth through the body. Hilary Neroni explains: "In the contemporary torture fantasy, truth lies in the tortured body and the torturer must use violence to rip away the fictions that hide it."[1] For Neroni, the production of fiction in television shows such as *24* is not the path toward the truth; rather, torture enacted on the vulnerable body is the only means to discover truth. Similarly, in *Phone Booth,* the Caller threatens Stu to get him to confess his sins, to speak the veracity of his affair to Kelly. The only means of uncovering the truth is through Stu's vulnerable body, which is sadistically confined in the phone booth.

But there is an alternative to ascertaining information that does not resort to the ideology of torture. In comparing the television series *Alias* (2001–2006) to *24,* Neroni explains that the shows differ in their methods of acquiring information. For Neroni, torture is less effective in *Alias* as a means of manifesting information. The character Sydney Bristow (Jennifer Garner) relies on performing fictional scenarios "as the most successful way of completing the tasks necessary for the preservation of national security."[2] Neroni explains that Sydney "recognizes herself as a desiring subject, and, at the same time, she sees others as desiring subjects as well."[3] Sydney completes her missions by making herself desirable and staging fictions rather than employing torture.[4] This is certainly the case in the 1980s Cold War thriller television series *The Americans* (2013–2018). Elizabeth (Keri Russell) and Philip Jennings (Matthew Rhys) are KGB officers posing as an American couple living in the United States. A major part of their job is to procure information by dressing up as different characters. Like Sydney in *Alias,* Elizabeth and Philip rely primarily on fictional scenarios in order to fulfill their missions, which involve reading the victim's desire. Perhaps the biggest fiction they perform is when Philip marries Martha Hanson (Alison Wright), a lonely woman who works as a secretary for the FBI's counterintelligence agency. Philip must play the character of Clark Westerfield in order to gain access to the FBI. Philip understands that for the mission to succeed, truth will be gained through the lens of desire rather than the terrain of torture. As such, Philip plays on Martha's desire in order to lure her into his trap.

The science fiction fantasy thriller *10 Cloverfield Lane* is far from the mission or espionage narratives of *Alias* and *The Americans.* Yet playing on the subject's desire is key to the film's narrative tension within its confined setting. *10 Cloverfield Lane* is a follow-up to Matt Reeves's alien invasion film *Cloverfield* (2008). It tells the story of a young woman named Michelle (Mary Elizabeth Winstead) who is held captive in a fallout bunker by Howard (John Goodman), a man who murdered a young girl named Brittany two years earlier. After surviving a car crash, Michelle awakens from a coma in Howard's bunker, which is located on a farm forty miles outside of Lake Charles, Louisiana. Michelle discovers that Howard rescued her from the accident and has since cared for her. Also living in the bunker is Emmett (John Gallagher Jr.), who talked Howard into letting him into the bunker after seeing a red flash outside. While Michelle was unconscious, Earth had been invaded by aliens. According to Howard, the planet may no longer be habitable, and the only way to survive is to remain in the bunker.

My claim is that Howard keeps Michelle alive in order to resurrect the fantasy of his daughter, Megan.[5] Michelle learns that Megan was, in fact, Brittany, who was kidnapped and murdered two years ago. In order for Michelle to plan her escape, she must play the role of Megan. Similar to Brandon and Phillip hiding a corpse in the trunk in the penthouse living room in *Rope,* Michelle's lie has a close correlation to a functioning reality within Howard's bunker. By adopting the figure of Megan, Michelle normalizes the bunker's confined space, thus keeping Howard's obscene underside at bay. By not performing Howard's fantasy, Michelle resurrects a nightmarish (excessive) side of him that could threaten her life. In order to trick Howard and escape the bunker, Michelle must resort to logic and reasoning. Similar to *Alias* and *The Americans,* Michelle's plan involves attracting Howard's desire through a fantasy scenario, luring him into a trap in preparation for her and Emmett's escape. Most importantly, Michelle and Emmett's secret corresponds to their surplus-knowledge (excess), which they must keep contained in order to sustain the fantasy. The combination of Howard's unreliability and Michelle and Emmett's lie drive the suspense and narrative tension within the bunker's confined setting.

Desire and the Missing Piece

The halfway mark of *10 Cloverfield Lane* involves a comical moment with Emmett working on a picture puzzle of a cat scuba-diving in a fishbowl. He connects the last piece only to discover that there are missing pieces. Working on the puzzle certainly underscores the different ways in which Michelle and Emmett try to pass the time in the bunker. Of course, the cat in the fishbowl speaks directly to Michelle and Emmett's entrapment. The cat's scuba-diving gear also alludes to Michelle's makeshift hazmat suit, which saves her when battling the aliens at the climax of the film. Perhaps more importantly, the puzzle's missing pieces are proxies for the uncertainty and unreliability of Howard. Indeed, Howard's motivations are not made clear to Michelle, Emmett, or the viewer. Michelle and Emmett are constantly shifting their allegiance to him. The missing pieces of the puzzle not only suggest the passing of time within the bunker's confined setting, but also represent Howard's untrustworthiness.

Perhaps more importantly, the missing pieces of the puzzle address the allure of what Lacan terms *objet petit a* (the object cause of desire). For Lacan, subjectivity is constitutive of lack. The subject's entry into the symbolic order comes with the prohibition of enjoyment. The symbolic order is grounded on regulating enjoyment. In *Talk Radio,* Barry's ethical action to speak on controversial topics not only breaks with broadcast radio's standards and practices, but also defies the prohibition of enjoyment that regulates the symbolic order. To enjoy obscenely, as Barry does, draws attention to one's excess. Barry sticks out because he enjoys too much in his talk on controversial topics. In the same way, Brandon cannot contain his satisfaction during the dinner party, knowing that David's dead body is hidden in the trunk in the living room in *Rope.* Yet it is Brandon drawing attention to his enjoyment that piques Rupert's desire to investigate the penthouse and find what is in the room more than the room. It is Brandon's obscene enjoyment that ultimately leads to his and Phillip's demise. The subject sacrifices enjoyment for entry into the symbolic order.

Yet the subject always carries a remainder of enjoyment—a kernel that becomes the subject's object cause of desire. As Slavoj Žižek explains, "the point of Lacan's concept of surplus-enjoyment: the very renunciation to *jouissance* brings about a remainder/surplus of *jouissance*."[6] The subject relinquishes *jouissance* for access to the symbolic. But the subject is tainted by the loss of *jouissance*—a piece of excess (surplus-enjoyment) that one can never get rid of.

Becoming a part of the symbolic constitutes the subject of desire. Sustaining one's desire is the fact that desire can never be satisfied due to the unattainability of the object cause of the desire. *Objet petit a* (the lost object) holds the answer for desire. But the paradox is that *objet petit a* never existed from the start, which is why desire has no escape from its excess. For Lacan, when the subject enters the symbolic order, desire is directed to the big Other: "desire is the desire of the Other." But the big Other does not have access to *objet petit a.* The symbolic functions on this shared absence of the object cause of desire. Indeed, the object cause of desire is the missing piece of the puzzle. The object cause of desire specifies an absence that elicits the subject's desire. That is, the logic of desire operates by the subject not obtaining the lost object. Yet the subject's inability to locate the lost object is paradoxically the source of his or her enjoyment.

The opening sequence of *10 Cloverfield Lane* depicts the logic of desire by emphasizing incomplete information to the viewer. The first image is a long shot of the river as the camera dollies backwards, moving through the window and ending inside Michelle's apartment. We see a number of objects in her apartment to paint a picture of her character, particularly her interest in clothing design. The absence of narrative sound and a fragmented editing style pose questions rather than supply answers. At one point, Michelle speaks on the phone with hesitation. Her lips and body language suggest that Michelle is leaving her boyfriend. As she exits the apartment, the image zooms in on a set of keys and a ring. Certainly, Michelle's packing her belongings puts us in Hitchcock terrain, as we are prompted to remember Marion Crane's (Janet Leigh's) escape from Phoenix after stealing her boss's client's money in *Psycho.* To be sure, like Marion, Michelle is a woman on the run who meets with a violent, halting force. A wide shot shows Michelle driving through a rural area, offering a sense of vastness compared to the city. She pulls up to the gas station as a truck suspiciously pulls up close behind her car. Similar to Steven Spielberg's road thriller, *Duel* (1971), a clear view of the driver is never given. The bodiless driver correlates to the gaze as an unknowable force that renders the space with uncertainty. Not unlike the suspicious driver in the parking lot of WGAB that opens *Talk Radio,* the unseen driver of the truck in the gas station reveals something that protrudes or sticks out. This surplus-knowledge, like the bucket that will not stand upright in the opening scene of *The Passion of Anna,* or the haunting and forbidding opening of *The Shining,* transforms objects and everyday actions into an uncanny state. These obstructions not only realize our desire of looking, but also lay a trap for our encounter with the gaze. As Michelle drives away, she receives a call from her boyfriend Ben (voiced by Bradley Cooper), who is upset that she left him. After the call, a vehicle crashes into Michelle as her car spins out of control. The film abruptly cuts to its credits and back to the accident as Michelle's car lands in a field. After the credit/car crash sequences, Michelle awakens in Howard's bunker with a broken leg.

The film's opening generates a number of questions, particularly the identity of the person who crashed into Michelle, and how she arrived at Howard's bunker. The movement from Michelle's apartment to the bunker is a truncated trajectory of events that follow the logic of desire in posing a number of questions without answers. The accident not only incites our desire to know more, but also creates a mystery about why Howard rescued Michelle. How did she get to the bunker? Is Howard the person who hit her? Is Howard trustworthy?

What Do You Want?

Perhaps the biggest mystery at the start of *10 Cloverfield Lane* is whether the planet has, in fact, been invaded by aliens. Certainly, one's knowledge of the invasion in *Cloverfield* offers insight into this question. As such, desire operates by prompting a number of questions without answers. The "missing scenes" that open *10 Cloverfield Lane* speak to the film's ambiguity, which stimulates our desire for the answer. Just as *Cloverfield* never supplies the viewer with a clear answer as to who the aliens are and why they have invaded the planet, *10 Cloverfield Lane* generates its mystery and suspense by both confining the viewer to Michelle's point of view and not showing the invasion itself. Of course, this is not new territory in the sci-fi/fantasy genre. A number of recent television series—particularly zombie and vampire narratives—often begin with a missing scene that would explain the reasons for the invasion, such as Rick Grimes (Andrew Lincoln) of *The Walking Dead* (2010–present), who awakens from a coma in a hospital and discovers that he is now living in a zombie apocalypse. In *Van Helsing* (2016–present), Vanessa Van Helsing (Kelly Overton) comes out of a coma to discover that she is living in a vampire plague and has the ability to bite vampires and turn them back to human form. In both cases, we are not privy to the origin of the apocalypse or plague. The missing scene in both shows' dystopian universes is *objet petit a,* not only because it is the mystery that generates our desire to know more, but also because its absence paradoxically stages various obstacles that these characters must battle for survival. In the same way, we are in the dark about Howard and the aliens as much as Michelle is. Like the conditions of Grimes and Van Helsing, Michelle's blackout denies us access to the missing scene.

When Michelle awakens from the car accident and discovers that she is held captive in a room, her instincts kick in as she plans to attack Howard. Noises are heard off-screen as Howard enters the room. Like Annie in *Misery* and Old Nick in *Room,* Howard is revealed in fragmentation. This partial view speaks not only to Howard's power, but also to the viewer's inability to fully render the room's setting. Michelle asks what he wants. When Howard's face is finally revealed, he responds to Michelle's question: "I'm going to keep you alive." Indeed, Howard's response speaks directly to the relationship between fantasy and desire. Fantasy establishes the coordinates of desire. Through the work of fantasy, one can have an imaginary relationship with one's object cause of desire. Howard is keeping Michelle alive in order to sustain his fantasy of Megan. Michelle will become the object that stands in for Howard's object cause of desire.

After Howard leaves, Michelle uses her crutch as a weapon by sharpening its end. She sets a fire in the air vent and positions herself in attack mode. Howard returns to the room and Michelle attacks him, which fails to physically harm him. He drugs Michelle and chains her to the wall. Later, he returns with food and explains that he saved her. He tells Michelle that she is safe in the fallout bunker because there was an attack—"possibly nuclear assault." He connects the alien invasion to the Russians as the possible culprit, calling them the "Russkies," slang used during the Cold War. Howard explains to Michelle that he built the bunker under his farmhouse: "I've prepared for this," he says, smiling with delight. Indeed, Howard's smile speaks to his obscene enjoyment, confirming that his conspiracy theories have been proven right. Here, Howard has a close connection to Forester in *Falling Down* and the Caller in *Phone Booth*—all three characters are depicted as nightmarish men who resist social progress and lament the past. Not unlike Forester's license plate that reads: "D-FENSE," Howard explains that you always have to be prepared for the worst. Like Forester, Howard was involved with military defense, working with chemicals to launch satellites into orbit. Certainly, the bunker reminds one of the concerns of global nuclear war and radiation fallout during the Cold War era. Although Michelle's reaction suggests her skepticism about Howard's conspiracy theories, they are proven correct at the end of the film.

A loud crash is heard off-screen as we are introduced to Emmett, a man of the same age as Michelle. From the start, Emmett is revealed to be clumsy—a trait that will come back to haunt him when planning their escape. Howard rescued Emmett, allowing him to escape into the fallout bunker during the alien invasion. Emmett has known Howard for a long time. He even helped Howard build the fallout bunker. Emmett tells Michelle that Howard is correct—she is safe in the bunker—although she is not entirely convinced. But for viewers of *Cloverfield*, Emmett is certainly right about the invasion. Michelle asks: "How do we get out of here?" As Emmett is about to tell her about the attack, Howard unexpectedly appears. Indeed, Howard is always watching and listening—which will prove fatal for Emmett later in the film.

Howard shows Michelle to the living quarter of the bunker while a jukebox plays 1950s music. The camera moves through the common area to reveal that Howard has created a living space akin to 1950s décor. Here, the style of the fallout bunker closely corresponds to Howard's stasis in time and his resistance to change—particularly in his view of women as homemakers. Perhaps more importantly, the bunker's 1950s décor harkens back to an innocent time—motifs that conservatives jumped on in the 1980s and 1990s in bolstering television shows such as *The Donna Reed Show* and *Leave It to Beaver* (1957–1963) for their positive and didactic portrayal of family values.[7] For Howard, the bunker serves as a peaceful scenario—a fantasy without its obscene underside, where men are in charge and women are in a subservient position. Howard reinforces this hierarchy when he tells Michelle that she will learn how to cook. Not unlike Annie in *Misery*, there is a dark and frightening side to Howard. Like Annie, who presents herself as a puritan to Paul (even as she unpredictably lashes out with verbal assaults), keeping Howard's obscene underside submerged involves sustaining his fantasy of the supposed innocence of the 1950s and the traditional roles assigned to men and women as depicted in prime-time television series. To be sure, when Michelle almost slips, Emmett tries to help. Howard yells at Emmett: "Keep your hands to yourself. No touching!" Emmett backs off. Howard has strict rules in the bunker. Preventing any form of intimacy between Michelle and Emmett not only alludes to his conservative values, but also sustains and protects his fantasy of Michelle as Megan.

Michelle is not convinced that Howard is reliable. Not unlike Rupert, who probes Brandon and Phillip in *Rope*, she recognizes something in him more than him—that he is concealing information. During dinner, she sees keys attached to Howard's jeans. To get access to the keys, she creates a fake conversation with Emmett. Howard becomes frustrated because he is not included in the conversation. Howard slams his fists on the table and shouts: "I know what a traitor looks like," suggesting that he can read Michelle's desire. That is, Howard recognizes the excess of her fake conversation with Emmett. Again, this will prove fatal for Emmett, who is unable to contain his excess and prevent Howard's obscene underside from manifesting later in the film. Howard forces Michelle to apologize, asserting that he is a disciplinary force as both a rule follower and the "man of the house." Michelle apologizes while clandestinely stealing his keys. As they continue to eat, Michelle grabs a bottle, smashes Howard in the head, and flees toward the stairs. But like her first attack on Howard, Michelle's escape comes to a halt. Howard is correct—there is something polluting the air. When Michelle is about to leave the bunker, Howard's neighbor Leslie (Suzanne Cryer) appears outside the door window. Leslie's face is contaminated as she begs Michelle to let her in to the bunker. Howard yells not to let Leslie in because she will contaminate the bunker. Michelle surrenders and returns the keys to Howard. When Michelle returns to her room, she has a conversation with Howard and learns that he had crashed into her because he was panicking about the invasion. He apologizes to Michelle. Later, Michelle stitches Howard's head wound. She knows that she has a potential weapon in the stitching needle, yet she does not attack him again. As such, restoring order to the bunker's confined setting is evident in how objects switch from tools to weapons and vice versa. When Michelle resists the temptation to use the needle as a weapon, she surrenders her desire to escape the bunker, accepting the truth of her situation. Howard requests that Michelle take Megan's clothes. Once again, we are in Hitchcock territory as one is reminded of Scottie reconstructing his fantasy of Madeleine (Kim Novak) in *Vertigo.* Howard explains to Michelle that Megan's mother turned against him and moved to Chicago. Here, Michelle literally sutures her relationship with Howard by stitching his wound. At the same time, Michelle restores Howard's fantasy, unbeknownst to her as a stand-in for Megan/Brittany. Michelle, so to speak, closes up Howard's excess. She both normalizes Howard and restores his bunker into an idyllic setting associated with 1950s nostalgia.

Fiction within Fiction

Upon Michelle's learning that Megan was Howard's daughter and her realization that it is not safe to leave the bunker, Howard suddenly appears to be trustworthy to her and Emmett. When the bunker's ventilation system breaks down, Michelle's loyalty towards Howards changes. Michelle is the only one who can fit through the air duct to reset the system. Snaking her way through the duct, she reaches the space where the ventilation is housed. After resetting the machine, Michelle notices a ladder that leads to an area with a skylight. Michelle climbs the ladder and reaches the window, which is partially shaded by a covering. Looking closely at the window, she notices human-made scratches at the edge of the covering. She slides the shades and discovers that someone has scratched "help" in blood. Michelle's look of horror is analogous to Lacan's reading of Holbein's *The Ambassadors.* Like the stain at the bottom of *The Ambassadors,* the small scratches on the side of the window arrest Michelle's looking with anxiety. Moving her head slightly (looking awry), Michelle encounters the gaze as the stain is revealed to be the word "help." Not unlike Brandon and Phillip's penthouse window in *Rope* that offers us an "Apollonian" view of the cityscape, the bunker's skylight generates a peaceful and comforting perspective for Michelle. When Michelle reads the message, however, the window loses its transparent effect, creating a "Dionysian" effect as the object looks back at her. Indeed, the message captures Michelle's and the viewer's desire as well as the chain of meanings that she pieces together in solving the mystery of Howard.[8] As Michelle climbs down the ladder, she steps on an object, which is revealed to be an earring with traces of blood. Her expression turns to horror as she realizes that the earring belonged to Megan, the girl in the picture that Howard had shown her. She concludes that the owner of the message written in blood was Megan. Speaking to Emmett about the earring and the message, Michelle learns that the girl in the picture was not Howard's daughter, but Brittany, who had gone missing two years ago.

Michelle realizes that she has become, in the way Slavoj Žižek describes Judy in *Vertigo,* a "copy of copy."[9] This is what Scottie horrifically discovers at the end of *Vertigo.* Gavin Elster (Tom Helmore) hired Scottie to follow and investigate his wife Madeleine. He tells Scottie that she has been haunted by her long-dead relative Carlotta Valdes and believes that she may be thinking of committing suicide. Unbeknownst to Scottie, he is investigating a "copy" of Madeleine (played by Gavin's mistress Judy). Near the halfway point in the film, Scottie and Judy (performing as Madeleine) unexpectedly become attracted to each other. Sticking to the plan, Judy (performing as Madeleine) pretends to commit suicide to cover up the murder of Elster's wife. In the second half of the film Scottie unexpectedly meets Judy, who looks strikingly like Madeleine. He dresses Judy to look exactly like Madeleine. Scottie does not know that he is, in fact, creating a copy of a copy of Madeleine. For Žižek, the "imitation of imitation" is where "symbolic truth emerges."[10] This is the horror that Scottie discovers at the end of the film: namely, he was set up by Elster. Scottie was nothing but a pawn in Elster's murderous plot. Similarly, Michelle is unknowingly imitating the role of Brittany who went missing, or was believed to be kidnapped, two years ago. Michelle and Emmett horrifically discover that Brittany is a substitute for Megan in the photo. As such, the truth emerges when they encounter the "copy of the copy." This is made evident when Michelle shockingly learns that she is wearing the same "Paris Je T Aime" (Paris I Love You) shirt as Brittany/Megan in the photo (see figure 7.1). Howard now dresses up Michelle as Brittany/Megan. This new information requires that Michelle and Emmett come up with a plan of escape immediately. Not unlike *Misery* and *Room*, Michelle and Emmett's plan must not involve physically fighting Howard, but playing on his desire. As such, they cannot awaken his excessive and obscene side as a child abductor and murderer.

The earring not only uncovers Howard's lie, but also reveals that Brittany is the real of Howard's desire. What Michelle discovers is the missing piece of Howard's traumatic kernel—his obscene enjoyment as a kidnapper and murderer. Michelle's new knowledge of Howard recalls a scene in *Misery* when Paul finds newspaper clippings of Annie's murder trial. Paul shockingly learns that Annie was accused of murdering babies when she was a hospital nurse. Yet Paul must continue to perform Annie's fantasy as her favorite writer while preparing his escape. Likewise, Michelle must perform Howard's fantasy in order to keep his obscene underside at bay. Not unlike *Room*, in which Joy has Jack play dead as a way to trick Old Nick, or Paul in *Misery*, who must write a new novel that resurrects the character of "Misery," Michelle must enact Howard's fantasy of Megan in order to sustain normalcy within the bunker. Her escape plan involves her seamstress skills, which help her create a hazmat suit out of a shower curtain. Once the suit is ready, she and Emmett will take the gun from Howard, tie him up, and one of them will escape and call for help. To do so, they must read Howard's desire by staging a fiction within a fiction. But they must not draw attention to the excess of their lie. That is, Michelle and Emmett must not display any signs that they are harboring a secret. They must contain their surplus-knowledge and maintain the status quo within the bunker. Similar to the ideas of the *Kammerspielefilme* in *Rope*, the confinement of space puts under a microscope not only objects within the room, but also the characters' gestures and body language. If Michelle or Emmett reveal something that sticks out, they will awaken a dark and nightmarish side of Howard, which is exactly what happens when Emmett is caught in a mousetrap during a game of charades.

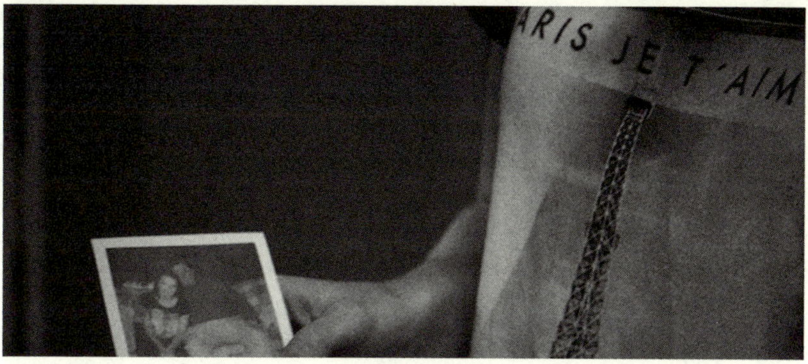

Figure 7.1. ***10 Cloverfield Lane*****. Michelle wears the same shirt as Brittany in the photo.**

In writing about Alfred Hitchcock's *Murder!* (1930), Alenka Zupančič links the play-within-a-play narration device to the logic of desire in the whodunit narrative—what she describes as the "play-scene-genre." In a traditional sense of the detective or whodunit genre, the crime is excluded from the narrative. The detective's job is to gather facts, clues, and data, and deduce what has happened. In solving the case, the detective moves from non-knowledge to knowledge. The detective is our surrogate in the quest for knowledge. Zupančič points out that Hitchcock did not care for the whodunit genre. By creating a play within a play, Hitchcock was able to stage something different from the traditional whodunit scene. Instead of revealing the murderer's identity in *Murder!* Hitchcock creates a scene in which the murderer Fane (Esme Percy) auditions for Sir John's (Herbert Marshall) play, which happens to be on the subject of murder. Fane realizes during the audition that Sir John has lured him into a trap. Knowing that he has betrayed his guilt for murdering the young actress Edna Druce, Fane kills himself during his trapeze act at the climax of the film. Fane never verbally admits to Sir John that he is the murderer. Instead, he leaves Sir John a letter, demonstrating that the play scene produced an indication of his guilt. Sir John's mousetrap underscores Hitchcock's bomb theory by allowing viewers to take part in his plan. As Zupančič explains, "The mousetrap captures not only the murderer's guilt, but also our desire—and this is what makes it so fascinating."[11] Drawing on Lacan's notion that every truth has the structure of fiction, Hilary Neroni explains, "The implicit claim of *Alias* is not that truth itself has a fictional status, that it is simply a construction, but one must use fictional constructions to find it."[12] Just as Sir John creates a fantasy to capture Fane's guilt in *Murder!* Neroni explains that Sydney in *Alias* creates a scenario that speaks to the victim's desire in accessing the truth.[13] Not unlike the climax of *Rope*—when Rupert exposes Brandon and Phillip's lie, which collapses the peaceful setting of the penthouse space—once Fane realizes he has been set up, his mannerisms become creaturely and distorted to depict his excess as an indication of his guilt. As such, Fane's protracted movements demonstrate the post-effects of the gaze.

In the same manner as in *Murder!* a play-scene captures Emmett's desire (as well as ours) during the game of charades. The phrase Emmett has is "little women." He offers Howard a number of clues to say the word "women," but Howard can only say "girl" and "little princess." This moment clearly speaks to Howard's fantasy of women as subservient to men. Not unlike Fane's bizarre mannerism when he is caught in Sir John's mousetrap, the word "women" causes Howard to become strangely uncomfortable. Enunciating "women" is traumatic for Howard because it forces him to face the real of his desire. During Howard's turn, he reads the card and offers the following verbal clues to Emmett: "I know what you're doing. I see what you're doing. I know what you're up to." Like Fane, Emmett becomes flustered, telling Howard he does not know what he is getting at. Howard continues by stating: "I see you when you're sleeping. I know what you're doing." Emmett begins to crumble, thinking that Howard is not playing the game but literally telling him that he knows about their escape plan. Michelle realizes the clue and proclaims: "Santa Claus!" Indeed, Emmett's indication of guilt has been recognized by Howard. Whereas Michelle is able to contain her surplus-knowledge by thinking rationally, Emmett cannot maintain the lie. Not unlike Phillip in *Rope*, who begins to shows signs of guilt during the party for murdering David, Emmett draws attention to his excess by his inability to perform the lie in planning the escape from the bunker. Also, not unlike Sir John trapping Fane's guilt during the audition, the game of charades turns an ordinary and everyday activity into something terrifying.

Howard, however, gives no indication that he has trapped Emmett's desire. And so for Michelle, Emmett, and the viewer, the plan has not been compromised. But this is not the case. After the game, Howard asks Emmett and Michelle to help him move a barrel into the bathroom. Similar to Annie in *Misery* explaining the ankle-smashing practice of "hobbling" once used in African diamond mines for those who stole the goods, Howard says that the barrel is full of perchloric acid, which helps shoot naval satellites into orbit. The chemical instantly dissolves biological elements, including humans. Emmett asks nervously why Howard is showing them the barrel. Howard responds by saying they have to get rid of the waste in the bunker, again trapping Emmett's desire. They move the barrel into the bathroom. Indeed, the waste that Howard is removing is Emmett—the thing that is getting in the way of his fantasy of Michelle as Megan. Howard then reveals the scissors that Emmett stole. He tells them that he knows what they are up to, proving that Howard is always watching. Emmett apologizes to Howard, saying that he was planning to steal his gun. Emmett explains that he wanted to show Michelle that he is a real man. Although Emmett has not demonstrated his skills to outwit Howard, his explanation speaks to Howard's fantasy of a strong and rugged male. Yet we are unsure whether Emmett is telling the truth about his feelings for Michelle. Nevertheless, Howard accepts his apology as Michelle and Emmett sigh with relief. Howard then retrieves his gun and shoots Emmett point-blank in the head.

Both Howard's revealing the scissors and Emmett's death operate as a traumatic encounter with the gaze. Howard's discovery of the scissors realizes our investment in the narrative that captures Michelle's, Emmett's, and our desire. Similar to Jeff caught spying on Thorwald in *Rear Window,* the reveal of the scissors realizes a blind spot in our looking. This moment demonstrates not only how our desire is caught within the frame of perception, but also the importance of the film's construction of a fantasy space of respite before the shocking reveal of the scissors. After the game of charades, we believe that Howard has not figured out that Michelle and Emmett are planning an escape. Once Howard calls them to the living room to move the barrel, fantasy and desire intersect, producing shocking results.[14] Because Howard knows that Michelle and Emmett were trying to deceive him, a nightmarish side of him emerges, resulting in Emmett's death. Just before Howard shoots Emmett, the image cuts to a shot of Michelle as she sees the gun come into frame. We do not directly see Emmett's death, only Michelle's horrified reaction. This blind spot in our looking realizes our desire of looking, laying a trap for our encounter with the gaze. Just as Fane expresses creaturely and distorted movement after being caught in Sir John's mousetrap in *Murder!* the post-effect of the gaze for Michelle is captured in the ringing sound after the blast of the gun. The post-effect of the gaze depicts the collapsing of the fantasy's screen to filter the real. The effect of the real is captured in the drop in audio, which interiorizes Michelle's point of view, as reality becomes distorted and unhinged. Faint sounds of Howard's dialogue can be heard as he attempts to comfort her. The drop in audio connects to the film's first scene in Michelle's apartment, which relies on body language and gestures as forms of communication. Not unlike the crippling effect of cinematic space in the final tracking shot of *Rope,* the zoom that engulfs Andreas at the end of *The Passion of Anna,* or Stu drugged in the ambulance at the end of *Phone Booth,* the post-effect of the gaze and deformation of space after Emmett's death are enhanced by the audio register.

For Howard, however, Emmett's death allows him to continue to enjoy Michelle as his fantasy object. For Michelle, she must put her plan into action and escape the bunker alone.

Desire and Fantasy, Vertical and Horizontal Movement, VFX

After Emmett's death, a number of images are shown of the bunker: the stairway leading to the exit, the living room, Michelle's room, and the storage area where Emmett slept. These images are moments of lull for us not only to reflect on the death of Emmett, but also to bridge us into the film's final act. Moreover, these images operate as pieces of a jigsaw puzzle—the puzzle of Howard that has now been solved as we see Michelle upset, sitting in Emmett's sleeping space. Howard is heard off-screen approaching. He holds an ice-cream cone and a bowl of ice cream. He is not shown in a full shot—reminding us of his unpredictability. He attempts to comfort Michelle as he tells her that "we can do whatever we want." The rules that he so strongly enacted have now disappeared. As Howard heads to the kitchen to cook dinner, Michelle returns to her room and prepares her hazmat suit by sealing it with duct tape. But before she can escape, Howard returns and tells her supper is ready. He senses something is wrong with Michelle, which leads him to find the hazmat suit under her bed. Michelle runs to the door and locks Howard in her room. Michelle quickly makes her way to the living room. She enters the bathroom and shockingly sees the perchloric acid dissolving Emmett's body. As she grabs the freeze spray from the drawer, Howard reappears. He is upset that Michelle has not shown him respect for saving her, as he says: "This is how you repay me?" Michelle knocks over the barrel as Howard falls into the perchloric acid. As Michelle escapes, the chemicals dissolve a lamp chord, setting a fire in the bunker. Michelle packs her hazmat suit and heads for the exit, but is stopped by Howard, whose face is deformed from the chemicals. Indeed, Howard's metamorphosis into a monster coincides with the destruction of the bunker. Michelle knocks over a shelf of food, knocking out Howard. She escapes through the filtration ducts as flames begin to engulf the bunker, killing Howard.

Having defeated Howard, Michelle must now battle her next obstacle: the aliens. Michelle escapes to the skylight where Brittany had scratched "help." She puts on the hazmat suit, breaks the lock using the freeze spray, and escapes from the bunker. She approaches Howard's truck to retrieve what's left of her belongings from the car accident. As she opens the door she rips the hazmat suit. Panicking, she sutures the rip with duct tape. She looks up and sees a flock of birds passing overhead. Realizing that the air is safe, she takes off her mask. But something arrests Michelle's looking. She sees a spaceship on the horizon, patrolling the area. Suddenly, Howard's bunker explodes, catching the ship's attention. The ship turns toward the direction of the explosion and deposits creatures onto the ground. Michelle frantically looks for the truck's keys, which she cannot find. She runs to Leslie's vehicle parked on the farm. She reaches the car and sets off its alarm, drawing the attention of the aliens. Michelle hides in a nearby shed, where she finds Leslie dead. While the aliens investigate the vehicle, Michelle finds Leslie's keys and turns off the alarm. The aliens approach the shed. Michelle escapes and runs toward a neighboring house in the distance. She stops as the mother ship hovers above the house. It begins to spray chemicals. Michelle runs back to Howard's truck and quickly puts on her mask. As she enters the truck, the mother ship sucks Michelle and the vehicle into the air. Michelle finds the bottle of liquor she took with her at the beginning of the film. She creates a Molotov cocktail and throws it into an opening of the ship. The alien ship explodes, dropping the truck to the ground, mirroring Michelle's car crash at the start of the film as the image cuts to black. Michelle awakens as the alien ship crashes in the distance. She enters Leslie's vehicle and drives away, crashing through a mailbox with the address of 10 Cloverfield Ln. An overhead shot tracks Michelle as she drives along, mirroring a shot that began her journey at the start of the film. Michelle turns on the radio and learns that the military has taken back the southern seaboard. The broadcast announces a safe zone located in Baton Rouge. But they are looking for those who have battle or medical training to assist people in Houston. Michelle slams on the brakes as she reaches a crossroads. She can either drive to the safe zone or to Houston. Michelle backs up the car and drives in the direction of Houston. A flash of lightning reveals a spaceship hovering in the sky as she drives into the distance, ending the film on an uncertain note.

10 Cloverfield Lane has many similarities to *Cloverfield*. Although *Cloverfield* is not confined to one space, as in the case of *10 Cloverfield Lane*, it is limited to Hud's (T. J. Miller) perspective. Viewers experience *Cloverfield* entirely from the perspective of a personal video camera, operated mainly by Hud. The camera documents the group's attempt to survive the monster's fury as they traverse the city in an effort to rescue Rob's (Michael Stahl-David) ex-girlfriend, Beth (Odette Annable), who is trapped in a collapsed building. Both films take what Dan Trachtenberg and J. J. Abrams describe as a "lo-fi" approach stylistically in order to produce "hi-fi" results.[15] (Hi-fi or high-fidelity more accurately reproduces the sound of its source. Lo-fi refers to lesser audio fidelity in recording its source.) In the case of *Cloverfield*, the amateur and improvisational quality (lo-fi forms) not only captures the group's frantic situation to produce hi-fi results, but also how personal media can inform the look and design of a film. For example, smartphones, mobile screens, and small digital cameras allow for the instantaneous recording of events, which can be quickly uploaded to the internet and shared with friends and family members through email and social networking sites. *10 Cloverfield Lane* also has a close correlation to lo-fi forms in the intimate spaces and close proximity of characters within the confined setting to produce hi-fi results. Just as we only see events through the camera lens directed by Hud as the vulnerable camera operator in *Cloverfield*, we are confined to Michelle's perspective in *10 Cloverfield Lane*.

Digital effects certainly help to enhance both films in achieving hi-fi results. This augmentation is particularly noticeable in that both films rely on vertical and horizontal movement as they build narrative conflict in relation to characters overcoming personal obstacles. Kristen Whissel explains that digital effects have multiplied contemporary cinema's "vertical imagination" in tracing opposing conflicts of extreme highs and lows. Whissel identifies characters defying forces of gravity as a "visualization of power," in what she terms "spatial dialectics." Many contemporary blockbuster films, according to Whissel, resist not only the laws of physics, "but also the spaces and times that define a fictional world's prevailing order."[16] For Whissel, the spatial dialectics of verticality can traverse historical inertia. Consider the dazzling scene in *Cloverfield* when Rob, Hud, and Lily rescue Beth from her penthouse building. Before the monster's attack on the city, Rob and Lily had broken up. Rob took a job in Japan, a decision that he wrestles with early in the film. After the attack on the city, Rob and his group of friends decide to find Beth rather than follow the military's order to leave the city. Here, the group must first horizontally traverse the space of New York City to reach Beth's penthouse building. Then they must ascend her building, which has collapsed sideways onto an adjacent building. Reaching the top of the building, they must cross the slanted rooftop to access Beth's penthouse, where they discover her pinned to the floor by a rebar. The group's horizontal and vertical movements clearly perform "polarized extremes," enhanced by the film's digital effects. Indeed, Rob's vertical movement to save Beth has personal meaning as the couple reunite. The spatial dialectics of the scene rupture and change the course of events for Rob and Beth. Certainly, the melodrama of this scene reminds us of many climatic sequences, such as King Kong's dramatic fall from the top of the Empire State Building, or Hans Gruber (Alan Rickman) falling to his death from the Nakatomi building at the end of *Die Hard*. Recent digital visual effects, however, have contributed to even greater aesthetic possibilities in characters achieving upward and downward movement, such as the blockbuster Marvel movies *The Avengers* (Joss Whedon, 2012) and *Dr. Strange* (Scott Derrickson, 2016).

Characters' dramatic ascent and descent not only follow Hollywood's melodramatic mode, but also intimately connect to the logic of desire and fantasy. Fantasy's appeal is that it can stage dramatic scenes such as the precipice ending of *Die Hard* or Hitchcock's Statue of Liberty scene in *Saboteur* (1942). Fantasy permits one to have a relationship with the object cause of desire, which digital effects can further enhance.[17] In *10 Cloverfield Lane,* the relationship between horizontal and vertical movement has a personal trajectory for Michelle and the theme of entrapment. The film begins with a horizontal pullback to reveal Michelle's apartment as we learn that she is leaving her boyfriend without talking to him face to face. Similar to the vista of Beth's penthouse in *Cloverfield,* the view from Michelle's apartment is spectacular. The next scene shows Michelle driving horizontally across the rural spaces until her accident halts her trajectory. While unconscious, Michelle descends into Howard's bunker—a space of doom, where Howard resurrects his fantasy of her as Megan. Part of Michelle's escaping the bunker encompasses her backstory involving a father and daughter at a hardware store. In a conversation earlier in the film, Michelle explains to Emmett that the father was in a hurry, yanking his daughter's arm. Michelle says that she wished she could have done something for the little girl, especially when she witnessed the father slap his daughter after she slipped on the floor. But Michelle did not help the little girl, as she says to Emmett: "And I wanted so badly to do something. To help her. But I do what I always do when things get hard. I just panicked and ran." Here, we learn that Michelle's father behaved the same way toward her. Certainly, Michelle leaving her boyfriend has a strong connection to her need to flee and avoid conflict. As such, horizontal movement for Michelle corresponds to a linear trajectory of her past. Similar to Andreas in *The Passion of Anna,* as explored in chapter 3, Michelle must traverse the fantasy in order to overcome and fully identify with her past of "no regrets." As explained in *The Passion of Anna,* Andreas stuffs away the shameful feelings of his past marriage by self-imprisoning himself on the island. At the end of the film, Andreas cannot identify with his past trauma (his symptom). Andreas has no character transformation as the zoom literally and *horizontally* digests him. Michelle, too, is in a state of confinement both personally (her familial past) and physically (the bunker). From this perspective, her escape from the bunker and battle with the aliens have a strong correlation to her overcoming her past. Facing death, Michelle defeats both Howard and the aliens through an upward trajectory. Yet this experience has transformed her. Whereas Whissel notes that vertical movement demonstrates the overcoming of historical forces, Michelle's ascent marks her overcoming her trauma by identifying with her symptom. The vertical movement ruptures Michelle's "historical continuity" as she breaks free from her abusive past.

Vertical movement demonstrates not only Michelle's transformation, but also how heights become associated with power. The ultimate test for Michelle is her battle with the alien ship. Similar to what occurs in *Cloverfield,* her catharsis is through an upward trajectory. At the end, Michelle chooses not to drive away from danger, but directly toward it. Michelle traverses the fantasy by identifying with her symptom of "no regrets." This, in turn, sets Michelle free as she turns toward the danger. Yet the film's ending leaves us wondering if she will take on the role of soldier or nurse in Houston. This conclusion reminds us of Sarah Connor's (Linda Hamilton) transformation at the start of James Cameron's *Terminator 2* (1991), as she takes up a masculine persona. Hilary Neroni describes Connor's transformation as embodying the contemporary violent woman in cinema. Whereas *Cloverfield* supplies viewers with wholeness in the romantic unification of Rob and Beth (which is often depicted in Hollywood melodramas), the ending of *10 Cloverfield Lane* leaves us with uncertainty. Neroni explains that "the love relationship makes each feel whole, which is to say, free from alienation and complete."[18] The contemporary violent woman, for Neroni, erupts the "complementarity" of the romantic union, which often allows "us to believe in the possibility of overcoming antagonism."[19] The climax of *10 Cloverfield Lane* supplies us with a resolution in Michelle's defeat of both Howard and the aliens. At the same time, her decision to drive to Houston—like Sarah Connor driving off into the horizon at the end of James Cameron's *The Terminator* (1984)—leaves us with unanswered questions and no romantic reunion.[20] Michelle's battle with the aliens certainly recalls the ending of *Alien,* when Ripley kills the alien aboard the escape shuttle. At the same time, the ending of the film denies the viewer closure as Michelle drives to Houston. The film leaves us with uncertainty—another missing piece of the puzzle that corresponds to the logic of desire.

Conclusion

127 Hours, *The Wall*, *Panic Room*, and Cyberspace

> *127 Hours* is like an exercise in conquering the unfilmable.
> —Roger Ebert

In an interview, filmmaker Danny Boyle discusses the process of adapting Aron Ralston's (played by James Franco) real-life survival story for the screen. In 2003, Ralston went hiking by himself in Blue John Canyon in Colorado. While Ralston was exploring a slit in the canyon, a boulder came loose, causing him to fall. The boulder pinned Ralston's right forearm to the side of the canyon. He was trapped for five days with no food, very little water, and no cellular phone. The only way Ralston could escape was to amputate his arm. In re-creating the slit of the canyon where Ralston was trapped, Boyle designed the set to limit movement for the production crew. According to Boyle, "There were only two ways in [into the slit of the canyon]—either through the top, or walking all the way around the back and then in—and it wasn't at all convenient for the equipment necessary for filming a movie, like cameras and lights. 'I told everyone to embrace it.'"[1] Boyle's choice to construct limits within the set of *127 Hours* returns us to a question posed at the start of this project: how do films that take place predominantly within one setting, such as *Rope*, *Room*, and *Locke*, make for an exciting film over a long period of time? As argued, the films explored throughout this project embrace cinematic excess by exposing the gaze as a knowable or unknowable force within the confined setting. The "unfilmable," as Ebert points out in his review of *127 Hours*,[2] is not only a challenge that filmmakers encounter when working within a limited setting, but also speaks directly to the logic of desire. Desire functions on absence (what we cannot see or know). Yet to be involved in a film's story world not only manifests our desire to see, but also lays a trap for our potential encounter with the gaze. The gaze manifests how our desire distorts the field of vision. To encounter the gaze not only realizes our involvement in the film's narrative, but also reveals the film's excess. The films explored throughout this study visualize the excess of the gaze as a spectatorship of shock and attraction within a confined setting. Moreover, these films demonstrate the narrative, aesthetic, ethical, social, and political possibilities of cinematic excess. Here, I would like to use *127 Hours*, *The Wall*, and *Panic Room* to bring together a number of points discussed throughout this study.

Limitations within the Vastness

Danny Boyle is known for his excessive and energetic style of filmmaking, as evident in films such as *Shallow Grave* (1994), *Trainspotting* (1996), *28 Days Later* (2002), and *Slumdog Millionaire* (2008). Boyle brings a similarly energetic quality to *127 Hours* (2010), even describing the film as an action film with a guy who cannot move.[3] This is apparent in his use of fast edits, shifting multiple camera angles, and handheld camerawork. Perhaps most notable is Boyle's employment of the split-screen format captured during the credit sequence. The screen is divided into three panes that shift upwards and downwards, while depicting crowds of people cheering and clapping at sporting events. We see images of people running a city marathon, swimmers racing, and the running of the bulls in Spain. These shifting images are juxtaposed against people praying, going to work, and vacationing on a beach. Aron Ralston subtly emerges by himself in the middle pane as he prepares for his trip to Blue John Canyon. Certainly, the split-screen format is characteristic of *Phone Booth* in the depiction of information as a database aesthetic. Here, *127 Hours* exposes the excess of the gaze as a knowable force in order for us to directly see life in motion as contingent and adrenalized. Whereas *Phone Booth* reveals an obscene and dark underside to telecommunication, screen culture, and news media sensationalism, *127 Hours* uses the split-screen format to depict crowds of people as a positive force. Yet Aron stands alone as he is sandwiched between the multi-screen panes of people. He appears spontaneously as an island unto himself.[4] As such, Boyle shows Aron's independence from others by giving him his own pane within the multi-screen imagery that starts the film. Here, the split-screen format and hyper-kinetic imagery are reminiscent of Godfrey Reggio's experimental film *Koyaanisqatsi* (1982), which translates as "life out of balance." This is certainly the case for Aron. When departing for the canyon, he does not leave a message for his friends or family. While preparing for his trip, his phone rings. But he does not answer it. The call is from his sister. On the voice message, we learn that Aron has not called or talked to his mother in a while and that she is worried about him. Aron is a thrill-seeking loner who does not rely on or need others. This is tested early on in his hike, when he meets Kristi (Kate Mara) and Megan (Amber Tamblyn), who are looking for an underground pool of water in the canyon. Aron takes them to the pool's location and they swim together. Afterward Kristi and Megan invite him to a party. Aron thanks them for the offer and abruptly takes off. As they watch Aron leave, Kristi says to Megan that he probably won't show up, suggesting his need to flee when it comes to emotionally connecting with others. When Aron becomes entombed in the canyon, we are forced to stay exclusively with him as we experience his transformation from loner to someone who is dependent on others. From this perspective, Aron is not that far from Michelle in *10 Cloverfield Lane* or Andreas in *The Passion of Anna*. All embody the lonely figure in relation to their physical and/or psychological entrapment.

127 Hours is not like confinement films such as *Misery*, *Room*, or *10 Cloverfield Lane*, where we wonder how the characters will overcome their captors. Rather, *127 Hours* assumes that we already know the true story of Aron Ralston. For example, when Aron is initially pinned to the boulder, he grabs his pocketknife and we believe that he is going to amputate his arm. Instead, Aron begins to the chip away at the boulder, hoping it will come loose and free him. Here, Boyle shows us a number of Aron's memories triggered by objects that set off very strong recollections of his past. For example, when the sunlight moves through the slit of the canyon, Aron extends his leg into a patch of light for warmth. The image cuts to Aron as a young boy, camping with his dad as they build a campfire. Throughout the film, Aron's memory triggers begin to form a pattern of his life and what led him to become a loner.

Indeed, as much as *127 Hours* is a survival narrative, it is also very much about Aron's letting go of his fantasy of not depending on the love of or need for others. Aron uses his video recorder as a confessional tool, to not only document his entrapment in case he should die, but to also express his remorsefulness to his family—to communicate his love to them. At one point, he apologizes for his selfishness, such as missing his sister's wedding. Not unlike *Phone Booth* and *Locke*, the slit of the canyon is a confessional space. Moreover, the boulder that entraps Aron has existential resonance. This is expressed when Aron emotionally says to the video camera, before amputating his arm, "I chose all of this. . . . This rock has been waiting for me my entire life. . . . Ever since it was a bit of meteorite. A million years ago. . . . There in space. It's been waiting to come here. Right, right here. I've been moving towards it my whole life." His video camera battery then dies. At this point, Aron amputates his arm. He escapes the canyon and is rescued by a family hiking. Not unlike Andreas in *The Passion of Anna* or Michelle in *10 Cloverfield Lane*, Aron is a lonely figure who is haunted by certain events of his past. Perhaps the most painful memory triggered during his entrapment is his breakup with his girlfriend. In an interview with the real-life Aron Ralston, he stated that he was "crushed to the core" after the breakup with his girlfriend in 2006.[5] But whereas Andreas clings to his fantasy of solitude until the very end of the film in *The Passion of Anna*, Aron is transformed by his entrapment. Aron achieves freedom not only by physically cutting off his arm, but also by confronting his traumatic past.

As argued, *127 Hours* suggests that audiences will have prior knowledge of Ralston's amputating his arm in order to escape the canyon. Having this "surplus-knowledge" of Ralston's entrapment, in certain ways, follows Hitchcock's bomb theory by rendering everyday action with uncanniness. Aron's arrival at the canyon is suspenseful because we know that he will eventually become trapped, turning the film into a survival narrative. This makes the amputation scene all the more disturbing. If we know the true story of Ralston, then we know that we will have to confront the decision to amputate his arm. Yet we are invested in Aron's survival and are therefore complicit in his decision. The scene is horrific and repulsive, which makes it very traumatic to watch. There are even reports of people fainting in movie theaters during this scene. Still, Aron's amputation of his arm is beautiful, not only because he survived this ordeal, but also because he has been transformed by the event itself. Indeed, *127 Hours* is a cinema of excess in Boyle's fast-paced editing, split-screen format, and handheld cinematography. It is a film that renders the gaze knowable within the confined space of the slit of the canyon, not only to depict Aron's entrapment, but also to show his transformation by the event itself. At the end of the film, Aron swims with his amputated arm, a scene that connects back to the beginning of the film when he swam with Kristi and Megan. Boyle stated that he wanted to start the film with water imagery. Certainly water is key to Aron's survival. But it also suggests fluidity as well as his rebirth. At the end of the film, when Aron emerges out of the swimming pool, he sees his family smiling at him. Through the limitations imposed upon him, Aron transforms into a subject who sees himself as a part of the world and dependent on the love of others. [6]

Know Your Enemy

Whereas *127 Hours* exposes the excess of the gaze as an overwhelming presence, Doug Liman's confinement thriller, *The Wall*, creates narrative suspense by rendering the encounter with the gaze as an unknowable force. It is a film where we encounter the gaze with traumatic results. Like *127 Hours, The Wall* takes place in an open and vast landscape. It is a sparse and minimalist narrative involving two American soldiers, Sergeant Shane Matthews (John Cena) and Sergeant Allen "Ize" Isaac (Aaron Taylor-Johnson), in the desert of Iraq. Matthews and Isaac are sent to investigate a pipeline construction site where eight contract employees have been shot and killed by an Iraqi sniper referred to as "Juba" (Laith Nakli). Surveilling the pipeline from a great distance, they conclude that it is safe to enter the site. While investigating the site, Matthews is suddenly shot by Juba. When Isaac goes to rescue Matthews, he is shot in the knee. Isaac painfully makes his way to a crumbling stone wall for protection. From this point on, the film takes place entirely behind the stone wall as Isaac tries to locate Juba's position while Matthews lays injured and unconscious out in the open. When Isaac calls headquarters for help, he learns that Juba has hijacked his radio signal. Isaac uses his other radio and discovers that Juba shot the antennae. Juba tunes his radio to Isaac's frequency, demanding that he talk to him. He wants to learn who Isaac is and why he came back to Iraq when the war is over. Not unlike the Caller in *Phone Booth,* if Isaac does not follow Juba's demands, Juba will kill Matthews, whom he has framed in his rifle's crosshairs.

Unlike *127 Hours* and *Phone Booth, The Wall* relies primarily on minimalist stylization. Like the first half of *Room,* the film employs low-key shifts to articulate cinematic space, such as the use of long takes and slow dolly shots. Yet it is Juba's disembodied voice (as Michel Chion's notion of the *acousmêtre*) that helps to create a spectatorship of uncertainty which entices our desire. Like the Caller in *Phone Booth,* Juba's presence is revealed through the crosshairs of his rifle. Juba is not only absent within Isaac's field of vision, but he is also an unreliable and unpredictable enemy. As Isaac figures out, Juba is "the ghost," the "Angel of Death," who is responsible for other killings in the desert. Both Isaac's and our inability to see Juba demonstrates the power of the *acousmêtre.* As explored in *Talk Radio, Phone Booth,* and *Locke,* the disconnect between voice and body is the excessive element that "sticks out" in the film, infusing the space with antagonism. As such, rather than employing hyper-stylized camerawork, Liman primarily relies on the separation of voice and body to unsettle our viewership.

Similar to the captive films explored throughout this study, Isaac must figure out a way to outwit Juba. Like Aron in *127 Hours,* Isaac must survive in the desert with no food or water. By mapping the trajectory of the bullet that hit his leg and by counting the number of times Juba fired his rifle at Isaac and Matthews, Isaac begins to narrow down Juba's location. At one point during his radio conversation with Juba, Isaac hears metal crashing in the background. Listening closely, Isaac identifies the banging of the metal on top of a large trash pile in the far distance. He believes it is Juba's location. Meanwhile, Matthews, assumed to be unconscious, interrupts Isaac's radio transmission with static to signal that he is alive. Isaac tells Matthews where Juba is positioned. Matthews subtly and slowly retrieves his rifle, trying not to draw Juba's attention and alert him that he is conscious. Using the passing of a sandstorm as a shield, Matthews loads his rifle and fires at the trash pile. Matthews drags himself across the desert floor as we believe that he has killed Juba. But as Matthews drags himself to the stone wall, Juba shoots and kills him. Here, at Isaac's lowest point, Juba demands to know the real reason why he came back to Iraq. We learn that Isaac harbors deep guilt for the death of his friend and fellow American soldier, Dean. He confides in Juba that Dean became trapped by an enemy sniper. Isaac tried to shoot the sniper but accidentally shot and killed Dean. Isaac emotionally breaks down and says that he lied about Dean's death to everyone. Not unlike Stu in *Phone Booth*, Ivan in *Locke*, Barry in *Talk Radio*, and Aron in *127 Hours*, the confined space of the stone wall becomes a space of confession for Isaac. Yet by confessing his guilt to Juba, Isaac overcomes this tragic event.

At the end of the second act of the film, Isaac is able to contact headquarters. But Juba intercepts the message and poses as Isaac. He tells headquarters that he and Matthews found nothing in their investigation. Juba requests that they pick them up because they are baking in the sun like potatoes. Listening in, Isaac knows that Juba is luring them into a trap. Shortly after, Ivan hears the helicopter approaching in the distance. In a last stand against Juba, Isaac breaks down the stone wall and fires at the trash pile. His act is both real and symbolic. No shots are fired back, and Isaac believes Juba is dead. The helicopter arrives and rescues Isaac. But as they are flying over the trash pile, Juba fires at the helicopter and shoots one of the soldiers and the pilot. Isaac yells to the other soldier that the sniper is in the trash pile. But it is too late as the helicopter crashes, ending the film with uncertainty. Here, *The Wall* shares a trope with the horror genre by employing the trick ending in the form of the gaze. Not unlike the alien that sneaks aboard the escape shuttle in *Alien*, or Carrie's hand jutting out the gravestone's pile of dirt at the end of *Carrie*, Juba's shooting down of the helicopter manifests a blind spot in our desire to see. The brief respite that the film offers after Isaac is rescued not only demonstrates how our desire distorts the visual field of perception, but also lays a trap for our encounter with the gaze. As such, to encounter the gaze demonstrates that our looking resides within the film, not as a transcendent spectator.

The ambivalent ending of *The Wall* not only denies us narrative closure, but also exposes the antagonism that classical narrative film structure often alleviates. As explored throughout this study, the excess of the gaze offers political and social insights, as in the case of *Green Room, Phone Booth,* and *Talk Radio.* Although *The Wall* establishes clear boundaries between Isaac and Juba, the fact that the enemy is not killed evokes the uncertainty of the Iraq War and the U.S. initiative to help rebuild Iraq's economy. Liman underscores this commentary by confronting the viewer with antagonism instead of narrative closure. Moreover, the film calls into question our understanding of (and empathy for) the enemy. Juba tells Isaac that he was a teacher in Baghdad. His school was destroyed by the U.S. military. Some of his students died, and he still feels pain from the shrapnel in his elbow. Juba tells Isaac that the stone wall that protects him once belonged to a school. Juba then became a sharpshooter trained by the United States. Juba not only speaks English, but also studied English literature—as we (and Isaac) learn by his references to Shakespeare and Edgar Allan Poe's "The Raven" and "The Tell-Tale Heart." Certainly, Poe's "The Tell-Tale Heart" speaks to Isaac's harboring of his guilt for accidentally shooting Dean. Not unlike Phillip in *Rope,* who becomes psychologically unraveled because he cannot contain his secret of murdering David, Isaac is haunted by the truth about Dean's death. As we learn, he carries Dean's broken scope with him. Here, the broken scope shows us two sides of the real as described by Žižek: the real is what resists symbolization and is the screen upon which to project our fantasies. On the one hand, the broken scope stands for trauma, horror, and guilt for mistakenly killing Dean. On the other hand, the broken scope as the screen of the real helps Isaac make sense of his guilt and shame over Dean's death.

Perhaps more importantly, Juba's reference to Poe is reminiscent of Poe's story "The Cask of Amontillado," where the character Fortunato is entombed alive behind a wall. Ironically, it is not so much that Isaac is trapped behind the wall that speaks to Poe's revenge narrative. Rather, it is Juba who is entombed—not only by the scars caused by the U.S. military in bombing his school, but also by virtue of his physical entombment in the trash heap. Still, our identification is aligned with Isaac, who is also wrestling with the scars of war, as he attempts to locate and kill Juba. In both cases, *The Wall* muddies our sympathy for the suffering both characters have endured from the war. As such, *The Wall*'s uncertain ending as the embodiment of the gaze forces us to focus on the trauma and instability of the war in Iraq, as well as our understanding of the enemy.[7]

Showing Too Much Space

Paradoxically, the confined spaces of *127 Hours* and *The Wall* are themselves situated in the open and vast spaces of the canyon and desert, respectively. By contrast, David Fincher's home invasion film, *Panic Room,* takes place almost entirely in a four-story brownstone/townhome (or "townstone," as it is called in the film)[8] in New York's upper West Side. The film relies on the exposure of the gaze as a knowable presence by showing the viewer too much space within the confined setting. The depiction of this excess of space not only reflects the vastness of the home, but also exploits the tensions of wealth, property, and class. The film begins with Meg Altman (Jodi Foster), recently divorced from her husband who is a pharmaceutical mogul, and her young daughter, Sarah (Kristen Stewart), viewing the "townstone" with two realtors, Lydia (Ann Magnuson) and Evan (Ian Buchanan). Like Ullman and Watson showing Wendy and Jack the Overlook Hotel at the start of *The Shining,* the showing of the property in *Panic Room* is also a tour for the viewer. Learning these spaces, such as the elevator and the vertiginous levels of staircases, plays an important role when the intruders break into the home. For example, the elevator, an excessive amenity for their home, saves Meg and Sarah from being captured by the intruders when they initially break into their home. When Lydia and Evan show Meg the master bedroom suite, she realizes that the room is smaller than the other bedrooms. Evan tells her that she is the first client to notice this, demonstrating Meg's awareness of space. As we learn, Meg is claustrophobic. Evan reveals that the master suite is built with a panic room, a safe space in case of an emergency. Evan explains that once the door to the panic room closes, no one can enter it from the outside. The panic room is encased in cement and thick steel. Here, Meg asks Evan if he ever read Edgar Allan Poe. Like Juba's citations, Meg's reference to Poe alludes to the "buried alive" narrative of "The Cask of Amontillado" and "The Premature Burial." And, similar to the amenities in Howard's bunker in *10 Cloverfield Lane,* the panic room is equipped with emergency kits, a public announcement system, a phone line, and a number of video surveillance monitors of various rooms within the home. Certainly, the surveillance monitors speak to the database culture and split-screen format as explored in *Phone Booth.* But surveillance monitors also reflect the manner in which the architecture of space is articulated in the film and its correlation to the illusion of the mastery of seeing. This is most notable in Fincher's elaborate use of the "all-seeing" moving long take.

Fincher employs the long take not only to guide us through the spaces of the home, but also to afford the viewer otherwise impossible perspectives for human eyes. Here, we are reminded of Fincher expressing why filming an entire story inside one house appealed to him: to construct a multilevel apartment where the camera "can go literally anywhere."[9] This is most notable in the long take of the intruders breaking into the house. The image begins with Sarah sleeping in her bed, then it glides out of her bedroom, and fluently descends the multiple levels of the stairs. The long take then moves through the first level of the home, stopping at three windows facing the street as a group of men arrive. Like *Misery, Room,* and *10 Cloverfield Lane,* the invaders/captors are mysterious, since we are unable to detect who they are and what they look like. The long take pans to the left and slithers inside the keyhole of the front door as one of the intruders, Burnham (Forest Whitaker), an employee of the home's security company, tries (unsuccessfully) to open the door with his keys. The camera moves out of the keyhole as the intruders go to the back door. The camera glides across the kitchen, moving across counters and past appliances. The long take reaches the back door, where the intruders find themselves (again) unable to gain access. The camera then moves upward through all of the floors of the home, stopping at a sky window, where we see the invaders track stealthily across the roof. The shot finishes in a closet with the intruders about to enter through a roof access panel. Similar to the cinematography in *The Shining,* the long take during the home invasion sequence embodies Joan Copjec's notion of the unattributable shot—a shot that cannot be connected to an observer but assures "that some others exist."[10] Similar to *The Shining,* the moving long take has a ghostly or spectral dimension in its ability to move through vents, walls, floors, and doors. Whereas the long tracking shots in *The Shining* suggest the lurking of a spectral figure, the intruder-like "all-seeing" long take in *Panic Room* is more characteristic of Tom Gunning's notion of the "cinema of attraction."[11] That is, the long take compels us to look on with captivation and awe, as we watch the mechanism and special effects of the shot defy the laws of empirical reality as it moves through impossible spaces for human eyes. As explained in the introduction, the elaborate long take in *Touch of Evil* entices our desire to see, by not only showing us the planting of the bomb in the trunk of the car, but also by obstructing our seeing as the car drives through the city. But, in the case of the intruder sequence in *Panic Room,* the long take defies impediments by having the camera—via special effects—transcend impossible access and usher us to places that otherwise would be potential barriers to our looking. The only obstruction during the sequence is our inability to clearly identify the intruders outside the home.

When Meg and Sarah discover that their home has been invaded, they frantically retreat to the panic room. They learn that the intruders are there to steal a large sum of money that the previous owner hid inside a safe in the floor of the panic room. Not unlike the confinement thrillers *10 Cloverfield Lane, Room,* and *Green Room,* the allure of *Panic Room* comes from not only wondering how Meg and Sarah can possibly survive when there is no escape route, but also how the intruders will force mother and daughter out of the panic room. Making matters worse, Sarah has diabetes and needs her glucagon syringe, which is in her bedroom. If she does not have her injection, she will die.

Indeed, *Panic Room* is a film that produces the gaze as a knowable force through its spectacular and expressive cinematography. This certainly does not evacuate the film's suspense. But the expressive camera and dark atmosphere draw considerable attention to the film's excessive presence. At the same time, the film's exposure of excess has a social dimension in terms of wealth, class, and property. As we learn during the tour of the home, the previous owner used the top floor for live-in help. Lydia tells Meg that the previous owner, who recently died, was a recluse, rich and paranoid. The home is obviously too big for Meg and Sarah. Even Meg has reservations about this. But as Lydia humorously says to her: "You will have another family. You could even have two families." After Sarah and Meg move into the house, there are spaces that are clearly not being used. This disjunction between lived space and empty and unused spaces helps to create uncertainty within the confined setting. As such, there is a ridiculously large surplus of space in the home for two people to inhabit.

Meg's wealth is set into relief by Burnham's working-class status. Burnham is a character defined by his tools and his expert knowledge of the mechanics of the house. As we have seen throughout this study, objects within confined settings are more likely to lose their primary purpose or meaning. For Burnham, his tools forgo their connection to his working-class status and become tools of criminality to break into the safe in the panic room. But his motivation to rob the safe does not mean hurting anyone. Here, the issue of class in relation to excess speaks to the logic of desire. As explored in *Misery, Room,* and *10 Cloverfield Lane,* characters must initially rely on logic rather than instinct in order to overcome their captors. In *Panic Room,* Burnham expresses ambivalence when he and his associates discover that Meg and Sarah have moved into the home earlier than expected. Their plan was to rob the panic room when the house was still empty. The other intruders are Junior (Jared Leto), who is related to the previous owner and has learned that the money is hidden in the panic room, and Raoul (Dwight Yoakam), a bus driver from Flatbush, Brooklyn. Junior and Raoul are willing to use violence if necessary. They operate on instinct and irrationality, making poor choices that ultimately result in deadly consequences. Even Jared Leto's cartoonish and excessive acting helps to embody his irrationality. By contrast, Burnham is rational and logical as he tries to figure out ways to get Sarah and Meg out of the panic room. Here, Burnham's moral ambiguity plays an important part in Meg and Sarah's survival at the end of the film. When Burnham finally accesses the panic room, he discovers that Sarah has suffered a seizure because of her diabetes. Meg had managed to throw the glucagon syringe into the panic room before Raoul locked her out. Burnham agrees to give Sarah her injection, telling her that he did not want the plan to go this way. The only reason he decided to rob them was to give his own child a better life. Instead of reacting negatively or acting violently toward Burnham, Sarah reads Burnham's embroidered name on his shirt and says: "Thank you, Burnham." As explored in *Misery*, *Room*, and *10 Cloverfield Lane*, characters must initially rely on logic rather than instinct in order to overcome their captors. In *Misery*, Paul plays on Annie's desire by performing the role as her favorite writer, which allows him to prepare for his escape. In *Room*, Joy and Jack have to construct a fictional death in order to trick Old Nick. In *10 Cloverfield Lane*, Michelle plays on Howard's desire by playing the role of his estranged daughter while planning her escape from the bunker. At the climax of *Panic Room*, when Raoul is about to kill Meg with a sledgehammer, Burnham, who has the chance to escape with the money, instead returns to the house and kills Raoul. As such, Sarah's compassion toward Burnham in the panic room played on his desire, which informs his decision to return to the house and save them by shooting Raoul in the head. When Raoul sees Sarah looking at him in the panic room, this is why he says: "Don't you look at me." Raoul knows that making eye contact with Sarah can potentially implicate his desire. By avoiding eye contact, Raoul sustains his commitment to the plan, even if it must involve violence.

Most of *Panic Room* takes place in the home and employs low-key lighting. By contrast, the final shot of Meg and Sarah sitting on a bench near the park is bright and colorful. But unlike the trick ending of *The Wall*, or the antagonism of the type provoked by the photograph of Jack from 1921 in *The Shining*, *Panic Room* does not leave us with ambiguity. This is most notable in the scene's long take dolly forward and zooming back shot that ends the film. The dolly forward and zoom back technique decompresses and widens the background while maintaining the size of the foreground. This technique speaks directly to Meg's transformation at the end of the film. The scene begins with Sarah reading a property listing, since they are now looking for another place to live. Meg responds: "Do we need all that space?" This suggests that the large space of the "townstone" has affected Meg. Her battle with the intruders indicates that she has overcome claustrophobia. In the final shot, the background of the park subtly expands the space behind Meg and Sarah. Here Fincher employs the dolly forward and zoom back shot not to create a vertigo effect, which is often used to express a character's heightened interior state, but rather to suggest Meg conquering her claustrophobia. Whereas the fantasy frame collapses at the end of *The Passion of Anna* as space caves in on Andreas, we have the opposite effect in the final shot of *Panic Room*. Meg's fantasy frame is assured by the dolly forward and zoom back shot to indicate that she has overcome her fear of entombed spaces. Indeed, *Panic Room* is a film that reveals the gaze as a knowable presence. Fincher correlates the excess of the gaze with an expressive cinematography. Its excessive treatment of the architecture of space not only reflects Meg's claustrophobia, but also speaks to the excesses and inequality of wealth. Yet the allure of the "townstone" is its location within the crowded space of New York City. As Lydia says to Meg early in the film: "I don't have to tell you this amount of living space is uncommon in Manhattan."[12]

Cyberspace and the Allure of Confinement Cinema

127 Hours and *The Wall* are examples of two recent films that involve confinement narratives. Films such as *Life of Pi, Gravity, All Is Lost, I Am Legend, The Martian* (Ridley Scott, 2015), *Captain Phillips, The Impossible* (J. A. Bayona, 2012), *Open Water,* and *Cast Away* (Robert Zemeckis, 2000) are just some of the films that have been released over the past several years and depict entrapment or characters marooned.[13] It is interesting to note that this surge of confinement movies has taken place during the emergence of cyberspace communication. Certainly, the conditions of digitization have transformed our everyday experiences of time and space, whether it is texting, FaceTiming a friend, or ordering a DVD on the web. But the collapsing of time and space has also informed the parceling and ordering of narrative information in cinema. Since the 1990s, a surge in nonlinear narratives in cinema has emerged. Films such as *Groundhog Day* (Harold Ramis, 1993), *Pulp Fiction* (Quentin Tarantino, 1994), *Memento* (Christopher Nolan, 2000), *21 Grams* (Alejandro González Iñárritu, 2003), *Eternal Sunshine of the Spotless Mind* (Michel Gondry, 2004), *The Constant Gardener* (Fernando Meirelles, 2005), and *Inception* (Christopher Nolan, 2010), to name but a few, are movies that forgo chronological storytelling. Scholars have attributed the increase in nonlinear narratives to everyday practices of digital media, such as surfing the internet, interactive video gaming, and time-shifting media.[14]

But what are the spatial implications of these films in relation to digital media and cyberspace? How has our engagement with virtual space shaped cinematic space since the emergence of the web? Just as we have seen a rise in nonlinear narratives, we have witnessed a swell in confinement cinema. This is not to suggest that nonlinear narratives and limited-space films are trumping the classical mode of filmmaking. The classical ordering of narrative time and space across multiple locations is still predominantly the way most films are presented. Nevertheless, the increase in confinement cinema offers some insights on digitization and cyberspace communication in relation to the logic of desire.

Unlike films such as *Room, 10 Cloverfield Lane, Panic Room,* and *The Wall, 127 Hours* does not pose the question of how Aron will escape. The film suggests that we know that he has to amputate his arm in order to survive. We quickly learn that because of the mass of the boulder pinning his arm, Aron only has one way to extricate himself. The enjoyment of the film lies in watching Aron arrive at this conclusion as he wrestles with his past. In the case of *Misery, Room, Phone Booth, 10 Cloverfield Lane, Panic Room,* and *The Wall,* our enjoyment comes in speculating how these characters will overcome their captors and escape their dire situations. These films are not only about survival, they are also puzzle narratives. Indeed, digital technologies have altered the relationship between the subject and the object of desire. As argued, desire is elicited by absence and lack. Movies entice our desire not by mastery, but by what we do not know. As I explained about *10 Cloverfield Lane,* the logic of desire involves searching for the missing pieces of the puzzle. That is, desire seeks resolutions to the questions posed by the film's narrative: Is Howard trustworthy? Have aliens invaded the Earth? As we saw at the end of *The Shining,* the photograph of Jack from 1921 leaves us with antagonism rather than closure. At the same time, the mysterious photograph entices our desire to rewatch the film, to see if we can find clues that explain the photograph's meaning. And certainly playback devices and on-demand streaming services enable us to rewatch *The Shining* at our leisure—to search and discover the secrets of the Overlook Hotel. As such, digital time-shifting devices greatly shrink the wait time in accessing movies and television shows. Moreover, on-demand services diminish the allure of the object of desire. As Todd McGowan explains, "on-demand technology has the effect of deflating the object by rendering it immediately accessible."[15] The speed with which one can access a movie impacts the logic of desire, because the gap between the subject and the object is so quickly fulfilled. The instant access afforded by digital technologies has the effect of diminishing the aura of the object (whether it is looking up the meaning of a word or streaming a movie on a mobile device). This was certainly the case with Ivan using his car technology to communicate with his family and employees in *Locke*. For McGowan, "atemporal" cinema (films that break with the linear unfolding of time so that we experience time directly) is a product of digital media and cyberspace. According to McGowan, these films reflect the logic of the drive, which "does not respect the forward movement of time but remains attached to repetition."[16] Whereas desire follows a linear ordering of events, drive is attributed to films that outright define chronology. These films, for McGowan, allow the subject to invest in the trauma of loss by experiencing time as contingent and antagonistic, not as ordered and linear.

Films such as *Panic Room*, *Misery*, *Room*, *Green Room*, *Phone Booth*, *10 Cloverfield Lane*, and *The Wall* elicit our desire because they evoke impossible situations for characters to overcome. The films impose an injunction that nothing is possible by backing their characters into a corner. Yet the impossibilities these characters must face stage the possibilities of their escape and survival. Films such as *Rope*, *Phone Booth*, and *10 Cloverfield Lane* not only creatively deploy excess in order to visually and audibly make for an engaging film within a confined location, they also pose questions that seem to have impossible answers to attract and elicit our desire. How will Phillip and Brandon get away with murder? How will Jack and Joy outwit their captor in *Room*? Certainly, movies that shift from multiple locations impose limitations in order to activate our desire. Otherwise, there would be no reason to watch them. But films with one or a few locations dramatically intensify the limitations imposed on both characters and the viewer. The limitation not only forces the filmmaker to come up with ways to spatially engage us, but also must attract our desire to see how they will sustain our interest in a narrative that works primarily within one location. It is not surprising that films that take place within a limited location—such as *Rope*, *Locke*, *Phone Booth*, *127 Hours*, and *The Wall*—are often referred to as experiments. This characterization attests to the challenges filmmakers face when working in one primary location.

If the recent surge in atemporal cinema is a product of the digital era, then we must appreciate the increase in confinement cinema as part of this development in relation to desire and the subject of loss. The increase in nonlinear narrative in cinema is intimately connected to digital technologies by shrinking the gap between the subject and the object of desire. Slavoj Žižek makes a similar point in his reading of postmodern cinema that "tells it all" in relation to subjectivity and the injunction to enjoy. As he poses the question, "what if, by way of 'filling in the gaps' and 'telling it all,' what we retreat from is the void as such, which, of course, is ultimately none other than the void of subjectivity (the Lacanian 'barred subject')?"[17] For Žižek, "filling in the gaps" and the freedom of a postmodern society to enjoy are the demise of the big Other, collapsing what he describes as "symbolic efficiency." Symbolic efficiency derives from the fiction or lie of the big Other. Yet our investment in the fiction of the big Other binds us together within the symbolic universe. This is most notable in how the big Other provides identities that we can take up in everyday life. I cannot say that I am a professor or lawyer without there being a consensus about what constitutes a professor or a lawyer. That is to say, the big Other *must also know* what a professor and a lawyer are: for example, passing a dissertation defense, or passing the bar exam.

Symbolic efficiency not only involves our collective belief in the big Other, but also the process of disavowal between vision and language. Žižek uses the examples of the mark or mask of a judge's insignia to explain this notion: "I know very well that things are the way I see them [that this person is a corrupt weakling], but none the less I treat him with respect, since he wears the insignia of a judge, so that when he speaks, it is the Law itself which speaks through him."[18] For Žižek, it is not just what our eyes see, but also the "words of the institution of the Law" that we believe when we respect the symbolic authority of a judge.[19] Shutting down the gap between the subject and object normalizes and avoids "the void of subjectivity." For this reason, the decline of symbolic efficiency or "short-circuiting" the gap between the subject and object has a dimension of enjoyment in relation to the logic of desire. The elimination of the gap between the subject and the object does not produce more enjoyment. By contrast, it is the prohibition and limitation in our investment in the big Other that enables us to enjoy.[20] The subject of desire requires that the object cause of desire always be missing. Yet it is the barrier to the primordial lost "thing" that paradoxically generates our enjoyment. It is this short-circuiting between subject and object that speaks to the allure of confinement cinema.

Confinement cinema seeks to reinforce the gap, to stress absence and loss by imposing a spatial limit upon both characters and the viewer. If we are losing the gap between the subject and object of desire because of digital technologies, then confinement cinema places emphasis on the gap by putting characters and the viewer into impossible situations narratively and *spatially*. Just as Joy and Jack are held captive in *Room*, we are trapped alongside them. This is not to suggest that films that are constantly shifting locations do not elicit our desire to see how the film will solve the problem it poses. Rather, it is the recent surge and allure of confinement cinema that speaks to our current technological moment. Our enjoyment is the spatial limitation, guessing how the characters will escape their situation, especially when they cannot access digital technologies to communicate with others, as in the case of Aron in *127 Hours* and Isaac in *The Wall.* Delaying the solution to the problems posed by the film enhances our spectatorship. What appears to be unsolvable (characters trapped in a panic room, a fallout bunker, a hotel, a phone booth, the slit in a canyon, or a crumbling stone wall) elicits our desire to see and hear. These films demonstrate that a single-setting narrative can be just as exciting as movies that shift among many locations. I have attributed this effect to Lacan's theory of the gaze and Michel Chion's notion of the *acousmêtre.* The gaze realizes our desire to see. Our encounter with the gaze shows how our desire distorts the field of vision. The gaze demonstrates that our desire to look is itself integrated into the film. Chion's notion of the *acousmétre* reveals our desire to hear (the invocatory drive) in the separation of voice and body. Both notions involve something excessive that stands out within the order of looking or hearing. As argued throughout this study, the manner in which excess is deployed within the confined location makes for a suspenseful and energizing spectatorship over an extended period of time.

Notes

Introduction

1. Quoted in Paul Guyot, "David Fincher—*Seven* & *Fight Club*," DVD Talk, https://www.dvdtalk.com/interviews/david_fincher_s.html.

2. Certainly one can argue that Cuarón's reason for not showing the bomb first is to capture the film's uncertain and dystopic futuristic setting due to two decades of human infertility, which has led to a breakdown in systems of government.

3. Slavoj Žižek, *Looking Awry: An Introduction to Jacques Lacan through Popular Culture* (Cambridge, Mass.: MIT Press, 1991), 90.

4. Also see Pascal Bonitzer, "Hitchockian Suspense," in *Everything You Always Wanted to Know about Lacan . . . But Were Afraid to Ask Hitchcock*, ed. Slavoj Žižek (London: Verso, 1992), 15–30.

5. Todd McGowan, *The Real Gaze: Film Theory after Lacan* (Albany: SUNY Press, 2007), 27.

6. See Joan Copjec, *Read My Desire: Lacan against the Historicists* (Cambridge, Mass.: MIT Press, 1994).

7. My analysis of Lacan's theory of the gaze as a knowable and/or unknowable force in confinement cinema is indebted to Todd McGowan's outstanding work involving the intersection of Lacan and cinema.

8. Jacques Lacan, *Seminar XI: The Four Fundamental Concepts of Psychoanalysis*, ed. Jacques-Alain Miller, trans. Alan Sheridan (New York: Norton, 1978), 53.

9. Ibid., 92.

10. Ibid., 101.

11. Henry Krips, "The Politics of the Gaze: Foucault, Lacan and Žižek," *Culture Unbound* 2 (2010): 91–102.

12. Lacan, *Seminar XI*, 38.

13. Slavoj Žižek, *The Fragile Absolute, or Why Is the Christian Legacy Worth Fighting For?* (London: Verso, 2000), 22.

14. Lacan, *Seminar XI*, 31.

15. Ibid., 85.

16. Ibid., 185.

17. McGowan, *Real Gaze*, 128.

18. Ibid., 163

19. Ibid., part 4.

20. Slavoj Žižek, *The Plague of Fantasies*, 2nd ed. (London: Verso, 2008), 84. Author's emphasis.

21. Also see Žižek, *Looking Awry*, 12–16.

22. McGowan, *Real Gaze*, 25.

23. For extended details on the split-screen format, see Anne Friedberg, *The Virtual Window: From Alberti to Microsoft* (Cambridge, Mass.: MIT Press, 2006), 200–19. See also Alexander R. Galloway's analysis of the "waning of montage" and the "logic of 'windowing'" in the television series *24* in *The Interface Effect* (Cambridge: Polity, 2012), 109–10.

24. Jennifer Friedlander, *Real Deceptions: The Contemporary Reinvention of Realism* (New York: Oxford University Press, 2017), 75.

25. See Slavoj Žižek's interpretation of *Full Metal Jacket* in *The Pervert's Guide to Ideology*, directed by Sophie Fiennes (New York: Zeitgeist Films, 2012).

26. McGowan, *Real Gaze*, 25.

27. Ibid., 44.

28. See Hilary Neroni's excellent analysis of *Saw* and *Hostel* in *The Subject of Torture: Psychoanalysis and Biopolitics in Television and Film* (New York: Columbia University Press, 2015).

Chapter 1

1. Quoted in Chris O'Falt, "How 'Green Room' Director Jeremy Saulnier and DP Sean Porter Created the Film's Gritty Look," IndieWire, April 19, 2016, http://www.indiewire.com/2016/04/how-green-room-director-jeremy-saulnier-and-dp-sean-porter-created-the-films-gritty-look-289694.

2. Quoted in Chris O'Falt, "Read the Very Personal Letter That Got 'Room' Director Lenny Abrahamson His Oscar-Nominated Gig," IndieWire, February 9, 2016, http://www.indiewire.com/2016/02/read-the-very-personal-letter-that-got-room-director-lenny-abrahamson-his-oscar-nominated-gig-24199.

3. Slavoj Žižek explains that the empty screen is one of the three dimensions of the real. Žižek notes that "the real is also and primarily the screen itself as the obstacle that always already distorts our perception of the referent, of the reality 'out there.'" Slavoj Žižek, *Enjoy Your Symptom! Jacques Lacan in Hollywood and Out*, 2nd ed. (New York: Routledge, 2001), 220–21. Also see Žižek, *Looking Awry*, 134–35.

4. See Todd McGowan, *Psychoanalytic Film Theory and the Rules of the Game* (New York: Bloomsbury, 2015), 70–75.

5. Matthew Flisfeder, *The Symbolic, the Sublime, and Slavoj Žižek's Theory of Film* (New York: Palgrave Macmillan, 2012), 98.

6. Žižek, *Looking Awry*, 86.

7. Antonio Gramsci, *Selections from "The Prison Notebooks" of Antonio Gramsci*, ed. and trans. Quintin Hoare and Geoffrey Nowell-Smith (New York: International Publishers, 1971), 323–33.

8. Quoted in Jacob Hall, "'Green Room' Director Jeremy Saulnier on Pat-

rick Stewart, Inept Heroes, and 'Full Frontal Gore,'" Slash Film, April 13, 2016, http://www.slashfilm.com/green-room-jeremy-saulnier-interview/2/.

9. Ibid.

10. Tom Gunning, *D.W. Griffith and the Origins of American Narrative Film: The Early Years at Biograph* (Urbana: University of Illinois Press, 1991), 17.

11. David Bordwell, Janet Staiger, and Kristin Thompson, *The Classical Hollywood Cinema: Film Style & Mode of Production to 1960* (New York: Columbia University Press, 1985), 50.

12. Ibid., 56.

13. Steven Shaviro, *Post Cinematic Affect* (Winchester, Eng.: Zero Books, 2010), 123.

14. Robert T. Wood, *Straightedge Youth: Complexity and Contradictions of a Subculture* (Syracuse, N.Y.: Syracuse University Press, 2006), 142.

15. Ibid., 143–46.

Chapter 2

1. Peter Wollen, "*Rope*: Three Hypotheses," in *Alfred Hitchcock Centenary Essays*, ed. Richard Allen and S. Ishii Gonzalès (London: BFI Publishing, 1999), 79.

2. François Truffaut, *Hitchcock/Truffaut*, rev. ed. (New York: Simon and Schuster, 1983), 342.

3. Ibid., 315.

4. See D. A. Miller, "Anal Rope," *Representations* 32 (fall 1990): 114–33; Robin Wood, "The Murderous Gays," in *Hitchcock's Film*, rev. ed. (New York: Columbia University Press, 2002); and Thomas J. Roach, "Murderous Friends: Homosocial Excess in Alfred Hitchcock's *Rope* (1948) and Gus Van Sant's *Elephant* (2003)," *Quarterly Review of Film and Video* 29, no. 3 (2012): 225–36.

5. Certainly, unwritten rules can mean different things in different cultures, such as greetings and etiquette. There is no written rule, for instance, that one must say "hello" when answering the phone, or say "God bless you" after someone sneezes. Yet many of us enact these unwritten rules in our daily interactions. And those who do not follow the unwritten rules tend to stand out, for example, wearing shorts and flip-flops to a Roman Catholic funeral. This is often what comedians tune into when writing jokes—exposing the unwritten rules that organize a given society. For example, in the *Seinfeld* episode "The Good Samaritan," Jerry (Jerry Seinfeld) suggests that they say "You are so good looking" after someone sneezes rather than "God bless you." The episode humorously violates an unwritten rule in Western society after someone sneezes. For a full theoretical account of jokes, see Todd McGowan, *Only a Joke Can Save Us: A Theory of Comedy* (Evanston, Ill.: Northwestern University Press, 2017).

6. David A. Cook, *A History of Narrative Film*, 2nd ed. (New York: W.W. Norton, 1990), 336.

7. Quoted in Bob Thomas, "Alfred Hitchcock: The German Years," in *Al-*

fred Hitchcock Interviews, ed. Sidney Gottlieb (Jackson: University Press of Mississippi, 2003), 158.

8. See both Patrick McGilligan, *Alfred Hitchcock: A Life in Darkness and Light* (New York: HarperCollins, 2003), 63; and Cook, *History of Narrative Film,* 336.

9. Wollen, "*Rope*: Three Hypotheses," 80.

10. Steven Jacobs, *The Wrong House: The Architecture of Alfred Hitchcock* (Rotterdam: 010 Publishers, 2007), 276.

11. Ibid., 268.

12. Ibid., 270.

13. Friedberg, *The Virtual Window,* 117.

14. Ibid., 117.

15. Quoted in Wollen, "*Rope*: Three Hypotheses," 78.

16. It is also important to consider Jeff's unease with his marriage to Lisa in relation to lack and desire. It is not until Lisa climbs into Thorwald's apartment that she becomes eroticized for Jeff.

17. See Miran Božovič, "The Man behind His Own Retina," in *Everything You Always Wanted to Know about Lacan . . . But Were Afraid to Ask Hitchcock,* ed. Slavoj Žižek (London: Verso, 1992), 161–77. Also see Slavoj Žižek, *Tarrying with the Negative: Kant, Hegel, and the Critique of Ideology* (Durham, N.C.: Duke University Press, 1993), 196–99.

18. Henry Krips notes that "not all anomalies in the visual field constitute moments of anxiety. For example . . . the sights of an actor in a film behaving 'out of character,' straining to ignore the fly that has blundered onto the film set and landed on his nose, may occasion viewer amusement rather than a distress." This, as Krips points out, raises a question of a politics of looking pertaining to the gaze. For more on this, see Krips's reading of Lacan's story of a boat trip he took with a group of fishermen as a young man and his encounter with the gaze. Henry Krips, *Fetish: An Erotics of Culture* (Ithaca, N.Y.: Cornell University Press, 1999), 102–8.

19. Cook, *History of Narrative Film,* 126.

20. Another example of the disruption of window transparency occurs during the dining scene aboard the Twentieth Century train with Roger Thornhill (Cary Grant) and Eve Kendall (Eva Marie Saint) in Hitchcock's *North by Northwest* (1959). The scene is filmed against the passing of the beautiful background of the Hudson River. Toward the end of the scene, the train begins to slow. Unbeknownst to Thornhill, as the train is about to stop, two police officers are seen exiting a police vehicle parked in the background seen through the train's window. Here, the sudden appearance of the law, combined with the slowing of the train, causes the window to lose its transparent effect as Thornhill learns that the state police are looking for him.

21. Ian Roberts, *German Expressionist Cinema: The World of Light and Shadow* (London: Wallflower, 2008), 5.

22. John D. Barlow, *German Expressionist Film* (Boston: Twayne, 1982), 66.

23. Lotte H. Eisner, *The Haunted Screen: Expressionism in German Cinema and the Influence of Max Reinhardt,* trans. Roger Greaves (Berkeley: University of California Press, 1969), 23.

24. Ibid., 23.
25. Quoted in Wollen, "*Rope*: Three Hypotheses," 80.
26. Also see Žižek, *Looking Awry*, 78.
27. Lacan, *Seminar XI*, 45.

Chapter 3

1. Maria Bergom-Larsson, *Ingmar Bergman and Society* (London: Tantivy, 1978), 103.
2. Ibid., 77.
3. Ibid., 78.
4. Peter Harcourt, "*A Passion* Analysis," in *Ingmar Bergman: Essays in Criticism*, ed. Stuart M. Kaminsky with Joseph F. Hill (London: Oxford University Press, 1975), 287. Author's emphasis.
5. See Žižek, *Looking Awry*, 139. Also see Slavoj Žižek and Glyn Daly, *Conversations with Žižek* (Cambridge: Polity, 2004), 119–21.
6. Egil Törnqvist, *Between Stage and Screen: Ingmar Bergman Directs* (Amsterdam: Amsterdam University Press, 1995), 16.
7. Marc Gervais, *Ingmar Bergman: Magician and Prophet* (Montreal, Que.: McGill-Queen's University Press, 1999), 100.
8. Ibid., 100–101.
9. Robin Wood, *Ingmar Bergman*, ed. Barry Keith Grant (Detroit, Mich.: Wayne State University Press, 2012), 188.
10. Ibid.
11. Ibid.
12. McGowan, *Real Gaze*, 115–21.
13. Ibid., 69–74.
14. Stig Björkman, Torsten Manns, and Jonas Sima, *Bergman on Bergman: Interviews with Ingmar Bergman*, trans. Paul Britten Austin (New York: Simon and Schuster, 1973), 255.
15. Vincent Canby, "The Passion of Anna," *New York Times*, May 29, 1970, http://www.nytimes.com/movie/review?res=EE05E7DF173FA62CAA4A4CC5B6799C8C6896.
16. Bergom-Larsson, *Ingmar Bergman and Society*, 104.
17. Laura Mulvey, *Death 24x a Second: Stillness and the Moving Image* (London: Reaktion Books, 2006), 67.
18. Ibid., 69–70.
19. Ibid., 79.
20. Ibid., 81.
21. McGowan, *Real Gaze*, 73.
22. Ibid., 74.
23. This is also because Mulvey does not acknowledge that Peter Brooks misreads the Freudian death drive in his analysis of narrative and drive. What Brooks does not consider in his analysis of narrative propulsion is that the death drive is the repetition of loss. See McGowan, *Real Gaze*, 223.

24. Žižek, *Looking Awry*, 40.

25. See Žižek, *Enjoy Your Symptom!* 207–9.

26. Mulvey, *Death 24x a Second*, 78.

27. See Slavoj Žižek, *The Plague of Fantasies*, 2nd ed. (London: Verso, 2008), 39–40; and Todd McGowan, "Fighting Our Fantasies: *Dark City* and the Politics of Psychoanalysis," in *Lacan and Contemporary Film*, ed. Todd McGowan and Sheila Kunkle (New York: Other, 2004), 145–72.

28. Bergom-Larsson, *Ingmar Bergman and Society*, 104.

29. It could also be suggested that cinema's hidden secret is not only the still frame, but the excess of the gaze, what Slavoj Žižek describes as a "primordial point of fixation (or freeze) in what we see in the gaze itself." Žižek explains that "the gaze not only mortifies its object, it stands itself for the frozen point of immobility in the field of the visible." See Žižek, *Plague of Fantasies*, 111.

Chapter 4

1. Lacan, *Seminar XI*, 106.

2. A number of interpretations have been offered on the meaning of the photograph. See Fredric Jameson, "Historicism in *The Shining* (1980)," in *Signatures of the Visible* (New York: Routledge, 1982), 112–34; Thomas Allen Nelson, *Kubrick: Inside a Film Artist's Maze* (Bloomington: Indiana University Press, 1982); and Roger Luckhurst, *The Shining* (London: BFI Book published by Palgrave Macmillan, 2013).

3. Slavoj Žižek, *The Fright of Real Tears: Krzysztof Kieślowski between Theory and Post-Theory* (London: British Film Institute, 2001), 35.

4. Ibid., 32.

5. Ibid.

6. Ibid., 36. Author's emphasis.

7. Ibid., 38.

8. Sigmund Freud, "The Uncanny," trans. James Strachey, in *The Standard Edition of the Complete Psychological Works of Sigmund Freud*, vol. 17 (London: Hogarth, 1955), 220.

9. Ibid., 246.

10. Ibid., 250.

11. Ibid.

12. Quoted in Michel Ciment, *Kubrick: The Definitive Edition* (New York: Faber and Faber, 2001), 186.

13. Ibid., 181.

14. Ibid., 185.

15. Joan Copjec, *Imagine There's No Woman: Ethics and Sublimation* (Cambridge, Mass.: MIT Press, 2002), 201.

16. Žižek, *Fright of Real Tears*, 36. Author's emphasis.

17. Copjec, *Imagine There's No Woman*, 212.

18. Lacan, *Seminar XI*, 84.

19. Copjec, *Imagine There's No Woman*, 210.

20. Krips, "Politics of the Gaze," 91–102.

21. The indeterminate location of the gaze closely follows Michel Chion's notion of *acousmêtre* (a cinematic voice that has not been embodied). "For the spectator . . . the filmic acousmêtre is 'offscreen,' outside the image, and at the same time *in* the image: the loudspeaker that's actually its source is located behind the image in the movie theatre." The *acousmêtre* is a voice that is at once inside and outside. Michel Chion, *The Voice in Cinema*, trans. Claudia Gorbman (New York: Columbia University Press, 1999), 23. Author's emphasis.

22. One is reminded of the credit sequence in Robert Aldrich's *Kiss Me Deadly* (1955). The film's opening credits roll in reverse, suggesting that Mike Hammer (Ralph Meeker), as well as the viewers, will encounter something that is incomprehensible: namely, atomic annihilation.

23. Copjec, *Imagine There's No Woman*, 216.

24. See chapter 6 in David Sterritt, *The Films of Alfred Hitchcock* (Cambridge: Cambridge University Press, 1993).

25. Žižek, *Enjoy Your Symptom!* 209.

26. The opposite could be said for the toilet-diving scene in Danny Boyle's *Trainspotting* (1996). Renton (Ewan McGregor) takes opium suppositories to combat his heroin withdrawal. Unexpectedly, the suppositories kick in and Renton is forced to use the "Worst Toilet in Scotland." Renton enters an extremely filthy bathroom, with brown smudges on the wall and a disgusting unflushed toilet. After Renton relieves himself, he dives head-first into the toilet to find his opium. Here, we have the reverse effect of the drain as preventing things returning from the "netherworld." As Renton passes through the drain, the water is beautiful and magical as he swims, searching for his opium.

27. Jeffrey Sconce, *Haunted Media: Electronic Presence from Telegraphy to Television* (Durham, N.C.: Duke University Press, 2000).

28. Ibid., 174.

29. Žižek, *Looking Awry*, 133.

30. The same could be said for Leonard "Gomer Pyle's" (Vincent D'Onofrio) monstrous transformation in *Full Metal Jacket*, when he kills Sgt. Hartman (R. Lee Ermey) and then himself. D'Onofrio explained that Kubrick wanted him to act "big," Lon Chaney big, for Pyle's final scene. See "Full Metal Jacket: Vincent D'Onofrio Interview," Stanley Kubrick Appreciation Society, May 29, 2017, https://www.youtube.com/watch?v=T05dkRjFZU4.

31. See Thomas Allen Nelson, *Kubrick: Inside a Film Artist's Maze* (Bloomington: Indiana University Press, 1982).

32. Luckhurst, *Shining*, 91.

33. Ciment, *Kubrick*, 181.

34. See Tania Modleski, "The Terror of Pleasure: The Contemporary Horror Film and Postmodern Theory," in *Film Theory and Criticism: Introductory Readings*, 7th ed., ed. Leo Braudy and Marshall Cohen (New York: Oxford University Press, 2009), 617–26.

35. Luckhurst, *Shining*, 91.

36. Mulvey, *Death 24x a Second*, 67.

37. Ibid., 26.

Chapter 5

1. Lacan identifies four partial drives: the oral, the anal, the scopic, and the invocatory.

2. Chion, *Voice in Cinema*, 21.

3. Susan J. Douglas, *Listening In: Radio and the American Imagination, from Amos n' Andy and Edward R. Murrow to Wolfman Jack and Howard Stern* (New York: Times Books, 1999), 285.

4. Quoted in Susan Mackey-Kallis, *Oliver Stone's America: Dreaming the Myth Outward* (Boulder, Colo.: Westview, 1996), 112.

5. Quoted in Chris Salewicz, *Oliver Stone* (New York: Thunder's Mouth, 1998), 56.

6. Douglas, *Listening In*, 289.

7. Ibid., 289.

8. Daniel Marcus, "The Wonder Years: Televised Nostalgia," in *How to Watch Television*, ed. Ethan Thompson and Jason Mittell (New York: New York University Press, 2013), 229–30.

9. Todd McGowan, *The End of Dissatisfaction? Jacques Lacan and the Emerging Society of Enjoyment* (Albany: SUNY Press, 2004), 14.

10. Chion, *Voice in Cinema*, 63.

11. Douglas, *Listening In*, 40.

12. Ibid., 41.

13. Sconce, *Haunted Media*, 63.

14. Another film noteworthy in this regard is Clint Eastwood's *Play Misty for Me* (1971), a film about a disc jockey (Clint Eastwood) who is stalked by Evelyn (Jessica Walter), an obsessive fan who always requests the jazz tune "Misty." I kindly thank Annalisa Weaver-Zox for pointing this out to me.

15. Don Kunz, "Oliver Stone's Talk Radio," *Literature/Film Quarterly* 25, no. 1 (1997): 62–67, 66.

16. Peter Biskind, *Seeing Is Believing: How Hollywood Taught Us to Stop Worrying and Love the Fifties* (New York: Pantheon Books, 1983), 101–59.

17. Also see Barry Keith Grant, *Invasion of the Body Snatchers* (New York: Palgrave Macmillan, 2010).

18. Kunz, "Oliver Stone's Talk Radio," 65.

19. McGowan, *The Real Gaze*, 57.

20. McGowan, *Real Gaze*, 57.

21. Ibid., 60.

22. Mackey-Kallis, *Oliver Stone's America*, 113.

23. Ibid., 113.

24. See Todd McGowan's analysis of ethical drive and happiness in the cinema of Michael Mann. *Real Gaze*, 57–60.

25. Also see Robert Kolker, *A Cinema of Loneliness: Penn, Stone, Kubrick, Scorsese, Spielberg, Altman*, 3rd ed. (Oxford: Oxford University Press, 2000).

26. Mackey-Kallis, *Oliver Stone's America*, 117.

27. Frank Beaver, *Oliver Stone: Wakeup Cinema* (New York: Twayne, 1994), 118.

Chapter 6

1. See chapter 2 in Sconce, *Haunted Media.*

2. Chion, *Voice in Cinema,* 63.

3. Ibid., 21.

4. J. M. Hayward, "The New Aluminum Telephone Booth," *Bell Laboratories Record* 34 (August 1956): 294.

5. Ibid.

6. Ibid.

7. Hitchcock's daughter Patricia Hitchcock met Cohen years later at a Directors Guild event and said that one of the projects that Hitchcock wanted to make was a film that takes place in a phone booth. See Larry Cohen, "*Phone Booth*: A 30-Year Project Wouldn't Hang Up," *Los Angeles Times,* March 30, 2003, http://articles.latimes.com/2003/mar/30/entertainment/ca-cohen30.

8. John Belton, "Technology and Aesthetics of Film Sound," in *Film Theory and Criticism: Introductory Readings,* 7th ed., ed. Leo Braudy and Marshall Cohen (New York: Oxford University Press, 2009), 333.

9. Ibid.

10. Ibid., 334.

11. Chion, *Voice in Cinema,* 21.

12. Ibid., 24. Author's emphasis.

13. Tom Gunning, "Heard Over the Phone: *The Lonely Villa* and the De Lorde Tradition of Terrified Communication," *Screen* 32, no. 2 (summer 1991): 184–96, 186.

14. Marsha Kinder, "Hot Spots, Avatars, and Narrative Fields Forever—Bunuel's Legacy for New Digital Media and Interactive Database Narrative," *Film Quarterly* 55, no. 4 (2002): 2–15.

15. Lev Manovich, *The Language of New Media* (Cambridge, Mass.: MIT Press, 2002), 109.

16. I thank Jonathan Lethem for providing me a copy of his excellent book on *They Live.* See Jonathan Lethem, *They Live* (New York: Soft Skull, 2011).

17. McGowan, *The Real Gaze,* part 1.

18. Chion, *Voice in Cinema,* 21.

19. For a full account of Althusser's notion of interpellation, see chapter 5 in Henry Krips, *Fetish: An Erotics of Culture.* See also Žižek, *Tarrying with the Negative,* 73–80.

20. Also see Matthew Flisfeder's excellent reading of desire and interpellation in *The Symbolic, the Sublime, and Slavoj Žižek's Theory of Film* (New York: Palgrave Macmillan, 2012), 144–46.

21. David Laderman, *Driving Visions: Exploring the Road Movie* (Austin: University of Texas Press, 2002), 2.

22. Ibid., 1.

23. Ibid., 248.

24. Ibid.

25. Chion, *Voice in Cinema,* 28. Author's emphasis.

26. Ibid., 27–28. Author's emphasis.

27. Thomas Elsaesser, "Tales of Sound and Fury: Observation on the Family Melodrama," in *Imitations of Life: A Reader on Film & Television Melodrama*, ed. Marcia Landy (Detroit, Mich.: Wayne State University Press, 1991), 75.

28. Roland Barthes, *The Pleasure of the Text*, trans. Richard Miller (New York: Hill and Wang, 1975), 66–67.

Chapter 7

1. Neroni, *Subject of Torture*, 143.

2. Ibid., 140.

3. Ibid., 141.

4. Neroni describes Sydney as embodying the "detective of the real," one who sees "the importance of irrationality, desire, and anxiety as markers of the subject and thus of truth," whereas "biodetectives" see procuring truth within the symbolic (and occasionally in the imagery), such as the ideology of torture at work in *24*. See Neroni, *Subject of Torture*, 128–33.

5. It is not made explicitly clear whether or not Megan is deceased. Howard first tells Michelle: "Megan's not with us anymore." Later, he tells her that her mother turned Megan against him, and then they took off to Chicago. Emmett also tells Michelle that Howard's family moved to Chicago.

6. Slavoj Žižek, *The Ticklish Subject: The Absent Centre of Political Ontology* (London: Verso, 2000), 291.

7. See chapter 1 in Michele Hilmes, *Only Connect: A Cultural History of Broadcasting in the United States*, 4th ed. (Boston: Wadsworth Cengage Learning, 2014).

8. See Krips, *Fetish: An Erotics of Culture*, 105–8.

9. Slavoj Žižek, *For They Know Not What They Do: Enjoyment as a Political Factor*, 2nd ed. (London: Verso, 2008), 16.

10. Ibid., 15.

11. Alenka Zupančič, "A Perfect Place to Die: Theatre in Hitchcock Film," in *Everything You Always Wanted to Know about Lacan . . . But Were Afraid to Ask Hitchcock*, ed. Slavoj Žižek (London: Verso, 1992), 84.

12. Neroni, *Subject of Torture*, 142.

13. Also see Jennifer Friedlander's reading of how fiction provides a pathway toward the truth in the films *Catfish* (Ariel Schulman and Henry Joost, 2010) and *This Is Not a Film* (Mojtaba Mirtahmasb, 2011) in *Real Deceptions: The Contemporary Reinvention of Realism* (New York: Oxford University Press, 2017).

14. The intersection of fantasy and desire in cinema is what Todd McGowan terms "the cinema of intersection." See part 4 in McGowan, *The Real Gaze*.

15. See Dan Trachtenberg and J. J. Abrams, "Commentary," *10 Cloverfield Lane*, directed by Dan Trachtenberg (Hollywood, Calif.: Paramount Pictures, 2016), Blu-ray.

16. Kristen Whissel, "Tales of Upward Mobility: The New Verticality and Digital Special Effects," in *Film Theory and Criticism: Introductory Readings*, 7th ed., ed. Leo Braudy and Marshall Cohen (New York: Oxford University Press, 2009), 835.

17. At the same time, the overload of digital effects can potentially cause anxiety, or what Hugh S. Manon argues is the lack of lack. See Hugh S. Manon, "Beyond the Beyond: CGI and the Anxiety of Overperfection," in *Žižek and Media Studies: A Reader,* ed. Matthew Flisfeder and Louis-Paul Willis (New York: Palgrave Macmillan, 2014), 184–97.

18. Hilary Neroni, *The Violent Woman: Femininity, Narrative, and Violence in Contemporary American Cinema* (Albany: SUNY Press, 2005), 87.

19. Ibid., 98.

20. In certain ways, Michelle follows some of Carol J. Clover's description of the "Final Girl" often depicted in horror films. For Clover, the Final Girl is typically the one who escapes the slasher who has murdered all her friends, such as Laurie (Jamie Lee Curtis) in John Carpenter's *Halloween* (1978). The final girl is often smart, young, and innocent. She is typically coded as masculine, such as Ripley in the *Alien* franchise. See Carol J. Clover, *Men, Women and Chain Saws: Gender in the Modern Horror Film* (Princeton, N.J.: Princeton University Press, 1992).

Conclusion

1. Quoted in Erin McCarthy, "Director Danny Boyle Confronts Extreme Survival in *127 Hours,*" *Popular Mechanics,* November 5, 2010, http://www.popular mechanics.com/adventure/outdoors/a6265/127-hours-movie-danny-boyle-survival/.

2. Roger Ebert, "*127 Hours,*" Robertebert.com, November 10, 2010, http://www.rogerebert.com/reviews/127-hours-2010.

3. See Josh Horowitz, "Danny Boyle Says 'The Wrestler' Inspired His '127 Hours,'" *MTV News,* September 2, 2010, http://www.mtv.com/news/1647109/danny-boyle-says-the-wrestler-inspired-his-127-hours.

4. See Patrick Barkham, "The Extraordinary Story behind Danny Boyle's *127 Hours,*" *The Guardian,* December 15, 2010, https://www.theguardian.com/film/2010/dec/15/story-danny-boyles-127-hours.

5. Ibid.

6. A film that works in an opposite fashion is Akira Kurosawa's ransom thriller, *High and Low* (1963). The film begins with Gondo (Toshiro Mifune), a wealthy executive of a company called National Shoes. Gondo plans to take control of the company. But in order to set up his leveraged buyout, Gondo mortgages his home. Just as he is about to put the plan into effect, a man calls (Takeuchi [Tsutomu Yamazaki]) and says that he has kidnapped Gondo's son, Jun (Toshio Egi). Takeuchi wants a ransom of $30 million—all the money Gondo borrowed to take over National Shoes. As Gondo prepares to organize the money, he discovers that it was not his son who was kidnapped, but his chauffeur's son, Shinichi (Masahiko Shimazu). At first Gondo is reluctant to pay the ransom, but eventually he decides to pay. The first section of the film takes place entirely in Gondo's home—predominantly in his living room, where a large window looks out over the city of Yokohama. This section of the film runs a little over fifty minutes as a chamber-play film. Like *Talk Radio,* Takeuchi can see

Gondo from below in the city, but neither the viewer nor Gondo can see Takeuchi, creating a space of uncertainty through the separation of voice and body. At the end of the film, after Takeuchi has been caught by the police, he asks to meet with Gondo before he is executed. At the prison, Takeuchi and Gondo are protected by a glass barrier. Kurosawa superimposes their faces on the glass to suggest the dangers of going it alone and detaching oneself from society. At the start of the film, Gondo sets a course of obtaining power for himself by controlling National Shoes. As Geoffrey O'Brien explains in his essay from the Criterion Blu-ray, the superimposition of Gondo's and Takeuchi's faces shows that the two have become one. Takeuchi, as O'Brien observes, "is a demon of isolation, defiantly cut loose from those indispensable ties of human contact that are measured throughout every frame of *High and Low* by a constant play of glances and postures." The last image of the film is Takeuchi's scream of pain as the barrier descends on Gondo. As such, Gondo has now achieved his solidarity in attempting to go it alone in his power grab of National Shoes. Yet the ending leaves us with uncertainty as Gondo remains alone in front of the barrier at the prison. Also see Mitsuhiro Yoshimoto's excellent reading of *High and Low* in *Kurosawa: Film Studies and Japanese Cinema* (Durham, N.C.: Duke University Press, 2000).

7. Another film worthy to note is Rodrigo Cortés's *Buried*, in which the truck driver Paul Conroy (Ryan Reynolds), working in Iraq, is attacked and later finds himself buried alive in a wooden casket. The captor leaves a cell phone in the casket in order for Paul to orchestrate paying a ransom of $5 million for his release. Working with Paul is Brenner (Robert Paterson) at the U.S. State Department. Brenner is able to find Paul's location through an insurgent. At the end of the film, Paul hears Brenner's team digging, telling him that they have found his location. But it turns out that the insurgent led Brenner to another contractor's burial site, Mark White, who was supposedly rescued by Brenner. Like *The Wall*, the film leaves us with antagonism and with the need to ponder its potential meanings in relation to the Iraq War.

8. It is interesting to note that "townstone" sounds eerily like "tombstone," alluding to the premature burial narrative. I kindly thank Annalisa Weaver-Zox for pointing this out to me.

9. Quoted in Paul Guyot, "David Fincher—*Seven* & *Fight Club*," DVD Talk, https://www.dvdtalk.com/interviews/david_fincher_s.html.

10. Copjec, *Imagine There's No Woman*, 212.

11. Tom Gunning, "The Cinema of Attraction: Early Film, Its Spectator and the Avant-Garde," *Wide Angle* 8, nos. 3 and 4 (fall 1986): 63–70.

12. Even the title sequence reflects wealth and power. The typography of the titles is grand and exuberant, positioned like a billboard against the buildings of New York City. See Lola Landerkic, "*Panic Room* (2002)," Art of the Title, November 29, 2016, http://www.artofthetitle.com/title/panic-room.

13. It is interesting to add that when talking to friends, colleagues, and students about my project, they would often recommend movies for my research, which attests to the recent surge in and awareness of confinement cinema.

14. See Allan Cameron's *Modular Narratives in Contemporary Cinema* (Lon-

don: Palgrave Macmillan, 2008); and Todd McGowan, *Out of Time: Desire in Atemporal Cinema* (Minneapolis: University of Minnesota Press, 2011).

15. McGowan, *Out of Time*, 28.

16. Ibid., 32.

17. Žižek, *Fright of Real Tears*, 148.

18. Žižek, *The Ticklish Subject*, 323.

19. Ibid., 323. Also see Mark Andrejevic, *Infoglut: How Too Much Information Is Changing the Way We Think and Know* (New York: Routledge, 2013), 12–15.

20. See Todd McGowan, *The End of Dissatisfaction? Jacques Lacan and the Emerging Society of Enjoyment* (Albany: SUNY Press, 2004).

Index